STRAWBERRY HILL

STRAWBERRY HILL

HORACE WALPOLE'S GOTHIC CASTLE

ANNA CHALCRAFT & JUDITH VISCARDI

F

FRANCES LINCOLN LIMITED
PUBLISHERS
www.franceslincoln.com

Frances Lincoln Ltd
4 Torriano Mews
Torriano Avenue
London NW5 2RZ
www.franceslincoln.com

Commissioned and edited by Jane Crawley
Designed by Ian Hunt

TITLE PAGE: *Detail from A Country Procession Passing Strawberry Hill, watercolour by Thomas Rowlandson, 1789*

THE AUTHORS WOULD LIKE TO THANK
The Paul Mellon Centre for Studies in British Art
whose generous support made it possible to include
colour illustrations and modern photography.

NOTES ON THE TEXT

Throughout the text quotations from Walpole's letters are from the Yale University Press edition of Horace Walpole's Correspondence. Full details of these volumes are given in the Bibliography. Individual letters are not referenced if the date and correspondent are given within the text.

Grammar, spelling and use of capitals in quoted material follow those in the original text or are those used by W.S.Lewis if the text is taken from the Yale edition of the Correspondence.

During the period over which Walpole wrote his letters the British calendar was realigned. Great Britain accepted the Gregorian Calendar in 1752 and Parliament eliminated eleven days between 3 and 13 December 1752. The use of o.s and n.s. within the footnotes denotes an old or new style date.

When it is used to describe Horace Walpole's decorative style, Strawberry Hill gothic is often differentiated from true gothic by the addition of a k. In this book it has been decided to omit the k.

MONEY IN THE EIGHTEENTH CENTURY

Prices written in: £ s. d. (pounds, shillings, pence)

¼	=	1 farthing
4 farthings	=	1 penny or 1d.
½	=	1 halfpenny
2 halfpennies	=	1 penny or 1d.
12 pennies	=	1 shilling or 1s.
20 shillings	=	1 pound or 20/-
21 shillings	=	1 guinea

Contents

1 Introduction 6

2 Setting the scene 14

3 The Waiting Room, China Closet and Refectory 22

4 The Hall, Staircase and Armoury 34

5 The Little Parlour and the Yellow Bedchamber 42

6 The Blue Breakfast Room, the Green Closet and the Family Bedchambers 50

7 The Library and the Star Chamber 62

8 The Trunk-ceiled Passage and the Holbein Chamber 72

9 The Long Gallery and the Round Drawing Room 80

10 The Tribune and Beauclerc Closet 94

11 The Great North Bedchamber 104

12 The Garden 112

13 Life below stairs 122

14 Strawberry Hill after Walpole 132

15 Lost and found 144

Chronology 153

Bibliography 154

Biographies 156

Acknowledgements 160

Index 161

Picture Credits 168

1 Introduction

'An Idea of an Age'

OPPOSITE *Detail from the East Front of Strawberry Hill (page 13), showing the South Front*

[1] Walpole, Horace, *A Description of the Villa of Horace Walpole*, Strawberry Hill, 1774, Storer Collection, Eton College Library ECL Cc114

[2] Walpole, Horace, *A Description of the Villa of Mr. Horace Walpole, at Strawberry-Hill, near Twickenham, Middlesex*, Strawberry Hill, 1784

[3] Scatcherd, J.,ed., *Ambulator or a Pocket Companion in a Tour Round London within the Circuit of twenty-five Miles*, London, 1800

THIS BOOK IS WRITTEN to mark the long awaited conservation and restoration of the seminal house of the gothic revival in England, Horace Walpole's Strawberry Hill. It seeks to tell the story of Strawberry Hill by taking the reader on a tour through the interiors with contemporary evidence from the letters and diaries of those who visited it in its heyday.

In the eighteenth century Strawberry Hill was about Horace Walpole's perception of gothic and today it is about our perception of him and his reasons for creating a gothic house. It is a house which invites the visitor to play detective, to judge for him or herself the owner's intention. It is a house in which much of the original material can still be seen, although sometimes in a fragmentary or disguised state. The eighteenth-century decoration is still there today awaiting discovery.

The house became famous as one of the curiosities to be visited on the tourist route, with so many visitors knocking on the door that early in 1774 Walpole wrote a guidebook, which he intended for his servants' use when showing visitors around.[1] Later in the same year he updated the guide and published it adding fresh information as he acquired new furnishings and paintings. In 1784 at his private printing press, the Strawberry Hill Press, he produced what was to be the first illustrated house guide, *A Description of the villa of Mr. Horace Walpole*

at Strawberry-Hill, near Twickenham.[2] Throughout his life he commissioned drawings and paintings to illustrate the house and garden, kept an accounts book and wrote hundreds of letters to his friends describing the progress of his building plans.

In 1800, three years after Walpole's death, a guidebook on visiting London houses was published, which described the changes made by Anne Damer who inherited the house.[3] Later in the nineteenth and twentieth centuries sale catalogues recorded the disposition of furniture, paintings and objects d'art, whilst early photographs recorded architectural changes. Documentary and pictorial evidence from both the eighteenth and nineteenth centuries ensure that Strawberry Hill is possibly the best documented house of the eighteenth century.

With new evidence coming to light, various facts are emerging which have not previously been identified. The most significant of these is Horace Walpole's use both of colour and of the absence of colour in creating an atmosphere of gothic mystery and horror. There also emerge practical, cultural and aesthetic differences between the way in which Strawberry Hill was shown to the family and friends of Horace Walpole and the way in which visitors holding tickets of admission were conducted over the house by his servants. Not only were many areas omitted from the public visit, with only one room being shown on the ground floor and none on the

second floor, but also these visitors used a different entrance and were admitted only as far as the threshold of certain rooms.

A house is known to have stood on the site since records began when it was listed as Strawberry hid Shotte. The present house, known locally as Chopp'd Straw Hall, was built in 1698 as a three storey lodging house. It was this tiny, unlikely and unpromising building which was rented in 1747, and later bought, by Horace Walpole as a shell for his Collection and a base for entertaining and amusing his friends. For nearly fifty years builders were employed at Strawberry Hill adding, building and changing as directed by the 'Committee on Taste' appointed by Walpole to arbitrate on the use and fashion of the gothic style. After Horace's death the house passed first to a Walpole second cousin and then to the Waldegrave family; eventually through marriage the ownership reached Frances, Lady Waldegrave, who made as great a mark on the building in the Victorian period as Horace Walpole

had done in the Georgian. She, like him, saw the house primarily as a focus for entertainment and a jewel-like setting for herself as hostess. She also built, but the great gift she bequeathed to Strawberry Hill was her respect for Walpole's house. She made architectural changes, used a different style of decoration, but her additions were made without destroying what was already there. After her death the house passed through various hands before the Vincentian Order of Roman Catholic priests bought it as a centre for Catholic education in 1923. Once again there were changes and additions including those made necessary by war damage. To understand and appreciate the magic Strawberry Hill exerts it is necessary to peel back the layers added by each of its owners and see each as the apogee of an idea, each period completing a different function but each, whatever the date, using cutting-edge technology to provide fashionable living and to attract and encourage debate. There are many anomalies and therein lies the interest in its archeology. Horace Walpole used new materials, had amazing ideas, but utilised these to reinvest the past with excitement. Both Georgian and Victorian gothic architecture grew from a style which recalled the past but which was also the epitome of modernity.

Strawberry Hill gothic, to which a 'k' is sometimes added to differentiate it from traditional gothic, has always been considered a decorative style. Horace Walpole himself coined the term 'gloomth' to describe the atmospheric warmth he experienced in underlit gothic spaces, but this is only scratching the surface of the term and the way in which it was applied to the decoration of Strawberry Hill. For him the gothic period stretched from the eleventh century to the Tudor dynasty, although for inspirational material he had a marked affinity with the Perpendicular period of 1330 to 1550. He knew the buildings of King's College, Cambridge, and Westminster Abbey and he remembered their interiors as cavernous spaces in which especial objects appeared through shafts of light. He knew also buildings like Old Saint Paul's Cathedral through engravings executed in a single colour. All of these sources would have reinforced a memory of dark interiors made exciting through the history of the events which had taken place within their walls. There were the great cathedrals of France and Italy seen on the Grand Tour and never forgotten, among them Rouen and Rheims. These were remembered as dark spaces broken by wells of blue light filtered through medieval stained glass manufactured from precious minerals including gold and lapis lazuli. In the cathedrals of Italy he would have experienced the very different embracing warmth of gothic interiors, lit by alabaster not glass, the light itself repeated in the physical warmth of the buildings standing in the Italian sun. There was another rare source of gothic, the remains of the brilliantly hued glass of the English gothic buildings which had survived Henry VIII, Edward VI and Cromwell's troops; buildings which held furniture such as the Glastonbury chair, evocative of fairy tale, and small objects of outstanding beauty. Gothic was a style in which momentous happenings took place which were better understood through the decoration which survived. Whilst Walpole embraced the new discoveries in science and technology he was determined not to allow previous historic periods to be forgotten.

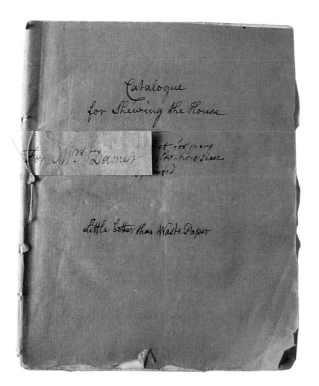

LEFT *Catalogue for Shewing (sic) the House, 1774 [A Description of the Villa of Horace Walpole] by kind permission of The Provost & Fellows of Eton College*

Walpole was assisted in his choice of style and sources by what he called a 'Committee of [or on] Taste'. In the early period of Strawberry Hill's goth-icising two of his great friends were part of this Committee: John Chute, who became responsible for much of the early building and was the antiquarian and heraldic influence on Walpole, and Richard Bentley, who concentrated on the interiors, furniture, and decoration. Later, others served on the Committee for short periods, but the house's unique quality and charm is mainly due to the vision of Horace Walpole, John Chute and Richard Bentley. At first they built a comfortable Thames-side villa in which to spend happy hours with friends. As they built and decorated they found how much could be attained through colour and light. They imbued the house with an element of surprise which they found pleasing and visitors found extraordinary. They created a house of great distinction.

The element of surprise was partly achieved because Strawberry Hill was so different in both its exterior and interiors to any other house visitors would have known and partly through an extraordinary and theatrical use of light and colour. Today this would be considered modern, but to the Georgian visitor it must have been staggering. Each room was presented with its own mood and all led to the Long Gallery with its spectacular ceiling of papier mâché described by Walpole as, 'richer than the roof of paradise'.[4] Objects within the rooms were

[4] Letter Horace Walpole to William Mason, 11 October 1778

record the gothic detail of these early buildings before they were lost for ever. Walpole believed that the houses of the past not only recorded great periods of architecture but gave a nobility to the owners through the history of the objects they contained. Each sword spoke of the Crusades, each family portrait of dynastic achievement, each state bedchamber of a royal visit; these were all to be included in Strawberry Hill.

Many of the new houses were built according to rules of taste which required them to have a classical sense of symmetry, although gothic detailing might be added as a decorative device. When Walpole built Strawberry Hill he wanted to be creative, to lead, not to follow rules, and he could not do this by building in the classical style. He studied folios of engravings depicting the interiors, roofs, screens, tombs and ornaments of the great gothic cathedrals and abbeys and used them as source material for his house. These engravings, mostly executed by great craftsmen, were remarkably detailed and beautiful to look at in their own right. He loved both their beauty and the image of the past they evoked. However, they presented two insuperable problems for him: they lacked information on the materials used in the original buildings and they were drawn without scale. Strawberry Hill gothic therefore became a form in which the primary source was a work on paper, one in which the scale and building materials used often differed widely from that of the original building. Through the use of engravings as a source for the architectural drawings, the actual structure of the buildings and the function of the elements within them became less important.

What was Horace Walpole like? There is a contemporary description of him written by Laetetia Matilda Hawkins sometime before 1772:

> His figure was not merely tall, but more properly long and slender to excess; his complexion, and particularly his hands, of a most unhealthy paleness. His eyes were remarkably bright and penetrating, very dark and lively; his voice was not strong, but his tones were extremely pleasant, and, if I may so say, gentlemanly. I do not remember his common gait; he always entered a room in that style of affected delicacy, which fashion had then made almost natural; chapeau bras between his hands, as if he wished to compress it, or under his arm; knees bent, and feet on tiptoe, as if afraid of a wet floor.[5]

placed where they would create the greatest impact, and around the most significant objects Walpole created stories. These stories, designed to become legends, summed up his love of the past and his desire to capture the spirit of the gothic age before it was lost forever.

England in the eighteenth century was a place of leisure and relative calm after the replacement of the Catholic Stuarts by the Protestant Hanoverians. With leisure and political stability came economic wealth for the few. Much money was spent on building in the latest fashion with owners having their buildings recorded for posterity by fashionable artists who painted the house, the master, his wife and children, horses and dogs, in paintings designed to become a record of achievement. Within the houses the latest furniture would be arranged, decorated with gilding, chairs upholstered in Spitalfields silk and mirrors placed with candelabra in front of them to reflect the light. Fashionable taste dictated the use of materials which enhanced light. In many cases the newly built houses replaced older Elizabethan or Jacobean buildings which had been pulled down in a Georgian building boom. To a lover of English architecture and its heritage this was a disaster and Strawberry Hill, built copying designs of 'ancient' buildings, was an attempt to

5 Stuart, Dorothy M.,
Horace Walpole, Macmillan,
New York, 1927, p.207

Horace, or Horatio, Walpole, was born in 1717, youngest of the five children of Robert Walpole and his wife, Catherine Shorter. His father Robert was, in all but name, England's first Prime Minister and a man of whose achievement Horace was immensely proud. One of the many ways in which Strawberry Hill can be seen is as a tribute to the Walpole family, a family of Norfolk landowners who acquired wealth and renown through Robert's political acumen. Robert spent his money on building a great house in Norfolk symbolic of his power, Houghton Hall, and in the acquisition of paintings, eventually owning a fabulous collection. Horace grew up with a tradition of great art and patronage around him. From his mother he gained a love of ceramics and a desire to collect and own rare pieces.

He attended Eton College and then went on to King's College, Cambridge. At Eton he became friends with Thomas Gray with whom he set off aged twenty-two on the Grand Tour to France and Italy. The two young men could not have been more different in character: Walpole interested in the unusual and the travel experience, in people, parties and entertainment but tiring easily of too much sightseeing; Gray more studious and intellectual, painstakingly recording the buildings, sculptures and paintings they saw.

In Florence they stayed with Horace Mann, British Envoy to the Court of Tuscany, who was to become Walpole's most regular correspondent: Walpole wrote about 1,800 letters to him over the course of his life although they were never to meet again. From Rome Gray and Walpole journeyed south to the newly discovered Herculaneum, but on their homeward journey the two young men quarrelled and returned to England separately in 1741.

Walpole was returned to Parliament in the same year representing first a Cornish and later Norfolk constituencies, although he was always more interested in moving behind the scenes than in pursuing an active political career within Parliament. His life income had been secured by his father who ensured that three sinecures from the Crown were bestowed on his youngest son, a fourth being granted later. These, together, brought in about £5,000 annually. After his father's death in 1745 he inherited the lease of a house in Arlington Street, off Piccadilly, in which he lived when in town until 1779 when he moved to Berkeley Square. However, it was Strawberry Hill, into which he moved in 1747 (purchasing it two years later), that he considered his real home, the one to which he returned for Christmas, Easter and the summer each year, and in which he increasingly completed his writing.

He wrote over 5,000 letters to friends most of which, together with replies, are still extant. In them he set out to record the unimportant day to day happenings of society as well as historic events written as they took place, lest they too, like old gothic buildings, should be forgotten or misrecorded; his letters form a commentary on a vanishing way of life. He wrote on 30 November 1761 to Sir David Dalrymple, 'nothing gives so just an idea of an age as genuine letters; nay, history waits for its last seal from them'.

He wrote about everything: an account of George II's funeral in 1760, the coronation of George III the following year, of Cherokee Indians visiting Twickenham in 1762, of slavery, the war in America, the French Revolution, the Gordon Riots, of watching a balloon descent, of throngs of traffic and the problems of travel to London, the building of Richmond Bridge, of highwaymen, housekeepers, the difficulties of coping with a pregnant cook and an irascible gardener who refused to be pensioned off. He wrote about the pleasure and the difficulties experienced in building and decorating a house. From his letters we see him as a product of his age and at the same time as a man far ahead of his time – tolerant of idiosyncrasy, fiercely protective of freedom and independence and intolerant of cruelty. Some of the letters he wrote are among the greatest written in any language. His letters also show him to be an oddity, notably eccentric even in an age of eccentricity and an exponent of the class system. The letters show an enthusiasm for life rarely matched in literature, recorded with wit and humour. They are 'a good read'.

In addition to his correspondence he found time to write several essays including the influential, *The History of the Modern Taste in Gardening*; the novel from which all our gothic literature has sprung, *The Castle of Otranto*; *Anecdotes of Painting in England* (in four volumes, with a fifth volume on engraving); poetry; satire; a play, *The Mysterious Mother*; and he researched and for the first time questioned the guilt of Richard III for the infamous murder of the princes in the tower in *Historic Doubts on the Life and Reign of King Richard III*; he completed a history of the Hanoverian Georges. The work of which he said he was most proud was his *Aedes Walpolianae*, which was an inventory and description of his father's picture collection at Houghton. The best of what he wrote after 1757 was published at the private printing press he founded, the Strawberry Hill Press; political and controversial works were sent to an outside publisher.

He never married, but Strawberry Hill was always filled with cats, dogs and the children of friends, for whom he would compose enormously complicated and elaborate games to be played over periods of several days or even weeks. To his friends he was generous with both his time and his money. His father had been created Earl of Orford on his retirement from politics and Horace, outliving his brothers and nephew, inherited the title in 1791 to become 4th Earl of Orford.

He lived to be eighty but his health became progressively worse with age. His will was detailed and recorded his attempt to keep his Collection and most treasured possessions safe together at Strawberry Hill, which itself had become for him a cabinet of curiosities. It also recorded numerous small bequests to women, recognising their need for independence, giving them money which he specified was for their personal use, not to be given to their husbands, fathers or brothers. In this, as in so many other ways, he displayed an unexpected mind in advance of his time. Mrs Delaney, a fellow eighteenth-century letter writer, was in agreement:

[6] Letter Horace Walpole to John Pinkerton, 27 October 1784

[7] Hayden, Ruth, *Mrs Delany* (sic), *Her life and her flowers*, British Museum Press, London, 2000, p.39

[8] Cornforth, John, *Early Georgian Interiors*, Yale University Press, New Haven & London, 2004

[9] Letter Horace Walpole to Horace Mann written from Strawberry Hill, 27 April 1753

…When young I wished for fame, not examining whether I was capable of attaining it, nor considering in what lights fame was desirable. There are two sorts of honest fame; that attendant on the truly great, and that better sort that is due to the good. I fear I did not aim at the latter; nor discovered, till too late, that I could not compass the former. Having neglected the best road, and having, instead of the other, strolled into a narrow path that led to no goal worth seeking, I see the idleness of my journey, and hold it more graceful to abandon my wanderings to chance or oblivion, than to mark solicitude for trifles.[6]

…there is one error which most fathers run into, and that is providing too little for daughters; young men have a thousand ways of improving a little fortune, by professions and employments, if they have good friends, but young gentlewomen have no way, the fortune settled on them is all they are to expect – they are incapable of making an addition.[7]

The building of Strawberry Hill took place over nearly fifty years and as the house evolved the garden was planted and slowly crept to maturity. A widespread interest in botanical and ornithological books and illustration throughout these years meant that the influence of the garden on both landscaping and the decoration of the interiors increased over the period.[8] House and garden must be seen as one, each view with its planting planned by Walpole to enhance the enjoyment of his guests.

I have brought two of your letters hither to answer, in town there are so many idle people besides one's self, that one has not a minute's time: here I have whole evenings, after the labours of the day are ceased. Labours they are I assure you; I have carpenters to direct, plasterers to hurry, papermen to scold, and glaziers to help: this last is my greatest pleasure: I have amassed such quantities of painted glass, that every window in my castle will be illuminated with it: the adjusting and disposing it is vast amusement. I thank you a thousand times for thinking of procuring me some Gothic remains from Rome; but I believe there is no such thing

there: I scarce remember any morsal in the true taste of it in Italy. Indeed, my dear Sir, kind as you are about it, I perceive you have no idea what Gothic is; you have lived too long amidst true taste, to understand venerable barbarism. You say, "You suppose my garden is to be Gothic too." That can't be; Gothic is merely architecture; and as one has a satisfaction in imprinting the gloomth of abbeys and cathedrals on one's house, so one's garden, on the contrary is to be nothing but "riant", and the gaity of nature.[9]

Strawberry Hill is Horace Walpole's visible legacy; his letters, his specially commissioned watercolours depicting the house and his inventory or guidebook, together give us an understanding of the techniques in use in the eighteenth century and of the problems and pleasures experienced by a Georgian gentleman in furnishing and decorating his house in the gothic style.

This book will take the reader through the house as if accompanied by the Housekeeper and it will follow the eighteenth-century route which had been carefully devised in order to create surprise, awe and gothic horror.

ABOVE *East Front of Strawberry Hill, tinted engraving from a watercolour by Paul Sandby*

2 Setting the scene

'A little play-thing-house'

TWICKENHAM in the eighteenth century was a fashionable area where society figures could enjoy a second home in the country and yet still remain within easy reach of London. The river frontage between Richmond and Hampton Court was punctuated by country villas built to reflect a more leisured way of life. Alexander Pope lived there until his death in 1745, and his garden and grotto continued to be an attraction: Walpole commented that his ghost never left the river. Henrietta Howard, Countess of Suffolk and mistress to George II, owned Marble Hill, close enough to Strawberry Hill for daily visits when she and Walpole wanted to gossip. Artists, actors, writers and members of parliament all left the bustle and noise of London for the delights to be found along the Twickenham riverside, where their

houses were surrounded by market gardens and nurseries. It was rural but busy, with the wide and shallow Thames humming with traffic. Up and down river the hills of Richmond and Kingston sheltered the site, while the river itself watered it, making it ideal for growing strawberries and soft fruit, but at the same time leaving it prone to flooding after heavy rains. Walpole often referred to flooding in his letters and they are peppered with worries about the state of the weather and the tides.

Because the area was fashionable, it was difficult to find land there for development and the house rented by Walpole in 1747, and bought by him two years later, was on the last available site. It was a small cottage known to the local residents as Chopp'd Straw Hall, because it was rumoured that the builder, coachman to Lord Bradford, had only managed to pay for its building by using money entrusted to him for winter hay and had fed the horses on chopped straw instead. It had been completed in 1698 as a fairly insignificant timber framed lodging house, and was enlarged in the early eighteenth century to become a combination of two and three storey elements. Although described by Walpole as 'a small tenement', it had had several fashionable residents: Colley Cibber the poet and playwright, the Bishop of Durham (who probably extended it), Lord Carnarvon and Lord John Sackville, but by the time of Walpole's arrival in 1747, it was occupied by a Mrs Chenevix, well known as a famous toy woman who sold her beautiful 'toys' or *objets de vertu* in a shop in Charing Cross.

> …[I] may retire to a new little farm that I have taken just out of Twickenham. The house is so small, that I can send it to you in a letter to look at: the prospect is as delightful as possible, commanding the river, the town and Richmond Park; and being situated on a hill descends to the Thames through two or three little meadows, where I have some Turkish sheep and two cows, all studied in their colours for becoming the view. This little rural bijou was Mrs. Chenevix's, the toywoman à la mode, who in every dry season is to furnish me with the best rain-water from Paris, and now and then with some Dresden china cows, who are to figure like wooden classics in a library: so I shall grow as much a shepherd as any swain in the Astraea.[1]

The fact that he had rented the house from a purveyor of small but expensive trinkets caught Walpole's imagination and he used the idea of Strawberry Hill standing as a treasure in a toy shop window in several letters describing his new surroundings. Writing to his cousin, Conway, in 1747 he conveys how enchanted he is with the eccentricities of the house as well as its situation and neighbourhood.

> You perceive by my date that I am got into a new camp, and have left my tub at Windsor. It is a little play-thing-house that I got out of Mrs Chenevix's shop, and is the prettiest bauble you ever saw. It is set in enamelled meadows, with filigree hedges:
> "A small Euphrates through the piece is roll'd,
> And little finches wave their wings in gold."
>
> Two delightful roads, that you would call dusty, supply me continually with coaches and chaises: barges as solemn as barons of the Exchequer move under my window; Richmond Hill and Ham Walks bound my prospect; but, thank God! the Thames is between me and the Duchess of Queensberry. Dowagers as plenty as flounders inhabit all around, and Pope's ghost is just now skimming under my window by a most poetical moonlight. I have about land enough to keep such a farm as Noah's, when he set up in the ark with a pair of each kind; but my cottage is rather cleaner than I believe his was after they had been cooped up together forty days. The Chenevixes had tricked it out for themselves: up two pair of stairs is what they call Mr Chenevix's library, furnished with three maps, one shelf, a bust of Sir Isaac Newton, and a lame telescope without any glasses. Lord Jack Sackville predecessed me here, and instituted certain games called cricketalia, which have been celebrated this very evening in honour of him in a neighbouring meadow.[2]

The scale of the original house must have been particularly appealing to Walpole if he compared it with his father's house, Houghton, which was one of the largest houses built in the eighteenth century. It stood in a good position for both views and ease of travel, bordered by the road running between London and Hampton Court on one side, and the river and road to Kingston on the other. He wrote in his *Short Notes Of My Life*:

> In May 1747, I took a small house near Twickenham for seven years. I afterwards bought it by Act of Parliament (it belonging to minors) and have made great additions and improvements to it. In one of the deeds I found it was called Strawberry Hill.

[1] Letter Horace Walpole to Horace Mann written from Arlington Street, 5 June 1747 (o.s.)

[2] Letter Horace Walpole to Henry Seymour Conway written from Twickenham, 8 June 1747 (o.s.). This includes a quotation from Alexander Pope's *Epistle to Mr. Addison occaisioned by his Dialogues on Medals.*

This first purchase was of five acres of land which were added to slowly over the best part of fifty years as land became available, until Walpole eventually owned about forty-six acres. It is probable that the pace of the acquisition of land partly determined the footprint of the evolving building. Walpole had to cope with the problems of buying new land as and where it came up for sale, and at the same time with the presence of the roads and the river. These confines only enhanced the final result: a structure that was as irregular in plan as it was innovative in design.

This was a period when gentlemen were taking an increasing interest in building and acting as their own architects. Walpole decided to adapt the original Chopp'd Straw Hall rather than demolish it and start afresh, and his first alterations created a balanced, symmetrical elevation to the south 'front'. He added a bay to the central part of the elevation

with an even arrangement of windows to either side. At this stage the house would have looked fairly classical and fashionable; what was different was the use made of gothic elements – quatrefoil windows, ogee door and window detailing, pinnacles to give the house a fairytale skyline, battlements around the roof – all elements usually reserved for grand buildings, but here used to enhance a tiny house. However, all was not what it appeared to be; Walpole chose to build a timber frame construction with a roughcast finish – to look like stone but lacking in permanence.

In creating an entrance from the lawn for those arriving by water, Walpole was forced to move the stair of the Chopp'd Straw Hall house to the space to the north, thus creating a separate hall with another entrance facing the main road. The house then had two entrances: the formal public approach from the road eventually made through a monastic

ABOVE *Strawberry Hill in the nineteenth century, engraving by Jeavons from a watercolour by Tombleson*

courtyard, and the less formal entrance into the Little Parlour, a room designed for summer supper-parties, by way of the river and the gardens.

Walpole designed both approaches to Strawberry Hill in a way which would create the greatest impact on visitors; he made use of the natural landscape and its relation to the house to heighten the effect. On the side facing the road views of the house were manipulated by the asymmetrical plan and by the careful positioning of trees to give those approaching a sense of the picturesque and of antiquity. By the time he had finished building, the trees masked much of the house and left both the Great Tower and the Beauclerc Tower visually cut off from the rest, although both were in fact part of the main building. The impression received on approaching the house for the first time was that the towers were gothic follies placed elsewhere in the grounds and not part of the house at all.

By the 1760s visitors arriving from the road would have entered through a gate into a cloistered monastic space. There they would immediately have been confronted by an oratory containing a bronze 'saint' and stoups for holy water, whilst to their right they could have glimpsed, through an intricate stone screen, a Prior's, or Priory Garden filled with sweet smelling herbs and flowers. By the side of the Oratory was the Little Cloister and two front doors – one a servants' entrance and the other for Horace Walpole's friends and guests (see plan on page 21). Above the doorway hung coats of arms and over the cloister there appeared to be lancet windows. However at Strawberry Hill it was unwise to make assumptions: with only one exception, these windows were blind, painted in *trompe l'œil* to look like gothic ogee windows. These blind windows were positioned to give the maximum impact of a medieval castle, but were painted on walls on the inside of which Walpole wanted to hang paintings in rooms where light was to be kept to a minimum. The courtyard can best be appreciated by remembering that Walpole was not an overtly religious man, so the cloister, oratory, stoups, screen and saint were all purely for drama and effect – designed to conjure up the right mood before visitors entered the Hall. Although the effect was gothic in the extreme, it was made inviting by a number of brightly coloured plants in pots.

A large china tub on a small plinth, which eventually was moved to the Great Cloister, was placed where it could be seen by everyone as they arrived. A notice was attached to it with the information that this was the famous tub in which Selima the cat had been drowned. This gothic event had been marked by a poem written by Thomas Gray destined to make Selima famous and Walpole's Chinese tub the best known tub in the country.

Selima had in fact drowned at Walpole's London house, but the tub was moved to Strawberry Hill where it could be seen by visitors as they arrived and where it would provoke questions and comments, even perhaps a smile. It also had a second purpose. It was the fashion to have fish and weed painted on the inside of china tubs so that the fish would appear to move when the tubs were filled with water; Walpole's real fish might have been placed in it to amuse, and confuse, his London friends. Like the tub each object in the house would have a history, a story to be told and wondered at.

Before setting out for Strawberry Hill visitors would have been aware of Walpole's rules for visiting. These were drawn up in detail, printed at the Strawberry Hill Press in large numbers and distributed through printshops and coffee houses or wherever people might gather. No one was denied access if they had applied for a ticket in the prescribed way, but if anyone turned up expecting to be shown around the house without having applied for tickets they would be turned away.

Each party was issued with a ticket, signed by Horace Walpole, which read: 'To Mr. Walpole's House-Keeper at Strawberry Hill. Any Day between twelve and three, you may, on their delivering this Ticket to you, show my House to the four following Persons.'[3]

Public tours were generally conducted by Margaret Young, who was Walpole's housekeeper throughout the second half of his life. After the visitors had been admitted she would have joined them in the Waiting Room which led off the garden. As well as establishing when and how the public was to be admitted, Walpole also defined exactly what they were to see, what his servants would relate, which rooms the visitors would be allowed in and which route they would follow. This was printed in *A Description of the Villa*, which was first published as a guide for his servants' use and evolved into one of the most interesting and influential books of the eighteenth century – an illustrated guidebook describing the house plan, the rooms, their

[3] Walpole, Horace, Collection of all the Loose Pieces printed at Strawberry Hill, 1757–1789, Lewis Walpole Library, Yale University, 49 2506

ODE ON THE DEATH OF A FAVOURITE CAT, DROWNED IN A TUB OF GOLD FISHES

'Twas on a lofty vase's side,
Where China's gayest art had dy'd
The azure flowers that blow;
Demurest of the tabby kind,
The pensive Selima, reclin'd,
Gazed on the lake below.

Her conscious tail her joy declar'd;
The fair round face, the snowy beard,
The velvet of her paws,
Her coat, that with the tortoise vies,
Her ears of jet, and emerald eyes,
She saw; and purr'd applause.

Still had she gaz'd: but 'midst the tide
Two angel forms were seen to glide,
The Genii of the stream:
Their scaly armour's Tyrian hue
Thro' richest purple to the view
Betry'd a golden gleam.

The hapless Nymph with wonder saw:
A whisker first and then a claw,
With many an ardent wish,
She stretch'd in vain to reach the prize.
What female heart can gold despise?
What Cat's averse to fish?

Presumptuous Maid! with looks intent
Again she stretch'd, again she bent,
Nor knew the gulf between.
(Malignant Fate sat by, and smil'd)
The slipp'ry verge her feet beguil'd,
She tumbled headlong in.

Eight times emerging from the flood
She mew'd to every wat'ry God,
Some speedy aid to send.
No Dolphin came, no Nereid stirr'd:
Nor cruel Tom, nor Susan heard.
A fav'rite has no friend!

From hence, ye Beauties, Undeceiv'd,
Know, one false step is ne'er retriev'd,
And be with caution bold.
Not all that tempts your wand'ring eyes
And heedless hearts, is lawful prize;
Nor all, that glisters, gold.

ABOVE *Illustration for Thomas Gray's 'Ode on the Death of a Favourite Cat', engraving from a drawing by Richard Bentley*

decorations, the choice of colours and furnishings, together with an account of the furniture, wallpaper, carpets, paintings, glass, ceramics and objects from the Collection. Later Walpole gave his reasons for deciding to publish in a Preface:

> It will look, I fear, a little like arrogance in a private Man to give a printed Description of his Villa and Collection, in which almost everything is diminutive. It is not, however, intended for public sale, and originally was meant only to assist those who should visit the place. A farther view succeeded; that of exhibiting specimens of Gothic architecture, as collected from standards in cathedrals and chapel-tombs, and shewing how they may be applied to chimney-pieces, cielings, windows, ballustrades, loggias, etc. The general disuse of Gothic architecture, and the decay and alterations so frequently made in churches, give prints a chance of being the sole preservatives of that style.[4]

For the most important or interesting objects, or those closest to his heart, Walpole specified from whom he had obtained them, which collections or sales they had formed part of, and their historic worth. Engravings were commissioned to be produced from existing watercolours of the house so that, on leaving at the end of the tour, the visitor could have a momento – like a modern postcard or photograph. What had started life as a guide for Margaret's use developed into a more detailed inventory, until finally Walpole had a document which listed the entire contents of Strawberry Hill and included the provenance of many of them. He kept the *Description* regularly updated, keeping track of objects as he moved them around the house. Today it allows the twenty-first-century reader to visit Strawberry Hill in the footsteps of the eighteenth-century traveller, subject to the same amazement, enjoying the same objects and hearing the same stories as Margaret would have told them when guiding them through the house.

> …Apropos to matrimony; I want to consult your Ladyship very seriously: I am so tormented by droves of people coming to see my house, and Margaret gets such sums of money by showing it, that I have a mind to marry her, and so repay myself that way for what I have flung away to make my house quite uncomfortable to me. …Good night, Madam; my poor rheumatic shoulder must go to bed.[5]

[4] Walpole, Horace, *A Description of the Villa of Mr. Horace Walpole at Strawberry-Hill near Twickenham, Middlesex,* Strawberry Hill, 1784

[5] Letter Horace Walpole to Lady Ossory written from Strawberry Hill, 4 August 1783

INSTRUCTIONS TO PERSONS WISHING TO VIEW THE VILLA AND ITS COLLECTIONS.

Mr. Walpole is very ready to oblige any curious Persons with the Sight of his House and Collection; but as it is situated so near to London and in so populous a Neighbourhood, and as he refuses a Ticket to nobody that sends for one, it is but reasonable that such Persons as send, should comply with the Rules he has been obliged to lay down for showing it.

• Any Person, sending a Day or two before, may have a Ticket for Four Persons for a Day certain.

• No ticket will serve but on the Day for which it is given. If more than Four Persons come with a Ticket, the Housekeeper has positive Orders to admit none of them.

• Every Ticket will admit the Company only between the Hours of Twelve and Three before Dinner, and only one Company will be admitted on the same Day.

• The House will never be shown after Dinner; nor at all but from the First of May to the First of October.

• As Mr. Walpole has given Offence by sometimes enlarging the Number of Four, and refusing that Latitude to others, he flatters himself that for the future nobody will take it ill that he strictly confines the Number; as whoever desires him to break his Rule, does in effect expect him to disoblige others, which is what nobody has a right to desire of him.

• Persons desiring a Ticket, may apply either to Strawberry-Hill, or to Mr. Walpole's in Berkeley-Square, London. If any Person does not make use of the Ticket, Mr. Walpole hopes he shall have Notice; otherwise he is prevented from obliging others on that Day, and thence is put to great Inconvenience.

• They who have Tickets are desired not to bring Children.

ABOVE *North Front of Strawberry Hill, engraving by Godfrey from a watercolour by Marlow*

BELOW *Ground floor plan showing the Housekeeper's route for tourists visiting Strawberry Hill*

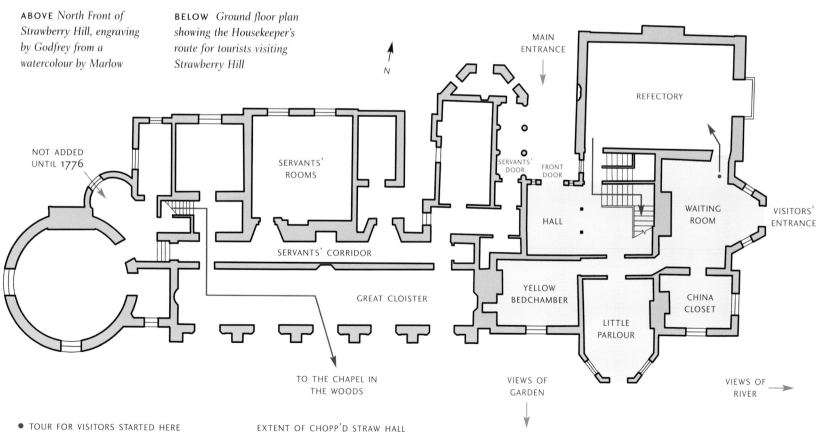

N

NOT ADDED UNTIL 1776

SERVANTS' ROOMS

SERVANTS' CORRIDOR

GREAT CLOISTER

MAIN ENTRANCE

SERVANTS' DOOR

FRONT DOOR

REFECTORY

HALL

WAITING ROOM

VISITORS' ENTRANCE

YELLOW BEDCHAMBER

LITTLE PARLOUR

CHINA CLOSET

TO THE CHAPEL IN THE WOODS

VIEWS OF GARDEN

VIEWS OF RIVER

● TOUR FOR VISITORS STARTED HERE   EXTENT OF CHOPP'D STRAW HALL

3 The Waiting Room, China Closet and Refectory

'Hoarding ideas for a future Strawberry'

OPPOSITE *Detail from*
The Three Ladies Waldegrave
(page 32)

[1] Victoria & Albert Museum
E. 558-1985

[2] The National Archives, Kew,
C101/20 p.11

[3] Gray, Thomas, 'Notes on
a tour through France and
Italy, 1739–1741, undertaken
in the years 1739–1741',
John Murray Archive

[4] Gray, Thomas, 'Journal of
the Grand Tour', Eton College
Library, ECL MS 413

[5] *The Letters of Thomas Gray*,
published by John Sharpe,
London, 1819

THE TICKET HOLDERS would have started their tour in the Waiting Room, '…a cool little hall where we generally dine, hung with paper to imitate Dutch tiles', as Walpole wrote to Horace Mann on 12 June 1753. Very little is known for certain about the room except that it had wallpaper of a small tile design in blue and white, enlivened by figures of Chinamen,[1] and that it contained a bust of the poet Dryden, from whom Walpole was descended on his mother's side. However after the death of Sir Robert Walpole in 1745 an inventory of his goods was drawn up, taking several years to complete, which listed both the general household goods and furnishings and the works of art which could be found in the various Walpolian houses.[2] One section of it is entitled 'carried to Strawberry Hill' and lists items of furniture which Horace Walpole must have found useful and used, at least at first, to furnish Strawberry Hill; later they may have been replaced. It is possible that the 'Two black Leather Settees, Seven Chairs Ditto' which are included in the inventory were placed in the Waiting Room. Robert Walpole appears to have furnished each Walpolian Waiting Room where he received tenants with black leather furniture; it would have been practical, hard wearing and would not have marked easily.

As Walpole's 'Rules for Visiting the House' stated quite clearly that visitors should not arrive before twelve noon and were expected to leave by three, it can be presumed that they arrived quite promptly. While they waited to start the tour with the housekeeper they would have been permitted, even encouraged perhaps, to peek into the China Closet and feast their eyes on the treasures within, but not to enter, because Walpole was terrified that some of his beloved ceramics might be broken by over enthusiastic visitors. The sight of the ceramics was expected to whet the appetite. The China Closet and the Waiting Room were linked thematically through pieces of Chinese porcelain on display and the use of the chinoiserie style tile-wallpaper design in the Waiting Room. The Closet was a tiny room and by looking into it the visitors first encountered two important design ideas used throughout Strawberry Hill. Both of them – the use of *trompe l'œil* and the concept of framing a view – stemmed from Walpole's memories of his Grand Tour.

Walpole and Gray recorded many of the experiences of their Tour. Walpole in the letters he wrote home to friends and Gray in a meticulously kept journal,[3] watercolours[4] and letters[5] to his mother. Gray did not comment on the interiors of the buildings they had visited in detail, but concentrated instead on the pictures, sculptures and objects they had seen. In so doing he was following the advice of the guidebook he had taken with him, which had been written by Jonathan Richardson and was intended for the young aristocrat, or

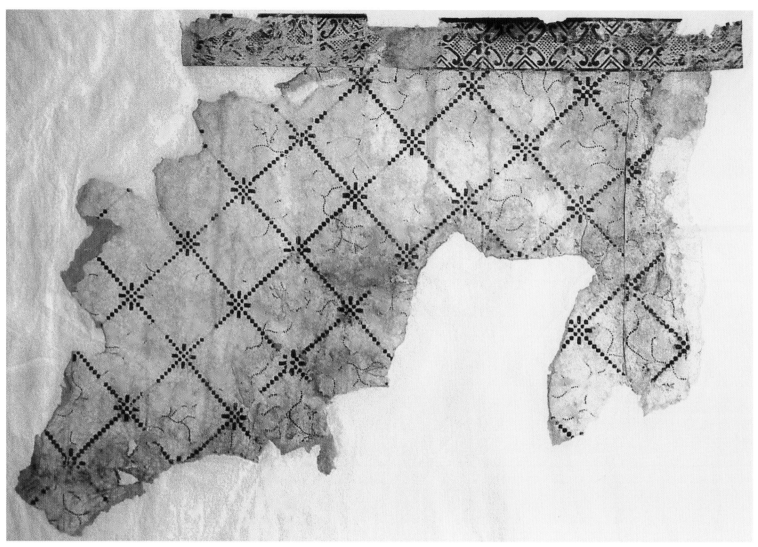

ABOVE *Fragment of eighteenth-century wallpaper found on the second floor of Strawberry Hill and similar to one hung in the China Closet. Each square is approximately two and a half inches wide*

[6] Richardson, Jonathan, *An Account of some of the statues, bas-reliefs, drawings, and pictures, in Italy, &c.,* London, 1722

[7] The National Archives, Kew, C101/20 p.29

[8] Gray, Thomas, 'Notes on a tour through France and Italy, 1739–1741, undertaken in the years 1739–1741', John Murray Archive

gentleman of leisure making the Grand Tour as the culmination of his education;[6] the guidebook would almost certainly have been known by Walpole as a copy was in his father's library.[7] Little space was given in Richardson's guide to plans of palaces or churches, nor was their decoration described, instead it listed the most important works of art in each city and the objects not to be missed by the visitor. Gray followed this guide and then encapsulated each city in his journal by noting its atmosphere and the way in which that had been achieved through its architecture and gardens. Much of what Gray described is reflected in Walpole's achievements at Strawberry Hill.

In his journal Gray described the approach to Genoa: 'Next the streets runs a row of marble columns of a regular order; between 'em are Statues Or Orange trees placed, & on them rests a frame of trellis-work, which is cover'd with vines or jessamine; these have a noble effect'.[8] On the lawn outside the China Closet and the Little Parlour

(the next door room) Walpole built a trellis-work screen against which he placed a row of orange trees in pots. Gray continued his description of a gallery they had visited with: 'another appointed arch that discovers to you either the gardens behind, or a Nich with a Statue, & Fountain; or some piece of painting in perspective to represent one or the other'. In the search for the sources that went into the making of Strawberry Hill, Gray's journals provide glimpses of vistas they had seen or memorable details which had been stored away and unearthed for use later; for what Gray wrote about Walpole would also have seen.

Memories of their visits to sixteenth-century villas around Rome were also squirrelled away by Walpole. He was especially interested in *trompe l'œil* and the way in which architectural elements could frame the views either inside or outside the house. What they had seen together and what influenced Walpole can still be seen today in any visit to Italian villas; *trompe l'œil* was used to bring the exterior –

gardens, birds, fountains, sea or sky – into the interior, an effect which married the two spaces and focused the attention of the visitor. Almost all the villa interiors visited by the two young men would have been decorated with frescoes in this way, although Richardson refers to very few examples in his guide:

> the larger picture is carry'd up above the top of the Frize being painted upon the turning of the Arch of the Vault; (for the ceiling is Such; 'tis flat but rais'd from the Side and End walls Archwise) And so much of these Pictures as is so rais'd inclos'd in a Cornish painted; and so contriv'd in Perspective as if one saw beyond into some farther Building.

With this 'contriv'd in perspective' Richardson draws our attention to the use of *trompe l'œil* and the framed distant and imagined view.

Trompe l'œil was used in the painting of the architectural wallpaper at Strawberry Hill, most notably in the Hall, and in the painting of the faux windows of the Long Gallery facing the road before the addition of the Great North Bedchamber. However the most striking example must have been the ceiling of the China Closet painted by Müntz, a Swiss artist, in 1758 or 1759, to resemble convolvulus flowers on poles. This decoration no longer exists but we have Walpole's description written to his friend Horace Mann on 27 January 1761:

> Three years ago I had the ceiling of my china room painted from one I had observed in the little Borghese Villa. I was hoarding ideas for a future Strawberry even in those days of giddiness, when I seemed to attend to nothing.

He had obviously been impressed by the ceiling in Italy and stored away the memory to use the idea almost twenty years later on the banks of the Thames: it must have looked wonderful. However, the mystery of its exact provenance remains unsolved and this is one of the many occasions when the visitor to the house, or the reader of Walpole's correspondence, can play detective. Which Borghese villa was it that provided the inspiration and does that villa's ceiling still exist?

Extensive use was made of *trompe l'œil* in the Italian villas visited by Walpole. In areas where china or plate were stored or displayed it was used to enhance the special relationship between the interior of the villa and alfresco dining. A fresco in the Palazzo del Te by Giulio Romano represents an alfresco credenza complete with an arched trellis of vines,[9] while in the covered loggia of the Farnesina in Rome Raphael painted awnings on the ceiling to make it appear open to the sky. The fresco copied the use of real awnings, hung over open loggias or enclosed courtyards where supper parties would have been held. Poorly lit rooms had trellises painted on their walls with flowered pergolas linking them to the surrounding garden, and in the Villa d'Este at Tivoli the walls were painted to enhance the views to the gardens beyond. Landscapes were even sometimes continued around the windows so that the interior landscape would merge with the real landscape of the garden or courtyard outside. Thomas Gray described doors to a small room in the Palazzo Corsini that had been painted 'on one side with views of ruins, and little figures' and with 'landscape on the other'.[10] There was no beginning and no ending, all was harmony and fun.

Apart from the painted interior decoration the architectural elements of the buildings were also carefully planned to frame the important views of the garden or landscape; at the Ducal Palace at Urbino brick battlements had been pierced with arches to frame views of the surrounding countryside. Gardens were designed with consideration for the views of the villa or palace from the garden as well as to how the garden might be viewed from within. The framing of views by the use of planting, or through windows, doorways or arches would direct the eye as well as enhance a feeling of mystery or discovery of what lay beyond. It was a theatrical use of architecture and landscape.

At Strawberry Hill Walpole used all these ideas. He used internal decoration to reflect the exterior views by hanging landscape and seascape paintings to mirror the garden and river views and to give an illusion that these paintings were windows on to the scenes outside. He also made use of planned vistas throughout the house to direct the eyes of visitors towards particular objects in his Collection and to orchestrate changes of mood. He had admitted to 'hoarding ideas'. The Grand Tour had excited him and it had opened up the possibility of 'painting' a house with light, using colour and idiosyncratic design details in building and decoration to create a mood: it had given him the idea of having fun and using his own creativity, not leaving all to a builder or architect.

[9] Strong, Roy, *Feast, A History of Grand Eating*, Pimlico, London, 2003

[10] Gray, Thomas, 'Notes on a tour through France and Italy, 1739–1741, undertaken in the years 1739–1741', John Murray Archive

The effect was recorded by Mary Hamilton in her Journal:

June 21st, 1784 (longest day): at half-past twelve I set out with Mr and Mrs Vesey for Strawberry Hill. …Mr Walpole was so obliging to take us through most of the rooms and opened the cabinets (which are not opened to the company who come to see

the house), which contain miniatures and various fine and curious things both modern and antique, …the whole style of this house is true Gothic, every room, boudoir, closet, gallery, etc. has painted glass windows, it is the most perfect thing of the kind in England I believe I may say in Europe. One ought to live in this house at least a month to see everything. It is filled with virtu. …At four o'clock we went down to dinner which was a very elegant one, incomparably well served; it showed the master of the house was a man of fortune and taste, accustomed to elegancies. …Mr Walpole carried us to a china closet filled with modern and old china…[11]

What would Mary Hamilton have seen in this tiny room little bigger than a cupboard, its content close to Walpole's heart? First, it was bursting at the seams – in fact, so much was stacked inside that 149 pieces would not fit in and had to be stacked outside in the Waiting Room; second, almost everything had a story attached to it. Some of the ceramics were family pieces which had been owned by the Walpole family in their Arlington Street house, including a 'square Dish with a Cock and Hen' and a 'white Ribb'd Tea Pot'.[12]

Six hundred and eighty-two pieces of porcelain, pottery and glass jostled for position against a background of terracotta floor tiles, white tiled walls with blue and white borders and the convolvulus painted ceiling. It would have been impossible to separate many of the individual pieces, but the overall effect would have been a feeling of rich texture. The only place where decoration would have been possible was the ceiling where the painted trellis of flowers opening to an imaginary sky would have lightened the space and completed the illusion of an Italian credenza. Light entered through a lancet window of painted glass which highlighted the chimneypiece, one of many in the house copied from gothic sources – this one modelled after a chimney at Hurstmonceaux, but with an extraordinary detail above resembling another window, in which a niche had been built. The chimney was painted and gilded and displayed the coats of arms of the prominent owners of the earlier Chopp'd Straw Hall; to these Walpole's own arms were added. Strawberry Hill was to be his 'seat'.

On top of the chimney, given pride of place and standing within the niche, stood a Saint-Porchaire ewer. It was Walpole's most important ceramic piece, a luxurious object demonstrating his desire to own rare and exciting objects which defined both his discrimination and his heritage. The sixteenth-century faience ewer stood about thirteen and a half inches high, richly decorated in an arabesque pattern, the handle in the form of a bare-chested man while the lip of the ewer portrayed a grotesque. The blue and green decoration of the enamel panels were probably applied using the same technique as that used for medieval tiles where clay slip was poured into a mould of a different coloured clay.[13] Walpole believed it to have been designed by Giulio Romano and the room around it must have been evocative of one of Romano's frescoes. The China Closet spoke of Italy.

Although other individual objects might have been important (and Walpole no doubt pointed out specific items to his friends), for the general public it was the display as a whole, the vast number of pieces and the overall impression created, that was paramount. The room, crammed with china and ceramics, was shown as a 'cabinet' representing the house, which would in turn itself be seen as a cabinet of curiosities for Walpole's many and varied collections: this was just the first of them. Walpole was stage managing his Collection. The display static, set up with fixed viewpoint from the door at one end, forced the visitor to look sideways into the room from which position the size of the Collection would have been astounding.

It has to be remembered that European china production was still in its infancy and the modernity of some pieces in the Collection therefore remarkable. The Meissen factory had only discovered the secret of its manufacture at the beginning of the eighteenth century; Walpole had many examples of Meissen which he called 'Saxon ware'. One piece is described by him in detail: 'A boy supporting a shell, finely modelled in red earth; the first sort of Saxon china before it was glazed or painted, and which was only given as presents by the elector: extremely rare'.

In England the Chelsea factory produced identifiable pieces from the 1740s onwards, specialising in figurines and shell-salts decorated with crayfish, modelled after earlier silver designs. Its trade card advertised: 'A Variety of Services for Tea, Coffee, Chocolate, Porringers, Sauce-Boats, Basons, Ewers, Ice-Pails, Terreens, Dishes and Plates of different Forms and Patterns, and of a great

Variety of pieces for Ornament in a Taste entirely new'. Walpole owned 'Two white saltsellers with crawfish in relief, of Chelsea china'. Patronised, as it was, by Queen Charlotte, Chelsea was the most fashionable English factory and it set the standard for the other manufacturers. It was, with Wedgwood, the English company most favoured by Walpole, although he continually also bought examples from other factories. Several pieces of china were probably kept in the Closet because of their interesting histories or because they had a connection to his friends, 'Twelve plates of Wedgwood's ware, with cameos of lady Diana Beauclerc'; he was to name one of the towers at Strawberry Hill after Diana. Many pieces of Sèvres

[11] For this and all subsequent extracts from this journal see Lewis, W.S., ed., The Yale Edition of Horace Walpole's Correspondence, Yale University Press, New Haven, 1937–83

[12] The National Archives, Kew, C101/20 p.28

[13] Coutts, Howard, 'Saint-Porchaire Ceramics', article ed. by Barbar, Daphne and Sturman, Shelley, National Gallery of Art, Washington, Hanover and London

BELOW *Late eighteenth-century ceramic biscuit figure*

BELOW RIGHT *Seventeenth-century tulip vase*

were bought by him on trips to Paris, although the grandest of these French pieces were displayed elsewhere, with only those for which no space was available housed in the China Closet. In old age Walpole added a handwritten note in his copy of *The Description* which simply said, 'More French Porcelain'. Was he tired of keeping individual records of his purchases or had he simply bought too much?

Almost all of the china in the closet was domestic and made for use, rather than figurines which were popular at the time, but which Walpole rarely bought. Large numbers of ceramic figures were produced as decorations to embellish the eighteenth-century dessert table. This practice so annoyed Walpole that in February 1753 he wrote a scathing article on their production and use, published in *The World*:

> The last branch of our fashions into which the close observation of nature has been introduced, is our desserts; …I see them a little in the light of a pantomime. Jellies, biscuits, sugar-plums and creams have long given way to harlequins, gondoliers, Turks, Chinese, and Shepherdesses of Saxon

china. But these, unconnected, and only seeming to wander among groves of curled paper and silk flowers, were soon discovered to be too insipid and unmeaning. By degrees whole meadows of cattle, of the same brittle materials, spread themselves over the whole table; cottages rose in sugar, and temples in barley-sugar; pigmy Neptunes in cars of cockle-shells triumphed over oceans of looking-glass, or seas of silver tissue; …Confectioners found their trade moulder away, while toymen and china shops were the only fashionable purveyors of the last stage of polite entertainments. Women of the first quality come home from Chenevix's laden with dolls and babies, not for their children, but their house keeper. …It is known that a celebrated confectioner (so the architects of our desserts still humbly call themselves) complained, that having prepared a middle dish of gods and goddesses eighteen feet high, his lord would not cause the ceiling of his parlour to be demolished to facilitate their entrée….[14]

The soft biscuit figures produced by both English and continental factories were placed among sweetmeats on the table where in candle-light it was difficult to tell which pieces were made of sugar and therefore edible, and which of porcelain. The fashion for having china moulded to resemble other objects soon spread to tureens and dishes shaped like bunches of asparagus or cabbages; these too Walpole eschewed.

As a man of the Enlightenment Walpole bought pieces of porcelain and examples of ceramics from around the world, building a representative Collection. It was this fact which was noticed by Mary Hamilton when she commented that the Closet was filled with both 'modern and old china'. In this way it was demonstrated in this small room, at the start of any visit to Strawberry Hill, that Horace Walpole was a cultured man, a collector of fine and interesting objects. The atmosphere was set for the rest of the tour. The visitor was ready to be entertained and amazed; the stage was set.

Tucked away in the far corner of the Waiting Room stood a narrow gothic door, possibly normally used as the servants' entrance to the Refectory or Great Parlour. After looking at the diminutive China Closet crammed with objects, the visitors next followed the housekeeper through this door into a cavernous space. The walls were painted to resemble

[14] Walpole, Horace, *Complete Works*, London, 1798

[15] Unpublished research, Dr Michael Peover

stucco and there was black furniture ranged around them, but otherwise the room was sparsely furnished. The contrast would have been dramatic and increased the element of surprise. It was the start of a sophisticated approach to interior design.

The Refectory, along with the Library on the first floor immediately above, formed part of a new two-storey wing completed in 1754. In keeping with normal eighteenth-century practice it was furnished as a parlour with the tables for dining only brought in by servants when they were needed. When completed it exemplified Walpole's desire to have a house which was gothic, yet at the same time fashionable and comfortable. He wrote in the Preface to his *Description*: '…In truth, I did not mean to make my house so Gothic as to exclude convenience, and modern refinements in luxury. The designs of the inside and outside are strictly ancient, but the decorations are modern.'

Two of Walpole's friends were members, with him, of a design committee which he had set up to rule on the inclusion or exclusion of objects for Strawberry Hill. One of them, Richard Bentley, provided the design for the gothic chimneypiece which stood in the centre of the longest wall of the room with settees flanking it which might have come from Sir Robert's Arlington Street house. In summer these were dressed in newly fashionable pink gingham case-covers, probably of a hard-wearing material. For the rest of the year, without the gingham, this was a dark, totally colourless room, lit by a simple gothic window (later altered to a bay) which had painted glass panes at the top. Most of the panes showed scenes of eating and drinking thus making a visual pun on the purpose of the room;[15] a few depicted religious scenes perhaps chosen to recall the biblical readings which would have taken place during meals in a true monastic refectory.

ABOVE *Parlour [Great Parlour or Refectory] at Strawberry Hill, watercolour, courtesy of the Lewis Walpole Library, Yale University. Reynolds' painting of The Three Ladies Waldegrave can be seen on the right above the chairs designed by Walpole and Bentley*

The cornice or frieze of the room had caused problems for the workmen in 1754. They had misunderstood, or never been told, what was meant by 'gothic'. Walpole had intended to make use of a design he had seen at Wroxton: '…The chapel is new, but in a pretty Gothic taste, with a very long window of painted glass, very tolerable. The frieze is pendent, just in the manner I propose for the eating-room at Strawberry Hill'.[16] In a letter written a few months later he expresses exasperation: 'The last time I went to Strawberry, I found the stucco men as busy as so many Irish bees, plastering up eggs and anchors for the frieze of the eating-room, but I soon made them destroy all they had done…'[17]

Walpole finally achieved a perfect marriage between the overall design of the room and the gothic furniture designed for it. A set of eight black chairs, with 'matted bottoms', which were designed by Bentley and Walpole together and made by William Hallett, were ranged against the walls. Their carved backs, based on the fretwork of gothic church windows, repeated the design which could be seen in the top of the Refectory window and also reflected, with only modest changes, the side panels of the chimney. The repetition gave the design harmony and integrity. This was also cutting-edge design – with the chairs, as the focal point of the room, determining the architectural detail. A table, also black and gothic and again designed by Bentley, stood against the far wall. The chair backs, with their gothic window tracery, would have thrown huge black shadows of lancet windows on to the stucco-papered wall when light fell on them from the window. The papered wall itself increased

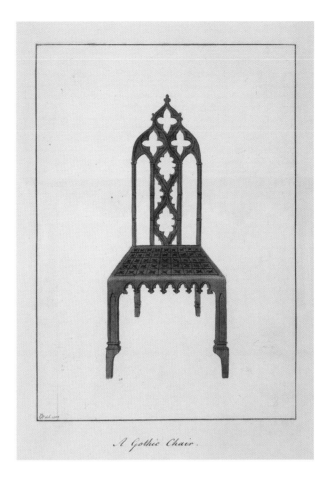

A Gothic Chair.

LEFT *A Gothic Chair designed for the Refectory by Richard Bentley and Horace Walpole, watercolour, courtesy of the Lewis Walpole Library, Yale University*

BELOW *A Gothic Table designed for the Refectory by Richard Bentley, watercolour, courtesy of the Lewis Walpole Library, Yale University*

A Gothic Table.

[16] Letter Horace Walpole to John Chute, 4 August 1753

[17] Letter Horace Walpole to John Chute written from Arlington Street, 30 April 1754

the unusual effect of the design, and doubtless provoked discussion. To further emphasise both the paper and the chairs, the dado rail of the room was built just at chair-seat height. Its low position would have made both the chairs and the room itself appear loftier while at the same time ensuring that any shadows on the walls created the greatest possible impact. This room is very special in the history of design. The manipulation of light here was similar to the use made of *trompe l'œil* elsewhere in the house.

Apart from Bentley's ultramodern furniture there were contemporary pieces acquired by Walpole equally deserving of comment: a Louis XV gilt-bronze and ebony mantel-clock, made in about 1766, with a movement by the great French clock-maker Julien Le Roy, stood upon a black-japanned bureau. The decoration of the clock-case was in the fashionable French style. It had been bought by Walpole on a trip to Paris in about 1766 as part of his winnings from a lucky lottery ticket. Above the clock

hung a Joshua Reynolds painting of Walpole's nieces 'The Three Ladies Waldegrave', with the black gothic chairs flanking it on either side. Right and left of the window hung two pier glasses in black and gold frames designed by Walpole. Even small objects placed around the room were devoid of colour: the design on a hunting-horn was shown in relief and a bottle was noted as 'white'.

It was traditional for great parlours to be hung with family portraits and more paintings by Reynolds and other artists hung around the room, almost all of them portraits of Walpole's friends or family. A Reynolds conversation piece of Walpole's three great friends, Dick Edgcumbe, Gilly Williams and George Selwyn, painted sitting in the Library of Strawberry Hill hung over the chimneypiece. These portraits were full of colour and seen against the black wood furniture would have seemed to people the room. The family could be seen as inheritors of the past, with Walpole himself a patron of both the arts and of modern design.

Joshua Reynolds was one of the artists he patronised. Reynolds was a few years younger than Walpole and a pupil of Thomas Hudson, whose work also hung at Strawberry Hill and who was a neighbour in Twickenham. Walpole sat to Reynolds in 1756 for a portrait which he intended as a gift for his illegitimate half-sister Mary, of whom he was fond. It was engraved and produced as a mezzotint by McArdell the following year. Walpole had ordered a 'private plate'; that is, one in which all of the impressions belonged to the sitter to be given as gifts or mementoes to friends, and were not for general sale. He was annoyed that Society got wind of the engraving and wrote a terse and angry note to McArdell ordering him to secure the impressions. Reynolds was paid forty-eight guineas for the portrait, the fee to include painting a copy which was despatched to Walpole's cousin, Francis Seymour Conway. In these portraits he chose to be painted both as a writer – holding a quill – and also as a connoisseur and collector – standing

beside an illustration of an engraving of one of his most precious objects, an ancient marble eagle found at the site of the Roman Baths of Caracalla in Rome.

Walpole favoured portraits at Strawberry Hill above other, more heroic, paintings and Reynolds may well have been chosen because he had the ability to endow his sitters with the ambience and heroic attitudes normally only found in history painting. In his ability to bring sitters of the eighteenth century to high fashion, while at the same time recalling the best of previous ages, he was close to Walpole's heart.

The last piece of furniture the visitors passed on following the housekeeper out of the room was Richard Bentley's strange black-framed jasper table with twisty legs and gothic points. A gothic design was carved on the frieze of the table and on entering the Hall the visitors would have found themselves in a space which was painted throughout with the same design as that found on the table.

4 The Hall, Staircase and Armoury

'The most particular and chief beauty'

OPPOSITE *The Staircase and Armoury at Strawberry Hill, engraving by Newton after a watercolour by Edward Edwards. The armour credited by Walpole as belonging to Francis I can be seen upper left*

VISITORS WITH TICKETS would have left the Refectory and been taken by the housekeeper up one flight of stairs and into the Blue Breakfast Room on the floor above. Up a second flight of stairs stood the Armoury, from which vantage point they would later view the Hall. Only those of Walpole's friends whom he showed around his castle himself would have seen, or more likely been invited to use, the other ground floor rooms which were kept as private apartments: the Hall, the Little Parlour and the Yellow Bedchamber.

The Hall, with its front door through which only personal friends would have entered, and its myriad of small doors, was one of the great focal points of Strawberry Hill, rising like a tower through the two, and in places three, storeys of the castle to the uppermost point where four grisaille quatrefoil glass panels were set in the roof. At night it was lit by a single candle in a japanned lantern suspended by a yellow and black cord from the central rose of the ceiling. This cast little light because the flame was shielded by an array of early glass. Illuminated by the candle were six doorways on the ground floor in addition to the front door. They were set within two minute, shadowy corridors, suggesting a mystery which in reality was non-existent: two of the doors were for service and storage and the others led to the Waiting Room, the Little Parlour, the Refectory and the Yellow Bedchamber. No

furniture of note dressed the Hall and it must have presented a surprising, almost shocking, image of welcome to the average Georgian guest as they entered through the front door.

The Hall was designed to be seen as an architectural space which would impart the mood of an earlier age. It offered a taster of what would be found in the other rooms of Strawberry Hill and it presented Horace Walpole both as an antiquarian and as an innovator; it linked the medieval castle and the past with new techniques and craftsmanship.

The walls were decorated in wallpaper which had been designed by Richard Bentley and copied from an engraving of Prince Arthur's chantry tomb in Worcester Cathedral. The use of wallpaper was not new but still infrequent enough to be seen as innovative, the more so because the tomb, and therefore the wallpaper itself, was of gothic design. It was partially the success of the Strawberry Hill Hall which led to the production and popularity of gothic wallpapers in other houses. Walpole described the effect to his friend in Florence:

> ...under two gloomy arches, you come to the hall and staircase, which it is impossible to describe to you, as it is the most particular and chief beauty of the castle. Imagine the walls covered with (I call it paper, but it is really paper painted in perspective to represent) Gothic fretwork: the lightest Gothic

ABOVE *Two fragments of wallpaper, 1791, painted by Cornelius Dixon of Norwich and discovered in the Hall at Strawberry Hill. The top fragment is about 18 by 11 inches*

[1] Letter Horace Walpole to Horace Mann written from Strawberry Hill, 12 June 1753

[2] Letter Thomas Gray to Thomas Wharton, 8 September 1761

[3] Letter Thomas Gray to Thomas Wharton, 22 October 1761

balustrade to the staircase, adorned with antelopes (our supporters) bearing shields; lean windows fattened with rich saints in painted glass, and a vestibule open with three arches on the landing place, and niches full of trophies of old coats of mail, Indian shields made of rhinoceros's hides, broadswords, quivers, long bows, arrows and spears – all supposed to be taken by Sir Terry Robsart in the holy wars.[1]

In 1753 the paper and the balustrade were both painted grey or stone colour, a shade which was inexpensive and did not discolour, but the task of finding a paper had presented Walpole's Committee of Taste with a problem. No gothic paper was available at the upholsterer's from whom Walpole normally purchased wallpaper. Later when Thomas Gray searched London for suitable wallpaper on behalf of a friend, he too could find no gothic paper for sale anywhere in the metropolis. The solution

chosen by Walpole in 1753 was to follow an established custom of the period and to buy blank, unpainted paper from Thomas Bromwich (whose company was at the Sign of the Golden Lyon on Ludgate Hill, and who was already supplying other wallpapers for Strawberry Hill) and then to have it painted to his own design by a paper-stainer; the paper-stainer chosen by Bromwich to replicate the tracery of Henry VIII's brother's tomb on the walls of Strawberry Hill, was named Tudor, which suggests Bromwich had a sense of humour.

It was not unusual to ask for a design to be made to order rather than buy a wallpaper off the shelf and there was a choice of either having it hand painted or of getting a special wallpaper block produced from the owner's design. The practice is recorded by Thomas Gray on a visit to Thomas Bromwich a few years later:

…I own I never yet saw any Gothic papers to my fancy. There is one fault, that is in the nature of the thing, and cannot be avoided. The great beauty of all Gothick designs is the variety of perspectives they occasion. This a Painter may represent on the walls of a room in some measure; but not a Designer of Papers, where, what is represented on one breadth, must be exactly repeated on another, both in the light & shade, and in the dimensions.[2]

In a few weeks he wrote again advocating the use of two famous books of engravings:

…if nothing there suits you, chuse in Dart's Canterbury, or Dugdale's Warwickshire, etc. & send the design hither. They will execute it here, and make a new stamp on purpose, provided you will take 20 pieces of it, & it will come to 1/2d or a penny a yard the more.[3]

Whenever a new design was required by a client London could provide the tradesmen needed to carve the blocks. Many of them were already employed carving patterns and then printing them on fabric for a busy market; London workmanship was unsurpassed. It was common practice for a pattern, even a complicated one, to be cut into a block, with the carver further embellishing the design by the insertion of rows or patterns of small brass pins or pegs. However, their design skills often lagged behind their carving ability.

The paper which they used was both durable and pliable, made from rags which sometimes came from

as far afield as America. The manufacturing process required a ready supply of water, which was one reason for the trade to grow up around London where Thames water could be used in the process and where roads, canals and the Thames itself made for easy transportation. The picking, sorting and cutting of the rags into strips was hazardous both because the rags often harboured disease and because lime was added to speed the pulpmaking process. The job was frequently assigned to women. The paper pulp was then cast into sheets of about 22 inches by 24 inches which had to be glued together to form lengths of wallpaper before being fixed to the wall. The paper-stainer was a highly skilled craftsman who had served an apprenticeship of at least seven years. His work followed after that of the block carver. Once engaged by a client he would not only print or paint the wallpaper but might also 'hang' it, a term which remains in use.

Battens were fixed to the top, bottom and sides of the wall and hessian or lining textile was fixed to the battens; this roughly followed the technique of hanging a piece of textile or tapestry. The textile absorbed irregularities in the plasterwork and the lengths of block printed or blank paper were attached to it. The batten was then covered with a decorative border. Cheap papers were frequently stuck directly to the wall, but better quality papers were normally properly hung. Each piece of paper was individually taxed, but somehow Horace Walpole managed to evade the duty, paying no tax on any piece of paper yet found at Strawberry Hill.

Walpole enjoyed coining and using unusual words and would refer to the quirky irregularities of space in Strawberry Hill as 'sharawaggi' (Chinese want of symmetry). There was no way in which regular blocks could be used to produce a wallpaper which would be both true to a design of the chantry

ABOVE *The Hall balustrade, designed by Richard Bentley and inspired by the Rouen Cathedral library staircase*

tomb, and at the same time could fill the walls, corners and angles of the Hall and Armoury.

At Strawberry Hill, Tudor the paper-stainer, working under the direction of Richard Bentley, added lowlights to give the design the appearance in *trompe l'oeil* of a genuine medieval tomb. The effect was further enhanced by the general low light level of the Hall and by the use of genuine medieval hexagonal tiles of rich terracotta on the floor; the tiles had been 'rescued' by Walpole from Gloucester Cathedral. The use of genuine old tiles abutting the *trompe l'oeil* walls imparted an increased appearance of reality. The use of *trompe l'oeil* by Walpole suggests a desire for economy, the need for speedy completion and a sense of fun.

To further enhance the effect a wooden balustrade was built, but painted to resemble stone, with an antelope carved from lime wood, once again painted in stone colour, adorning each newel post.The design element used on the balustrade was roughly based on one from Rouen Cathedral, but the chosen motif was artistically and fancifully applied to the Strawberry Hill staircase. Instead of simply repeating the design in a scale that could be multiplied to suit each landing, every element was stretched or condensed to fit its space; twisted to accommodate the stair-rise and then stretched and splayed out to be seen to great advantage on the uppermost landing. Later Bentley reused his design

as part of the decoration to the chimneypiece in the Holbein chamber, where it was once again manipulated and adapted to suit a particular position. It is precisely this playfulness in the way in which elements of design are used in the house which gives Strawberry Hill its special character, its lack of predictable order, its 'serendipity'. Walpole coined this word when writing the story, *The Three Princes of Serendip*, and its definition has come down to us as 'the ability to make happy and unexpected discoveries purely by accident' – which is what happens throughout Strawberry Hill. Nothing is what it first appears to be – timber and wallpaper replicate stone – and there is always a surprise through the next doorway or down the next short passage.

Very soon after completing the Hall Walpole commenced a round of country house visiting and went to Worcester Cathedral to see the building itself, complete with the tomb which had been used as a source. A letter was dispatched to Richard Bentley in September 1753 which highlights the problems experienced by the Committee of Taste in using seventeenth-century engravings as design sources: '...Prince Arthur's tomb, from whence we took the paper for the hall and staircase, to my great surprise, is on a less scale than the paper, and is not of brass but stone, and that wretchedly white washed...'

The realism of the stone-painted paper was enhanced by painted glass set either side of the front door. The glass was of two saints, which both added to the gloom by filtering light, and increased the medieval imagery. The glass suffered badly in 1772 and Walpole wrote to his cousin describing the accident at Strawberry Hill:[4]

Late Strawberry Hill, January 7, 1772
You have read of my calamity without knowing it, and will pity me when you do. I have been blown up; my castle is blown up; Guy Fawkes has been about my house; and the fifth of November has fallen on the sixth of January! In short, nine thousand powder-mills broke loose yesterday morning on Hounslow-heath; a whole squadron of them came thither, and have broken eight of my painted glass windows; and the north side of the castle looks as if it had stood a siege. The two saints in the hall have suffered martyrdom! they have had their bodies cut off, and nothing remains but their heads. The

two next great sufferers are indeed two of the least valuable, being the passage windows to the library and great parlour – a fine pane is demolished in the Round Room; and the window by the Gallery is damaged. Those in the Cabinet, and Holbein Room, and Gallery, and Blue Room, and Green Closet, etc. have escaped. As the storm came from the northwest, the China Closet was not touched, nor a cup fell down. The bow-window of brave old coloured glass, at Mr Hindley's, is massacred; and all the north sides of Twickenham and Brentford are shattered. At London it was proclaimed an earthquake, and half the inhabitants ran into the street.[4]

Although there were many explosions from the powder mills on Hounslow Heath, this particular one, in which three storage mills were ignited, produced shock waves which were recorded in Gloucester. The explosion had a significant effect upon the Strawberry Hill household, as described by Walpole to Lady Ossory when he returned to his Arlington Street house the following day:

Well! Madam, I am returned from my poor shattered castle; and never did it look so Gothic in its born days. You would swear it had been besieged by the Presbyterians in the civil wars, and that finding it impregnable, they had vented their holy malice on the painted glass. As this gunpowder-army passed on, it demolished Mr Hindley's fine bow-window of ancient Scripture histories; and only because your Ladyship is my ally, broke the large window over your door, and wrenched off a lock in your kitchen. Margaret sits by the waters of Babylon, and weeps over Jerusalem. I shall pity those she shows the house to next summer, for her story is as long and deplorable as a chapter of casualties in Baker's 'Chronicle'– yet she was not taken quite unprepared, for one of the bantam hens crowed on Sunday morning, and the chandler's wife told her three weeks ago when the barn was blown down, that ill luck never comes single. She is however very thankful that the China-Room has escaped, and says, God has always been the best creature in the world to her. I dare not tell her how many churches I propose to rob, to repair my losses.

The stairs were built wide and shallow, ideal for Walpole who had regular and severe bouts of gout. By moving the stairs when he first bought the house from their original position on the site of what became his Little Parlour, to the new hallway, a tower had been created which linked the early three-storey part of the house with the new two-storey Library and Refectory wing. Thus a variety of shadowy levels were created which exuded Walpole's 'gloomth' – a word he coined to describe the unique Strawberry Hill mixture of warmth and gloom, which together were intended to induce horror. On the flight of stairs leading to the Library Walpole gathered together an Armoury of mainly eighteenth-century weaponry; swords, shields and all the accoutrements of war displayed ready for use should Strawberry Castle be attacked. In a niche he stood a magnificent suit of armour, which had supposedly been fashioned by the great Italian gold and silversmith, Benvenuto Cellini for Francis I. So pleased was Walpole with the armour that he

BELOW *Lantern, watercolour by Richard Bentley, courtesy of the Lewis Walpole Library, Yale University. This lantern provided the only lighting in the Hall*

ABOVE *View of The Hall and Staircase at Strawberry Hill, watercolour by Richard Bentley, 1753, courtesy of the Lewis Walpole Library, Yale University*

at four o'clock as I was going to dine abroad. Your partiality to me and Strawberry have I hope inclined you to excuse the wildness of the story. You will even have found some traits to put you in mind of this place. When you read of the picture quitting its panel, did not you recollect the portrait of Lord Falkland all in white in my gallery? Shall I even confess to you what was the origin of this romance? I waked one morning in the beginning of last June from a dream, of which all I could recover was, that I had thought myself in an ancient castle (a very natural dream for a head filled like mine with Gothic story) and that on the uppermost bannister of a great staircase I saw a gigantic hand in armour. In the evening I sat down and began to write, without knowing in the least what I intended to say or relate. The work grew on my hands, and I grew fond of it – add that I was very glad to think of anything rather than politics – In short I was so engrossed with my tale, which I completed in less than two months, that one evening I wrote from the time I had drunk my tea, about six o'clock, till half an hour after one in the morning, when my hand and fingers were so weary, that I could not hold the pen to finish the sentence, but left Matilda and Isabella talking, in the middle of a paragraph. You will laugh at my earnestness, but if I have amused you by tracing with any fidelity the manners of ancient days, I am content, and give you leave to think me as idle as you please.'[5]

In this book, which quickly became the page-turning bestseller of the day, Walpole used the new novel form and added gothic horror. Set within a great medieval castle it has a complex plot revolving round an ancient prophecy that a usurper could rule the State of Otranto only as long as there was a male heir to succeed, or alternatively until the castle was no longer large enough to hold the ruler. The wicked villain and usurper, Manfred, tries to hold on to his illicitly acquired State by marrying his only son, Conrad, to the beautiful Isabella. On the eve of the wedding his son is found dead, crushed beneath a giant helmet – this is a brief résumé of the first page. The tale unfolds with virtuous maidens fleeing the attentions of Manfred, much hand-wringing and weeping, portraits walking out of their frames, skeletons, handsome peasants, and the ghost of the rightful ruler growing in size until he destroys the castle and fulfils the prophecy. Through the

acquired a suit of horse armour to display alongside it. The armour was the only large object in the Armoury and probably the only one which would have reflected light. The stairs continued upwards, past the Armoury, to a top landing on one side of which a door led to a small room which Mr Chenevix had used as a library.

It was about this same space at the highest point of the Hall that Walpole dreamed a strange, unearthly, dream in 1764:

I had time to write but a short note with "The Castle of Otranto", as your messenger called on me plot runs a frisson of horror increased by the chase through never-ending subterranean passages. Apart from its castle-courtyard, the Castle of Otranto was Strawberry Castle, and each movement the characters make can be traced within the house. It is as though Otranto has been shrunk to a suitable size to sit upon the shelf of Mrs Chenevix's shop.

Walpole first published the novel in 1764 anonymously, describing it as a translation from 1529 by the Italian, Onuphrio Muralto, Canon of the Church of St Nicholas at Otranto. Onuphrio Muralto was devised as a rather complicated verbal puzzle relating to the name Horatio Walpole,[6] but once the book took off and fear of ridicule was over, it was republished with Walpole's authorship acknowledged. 'I wrote the Castle of Otranto in eight days, or rather nights: for my general hours of composition are from ten o'clock at night till two

in the morning, when I am sure not to be disturbed by visitants. While I am writing I take several cups of coffee.' Although he affected to despise writers he wanted to be known as one. He described the book as 'an attempt to blend the two kinds of romance: the ancient and the modern.'[7] It was this which excited the public and gave rise to a genre, that of the gothic novel, which has never gone out of fashion; each generation shivering at primeval fears of the chase, lust, rape, spirits of the dead, darkness, loss and destruction. From Otranto it is a logical step to the film *Psycho*, and both started with Walpole's dream of 1764 about the staircase of Strawberry Hill.

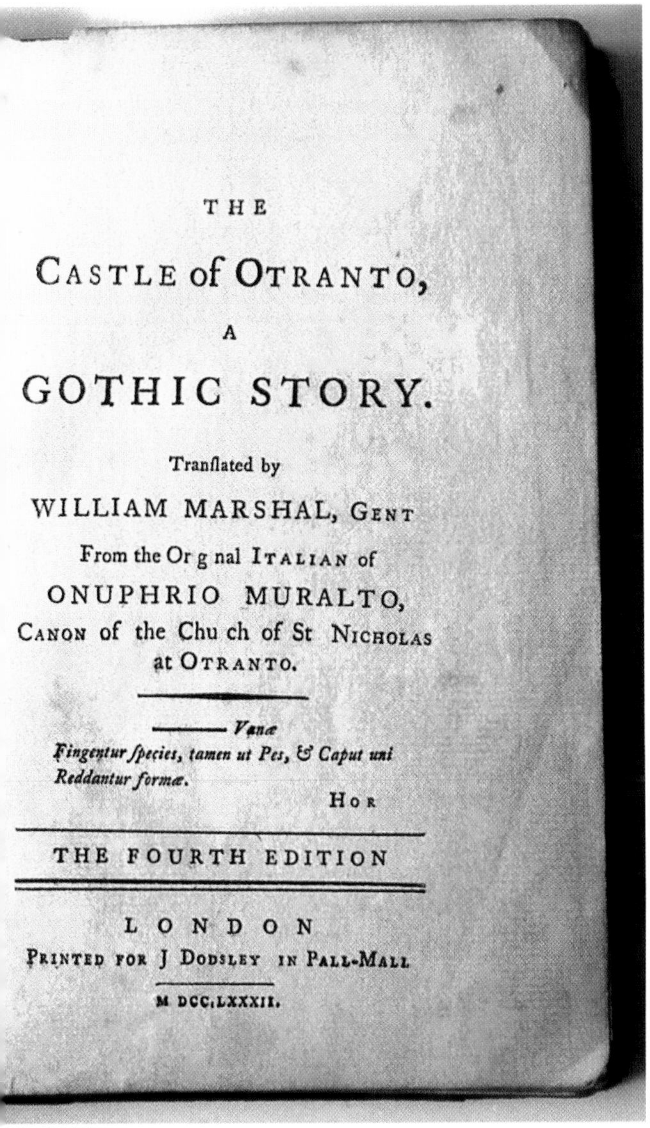

Walpole experienced the dream during a period when he was suffering from gout and it has been suggested that the contemporary description of him walking 'as if afraid of a wet floor'[8] might well describe the careful gait of a man with gouty feet. One of the standard remedies for gout in the eighteenth century was a prescription for laudanum. Could *Otranto* and the beginning of gothic horror have been inspired by a drug-induced nightmare?

Many of the ticketed visitors who came to Strawberry Hill came out of curiosity to see the author of *The Castle of Otranto*. It was from the Armoury that those with tickets would first have properly seen the Hall, and from that upper vantage point the whole glory of Walpole's Hall could be seen below – looking just like Otranto. The tiles, doorways disappearing in the gloom, heraldic beasts on the newel posts, narrow passages, stone-looking walls hung with arms could all have been part of the Italian castle. The Armoury confirmed Strawberry Hill as the creation of Horace Walpole; a place of entertainment, wonderment and fun, to be marvelled at, but with a serious intent.

> …I have the satisfaction of announcing to you the arrival of two great personages from France; one is, Mademoiselle Heinel, the famous dancer; the other, King Francis the First. In short, the armour of the latter is actually here, and in its niche, which I have had made for it on the staircase; and a very little stretch of the imagination will give it all the visionary dignity of the gigantic hand in armour that I dreamt of seeing on the balustrade of the staircase at Otranto. If this is not realizing one's dreams, I don't know what is.[9]

BELOW *Early copy of* The Castle of Otranto *by Horace Walpole, crediting it as an earlier publication written in 1529 and translated from the original Italian of Onuphrio Muralto*

THE

CASTLE of OTRANTO,

A

GOTHIC STORY.

Tranflated by

WILLIAM MARSHAL, GENT

From the Orginal ITALIAN of

ONUPHRIO MURALTO,

CANON of the Chuch of St NICHOLAS
at OTRANTO.

—— *Vanæ*
Fingentur fpecies, tamen ut Pes, & Caput uni
Reddantur formæ.
HOR

THE FOURTH EDITION

LONDON
PRINTED FOR J DODSLEY IN PALL-MALL

M DCC.LXXXII.

[5] Letter Horace Walpole to the Rev. William Cole written from Strawberry Hill, 9 March 1765

[6] Walpole composed an anagram of 'Horatio' but omitted the letters 'a' and 't'. When Onuphrio is formed from the remaining 'HORIO' the letters 'PUN' have to be found; 'PUN' is the explanation of the word game he was playing. In 'MURALTO' likewise, the word can be divided into two parts: MUR, French for wall and 'ALTO' meaning high and used in the same context as the imperial measurement of rod, pole or perch. Together he tells the knowledgeable reader that the author is Horace (Horatio) Walpole

[7] Walpole, Horace, Introduction to *The Castle of Otranto*, Strawberry Hill, 1764

[8] Laetetia Matilda Hawkins quoted in Stuart, Dorothy M., *Horace Walpole*, Macmillan, New York, 1927

[9] Letter Horace Walpole to Lady Ossory, 4 December 1771

5 The Little Parlour and the Yellow Bedchamber

'Elegance and taste'

OPPOSITE *Detail of an early sixteenth-century Flemish glass roundel of Noah's Ark, now in the Hall of Strawberry Hill*

THE TICKETED VISITORS standing in the vantage point of the Armoury and looking down below on the gothic passages appearing and disappearing in front of them, winding to right and left, would in fact have been looking at the conventional doors leading into the Waiting Room, from which they had started, and the Little Parlour and the Yellow Bedchamber, both of which were private rooms and which they could not enter.

The Thames flowed close to both rooms. As well as providing an ever changing view of the busy river traffic, it would also have brought some of Walpole's friends to the house; they could disembark and enter the Little Parlour from the garden, with the river forming a backdrop. A bay had been added to the earlier building, enhancing the views of river and garden and ensuring the maximum amount of natural light came into the private rooms of the house. In summer the Little Parlour was bathed in sunlight throughout the afternoon, a quite different effect from that in the Hall, Refectory and Armoury. Painted and stained glass, set within the upper lights of the windows, filtered the light and controlled its colour and strength. Armorial glass added to the colour and gave a sense of history. The glass in the lower section of the bay windows was left clear, enabling Walpole and his friends to look out at the garden with its changing scene and weather:

…I was prevented from finishing my letter yesterday, but what do you think? By no less magnificent a circumstance than a deluge. We have had an extraordinary drought, no grass, no leaves, no flowers… About four arrived such a flood, that we could not see out of the windows: the whole lawn was a lake, though situated on so high an Ararat: presently it broke through the leads, drowned the pretty blue bedchamber, passed through ceilings and floors into the little parlour, terrified Harry, and opened all Catherine's water-gates and speech-gates. – I had but just time to collect two dogs, a couple of sheep, a pair of bantams, and a brace of gold-fish; for, in the haste of my zeal to imitate my ancestor Noah, I forgot that fish would not easily be drowned. In short, if you chance to spy a little ark with pinnacles sailing towards Jersey, open the skylight, and you will find some of your acquaintance. You never saw such desolation!

A pigeon brings word that Mabland has fared still worse: it never came into my head before, that a rainbow-office for insuring against water might be very necessary. This is a true account of the late deluge. Witness our hands,
Horace Noah
Catherine Noah, her X mark
Henry Shem
Louis Japhet
Peter Ham, etc.[1]

[1] Letter Horace Walpole to Richard Bentley written from Strawberry Hill, 11 June 1755

ABOVE *Early Flemish glass roundel from the Blue Bedchamber*

Hall incorporated a piece of glass showing Noah's ark built on piers, steps leading up to it and Mrs Noah packing their trunks before sailing away on the flood. Walpole frequently wrote to friends bemoaning the weather, the flooding and being the owner of a leaky house.

The summer of 1783 was a wet one, upsetting Margaret who by that time had replaced Catherine as housekeeper:

> …The month of June has been as abominable as any one of its ancestors in all the pedigree of the Junes. I was literally half drowned on Sunday night. It rained through two stories and into the Green Closet at Strawberry, and my bedchamber was wet to its smock. The gutters were stopped or could not carry off the deluge fast enough. Margaret prayed to St Rainbow, but as he never appears till it is too late, we were forced to have recourse to mortal help and litter all the floors with hay to soak up the inundation.[2]

On entering the Little Parlour from the garden Walpole's friends might be serenaded by musicians engaged to entertain them by playing in the cloister which ran alongside the room. The music was heard inside the house and reinforced the first image of arcadian perfection set by the garden. The room cleverly merged the informal charm of the planting with an introduction to the monochromatic mood of gothic which friends would fully experience when they went into the Hall. The satisfaction Walpole experienced in achieving this balance is reflected in part of a letter written to Sir Horace Mann on 12 June 1753:

> …The opposite shore is a most delicious meadow, bounded by Richmond Hill which loses itself in the noble woods of the park to the end of the prospect on the right, where is another turn of the river and the suburbs of Kingston as luckily placed as Twickenham is on the left; and a natural terrace on the brow of my hill, with meadows of my own down to the river, commands both extremities. Is not this a tolerable prospect? You must figure that all this is perpetually enlivened by a navigation of boats and barges, and by a road below my terrace, with coaches, post-chaises, waggons and horsemen constantly in motion, and the fields speckled with cows, horses and sheep. Now you shall walk into the house. The bow-window below leads into a little

In 1755 Catherine was the housekeeper at Strawberry Hill and the other people mentioned in the letter were all in Walpole's service.

Flooding was a permanent worry to Walpole and although the name 'Strawberry Hill' implies that the house stood on high ground, the rise was slight and 'Strawberry Mound' would have been a more appropriate title. Walpole picked up and played with the image of the deluge and flood, placing painted glass in his windows which captured the spirit of Noah, while the lantern hanging in the

[2] Letter Horace Walpole to Lady Ossory written from Berkeley Square, 20 June 1783

parlour hung with a stone-colour Gothic paper and Jackson's Venetian prints, which I could never endure while they pretended, infamous as they are, to be after Titian etc. but when I gave them this air of barbarous bas-reliefs, they succeeded to a miracle: it is impossible at first sight not to conclude that they contain the history of Attila or Tottila, done about the very era.

The use of a stucco gothic wallpaper was described by Lady Luxborough writing to her friend William Shenstone in February 1751. The wallpaper of the Little Parlour would have looked somewhat similar:

> …As the frost is gone. …I hope your ink is thawed. …The proposal for stuccoing my little passage makes it come also to more than I expected. Moore (who has lately been at London) talks to me of a sort of stucco-paper, which I had never heard of; and says Lord Foley has done his Chapel in Worcestershire with it (the cieling at least). By his description, the paper is stamped so deep as to project considerably, and is very thick and strong; and the ornaments are all detached, and put on separately. – As suppose for example, it were the pattern of a common stucco-paper, which is generally a mosaic formed by a rose in an kind of octagon: it seems, in this new way one of these roses is to be bought singly; so you have as many in number as the place requires, which are pasted up separately, and then gilt: the ornaments for the cornices are likewise in separate pieces, and, when finished, cannot, I suppose, be known from fretwork. The difficulty, and consequently the expence, must be in putting up these ornaments, which as I understand, must be done by a man whom the Paper-seller sends on purpose from London…[3]

Over the wallpaper Walpole mounted a display of woodblock prints produced by John Baptist Jackson, an eccentric figure from Battersea. These prints, copies of Titian's paintings, were intended to remind his friends of their Grand Tour; the prints depicted an Italian landscape peppered with lagoons, canals and ruins. Early in the eighteenth century Jackson became interested in both printing and in the art of woodcarving. He first travelled to Paris to study and later continued to Italy where he worked in both Florence and Venice demonstrating skill in woodblock printing and engraving. He returned to

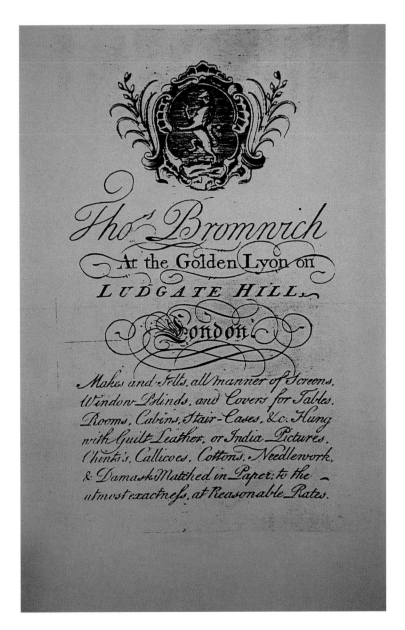

England in 1745 and started producing designs for printing patterns on to calico, later experimenting with various different techniques which could be used on wallpaper. In 1752 he placed an advertisement for his wares in the *Evening Post*:

> New invented PAPER HANGINGS, printed in Oyl, which prevents the fading or changing of the Colours; as also Landscapes printed in Colours, by J.B. Jackson, Reviver of the Art of Printing in Chiaro Oscuro, are to be had at Dunbar's Warehouse in Aldermanbury, London; or at Mr. Gibson's Bookseller, opposite the St. Alban's Tavern in Charles-street near St. James's-Square, and no where else.

ABOVE *Trade card of Thomas Bromwich*

[3] Luxborough, Lady, *Letters*, Dublin, 1776

Jackson produced a set of seventeen engravings, all copied from paintings by Titian, most of which had religious themes. Each one employed an advanced printing technique which used four separate blocks and several inks ranging from stone to black, with oil added to give permanency. This new method ensured there was great variety in shading which gave a sense of depth to each print. Pasting them directly on to the gothic stone-coloured paper of the Little Parlour increased their impact and theatricality. Jackson described the process:

> By this way of printing Paper the Inventor has contrived that the Lights and Shades shall be broad and bold and give great relief to the Figures; the finest Prints of all the antique Statues which imitate Drawings are introduced into Niches of Chiaro Oscuro in the Pannels of the Paper; these are surrounded with a Mosaic Work in imitation of Frames, or with Festoons and Garlands of Flowers with great Elegance and Taste. Saloons in Imitation of Stucco may be done in this Manner...[4]

Although Richard Bentley had originally intended to decorate the Little Parlour himself, he could not find the time and no other artist was specially commissioned by Walpole to design or paint the wallpaper, probably because it remained a private room and not one of the more important gothic interiors of the house; eventually Bromwich

[4] Entwisle, E.A., *A Literary History of Wallpaper*, Batsford, London, 1960, pp.23-4

[5] Letter Horace Walpole to George Montagu, 23 June 1750

[6] Letter Horace Walpole to Horace Mann written from Strawberry Hill, 27 May 1776

[7] Letter to Horace Mann, 12 June 1753

had to be called in to provide a workman to finish the wallpaper. Towards the end of Walpole's life the walls were rehung in 'sober brown'. The furnishings were carefully chosen for effect. An ebony table and eight matching chairs stood in the room, probably solid and uncomfortable to sit on; the room was used for supper, and upholstered chairs and soft furnishings would have retained the smell of food. In such a small crowded room the furniture must have made it a tight squeeze for any lady in a wide eighteenth-century costume. Was this deliberate? A way of emphasising the scale? Entering from the garden visitors would have thought themselves grown-ups in a toy house.

The chimneypiece of the Little Parlour was copied from an engraving of a tomb in Westminster Abbey and was surmounted by Walpole's arms. It was kept reasonably simple and had been designed by Richard Bentley, who had managed to find the time to finish the chimney design, although not to paint the walls of the room. As building and decoration in the house progressed the chimney-pieces became increasingly elaborate.

Of the three men most involved in deciding the design, building and decoration of Strawberry Hill, it was Bentley who was the infuriating figure possessed with a wonderful imagination but often impractical. He and John Chute were the main members of the group calling themselves the Committee of Taste, the final arbiter on all matters of taste always being Walpole himself. Bentley shared Walpole's passion for reviving an historic English style at Strawberry Hill which was at odds with the contemporary, more popular Palladian or Italian-style architecture, and it was he who shared most closely in Walpole's dreams of romance, love of theatre and sense of fun. His designs blend rococo wit with serious gothicism. Described by Walpole as 'a treasure of taste and drawing' he never had enough funds to live the life of independence he would have liked and frequently fell into debt, having to flee to Jersey in order to escape being dunned. Whenever he fled he had to leave his promised work incomplete. '...I have had another of your friends with me...' Walpole told George Montagu, 'whom I adore, Mr Bentley; he has more sense, judgement and wit, more taste and more misfortunes than sure ever met in any man'.[5]

John Chute, the other principal figure on the committee, had first met Walpole on the Grand

Tour; Chute retained a passion for classical architecture and symmetry even when working with great ingenuity on the plans for Strawberry Hill. He was at heart a true antiquarian and was more practical and architecturally competent than the other two men. On his death in 1776 a tribute from Walpole summed up the part he played: '…Mr Chute and I agreed invariably in our principles; he was my counsel in my affairs, was my oracle in taste, the standard to whom I submitted my trifles, and the genius that presided over poor Strawberry!'[6]

The rooms Chute designed transmit a sense of splendour and of being part of a lengthy English pageant, they are solidly rooted in good architectural design; Bentley's rooms achieve their effect through light and the use of carefully composed viewpoints as much as through structure. Later, when Walpole and Bentley had fallen out, other architects became involved; Robert Adam, Thomas Pitt, James Wyatt and James Essex, but it was the vision of Horace Walpole, Richard Bentley and John Chute which shaped Strawberry Hill.

Next door to the Little Parlour stood the Yellow Bedchamber, another of the early rooms, with a closet opening out of it. It was one of the few rooms at Strawberry Hill which underwent colour changes and fairly frequent redecoration. The use of yellow wallpaper, a pedestrian colour, suggested it was always intended to be an ordinary room for everyday use, not grand*. It soon became a very early print room. In 1753 it was, '…hung with yellow paper and prints, framed in a new manner invented by Lord Cardigan, that is, with black and white borders printed.'[7]

In the eighteenth century there was a craze for buying prints and using them for decoration. With unbounded enthusiasm for them in eighteenth-century society they were produced in large numbers covering every subject from religion to botany. Once published, they were copied and used by craftsmen in other fields. Frequently they were chosen for a particular decorative scheme not by subject, but by size. The chosen details being cut out and pasted on to paper before being varnished and finally hung on the walls. It was far-sighted tradesmen, like John Baptist Jackson, who started producing sheets of borders, ribbons, festoons, garlands of flowers, and bows ready for use. These only required cutting out and pasting around the print to form a frame. The prints used

in the Yellow Bedchamber were of the paintings which had been in the Walpole family collection, or prints which related to the Walpoles in some other way. The finished effect would have been that of a giant scrapbook on the walls telling the story of the family. The assembly of print rooms was a pastime enjoyed by both gentlemen and ladies, although professional paper-stainers could be brought in. Walpole's decorator, Bromwich and his partner, Legh, advertised in the 1760s on their trade cards that they could fit up a room with 'Indian pictures or prints'. The fashion took off and soon produced a market for wallpapers with the prints and frames already printed on the paper and ready for hanging. Jackson is credited with early papers in this style printed in distemper colours. New techniques in printing and the manufacture of paper made the style affordable and by its affordability it allowed choice.

ABOVE *John Chute, engraving by Greatbach after a painting by Müntz which originally hung at Strawberry Hill*

*Analysis has shown the paint to be composed of an expensive pigment, not the normal pigment used in the eighteenth century

BELOW *Modern reproduction of 'Shepherds and Sheep' print room wallpaper by Jean Baptist Jackson, courtesy of Cole & Son (Wallpapers) Limited*

[8] Cornforth, John, *Early Georgian Interiors*, Yale University Press, New Haven & London, 2004, p.207

[9] Cornforth, John, op. cit., p.246

Walpole was obviously pleased with the result and had other rooms decorated in the same style, although the Yellow Bedchamber was the only one in yellow, generally considered the most successful background colour. John Chute used the fashion in his own house in Hampshire, the Vyne, and Lady Cardigan had a massive eighty-two 'Indian pictures' pasted on her wall. Mrs Delaney wrote to her brother in 1751 describing the process:

> …I have received the six dozen borders all safely, and return you, my dear brother, many thanks for them. They are for framing prints. I think them much prettier than any other sort of frame for that purpose and where I have not pictures, I must have prints; otherwise I think prints best in books. The manner of doing them is to have the straining-frames made as much larger than your print as will allow of the border, the straining-frame covered with coarse cloth, the print pasted on it, and then the borders, leaving half an inch or rather less of margin round the print.[8]

A more general interest in prints stimulated a new interest in portraits and later the Yellow Bedchamber was redecorated with a grey spotted wallpaper and hung with copies of portraits of the beauties of the Stuart Court which Walpole had purchased at a house sale. It became known as the Beauty Room. In this period it was considered better to have a copy of a work by a great artist than a second-rate original painting and many copies were produced for Strawberry Hill. Jonathan Richardson noted the practice in 1752: 'A Copy of a very Good Picture is preferable to an Indifferent Original; for There the Invention is seen almost Intire, and a great deal of the Expression, and, Disposition, and many times good Hints of the Colouring, Drawing and other Qualities'.[9]

Over Richard Bentley's yellow and black gothic chimneypiece – drawn from his imagination rather

than from an engraving – hung a copy of Van Dyke's portrait of the Princes Charles and James with their sister Mary and their favourite dog. The chimney-piece was surmounted by five pinnacles similar to those on the roof of the house, which might have been timber or painted in *trompe l'œil*. All the furnishings remained unchanged: yellow silk and stuff damask with an ebony table on which Walpole placed a sandalwood and ivory writing-box and a pair of candlesticks. Because the room was furnished for everyday use rather than for viewing by a visiting public not a great deal is known about the contents or the changes, but it must have been a much used room getting shabby through wear and tear, because the decoration of the walls changed several times, which was unusual at Strawberry Hill.

ABOVE *Chimney in the Yellow Bedchamber; eighteenth-century engraving*

6 The Blue Breakfast Room, the Green Closet and the Family Bedchambers

'A charming effect'

OPPOSITE *Horace Walpole, engraving by Greatbach after a painting by Ecchardt*

BELOW *First Floor Plan showing the route taken by tourists when led by the Housekeeper*

THOSE VISITORS WITH TICKETS who had missed viewing the private rooms on the ground floor and had been shepherded instead up the stairs by the housekeeper, resumed their tour in the Blue Breakfast Room, where they were shown the first in a sequence of rooms in the South Tower each filled with brilliant colour and sunlight made more vibrant through being seen after the gothic darkness of the Refectory and Hall. On their way upstairs they would have passed a painting of Richmond Hill, a foretaste of the actual view to come. They stepped into a fashionable and beautiful room. Other rooms were presented as set-pieces from past periods, but the Blue Breakfast Room was right up-to-date in its decoration.

From an early age Walpole had admired and made copies of the paintings of Antoine Watteau which hung upon the walls of the family house in Chelsea.

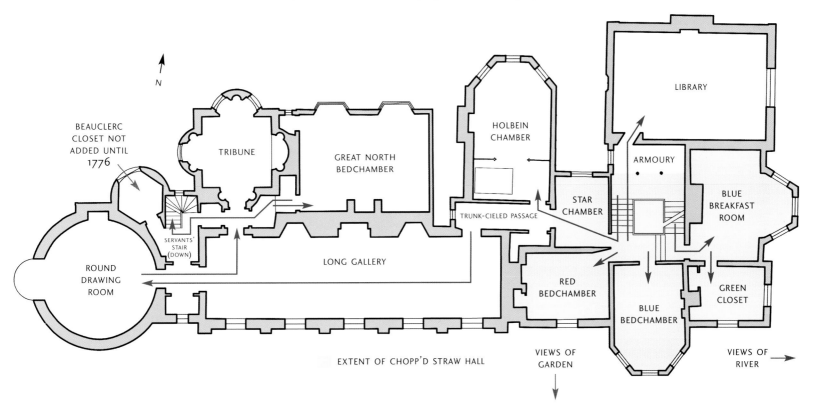

N

BEAUCLERC CLOSET NOT ADDED UNTIL 1776

TRIBUNE

GREAT NORTH BEDCHAMBER

HOLBEIN CHAMBER

LIBRARY

ARMOURY

STAR CHAMBER

BLUE BREAKFAST ROOM

TRUNK-CIELED PASSAGE

SERVANTS' STAIR (DOWN)

LONG GALLERY

ROUND DRAWING ROOM

RED BEDCHAMBER

GREEN CLOSET

BLUE BEDCHAMBER

EXTENT OF CHOPP'D STRAW HALL

VIEWS OF GARDEN

VIEWS OF RIVER

He enjoyed looking at paintings which depicted a period of leisure in which inappropriately clad men and women lounged about in sunny pastoral surroundings listening to music while time drifted by. In these paintings the arcadian mood is evoked through the tone and colours of the landscape. In a similar way in the interiors of rooms overlooking the gardens and river, colours were chosen to reflect the landscape, the green of the garden and the blue of the river Thames. The mood of tranquillity and harmony was first established in two rooms in the South Tower, the Green Closet, and the room next to it, the Blue Breakfast Room, and was then continued through some of the bedchambers. An idyllic way of life was conjured up, not always in keeping with the otherwise gothic theme of the house.

The atmosphere was described in Boydell's guidebook of 1796, *An History of the River Thames*:

> Here Strawberry-Hill, the villa of Lord Orford, very beautifully varies the advancing scene. Its pinnacles, rising from among the trees in which the building is imbosomed, and its Gothic windows that appear between the branches, compose a very pleasing and picturesque object, both as we approach and glide by it.

The Thames flowed to the south east, providing views from the house of the river traffic which changed with the tides. Clearly Walpole recognised the importance of the relationship of this section of the house to the landscape. In his early alterations two bays had been added to the house, one to the Little Parlour and the Bedchamber above and one to the Blue Breakfast Room, which enhanced the view and ensured that natural, ever-changing light entered these rooms throughout the day. Thus morning light would have filtered through the trees to the Blue Breakfast Room where deep blue glass was used as a setting for Flemish painted glass. The use of blue controlled both the strength and the colour of the light. It also increased the impact of the colours chosen for the upholstery and the furnishings. Walpole manipulated light, furnishings, and space to create that element of perceived serendipity that became Strawberry Hill. Colour-theming of rooms was regularly practised in the eighteenth century with blue as a fashionable choice, but not to the exclusion of all other colours. Walpole described the room in part of a long letter he wrote to Sir Horace Mann:

[1] Letter Horace Walpole to Horace Mann written from Strawberry Hill, 12 June 1753

[2] Walpole, Horace, *A Description of the Villa of Mr. Horace Walpole at Strawberry-Hill near Twickenham, Middlesex*, Strawberry Hill, 1784

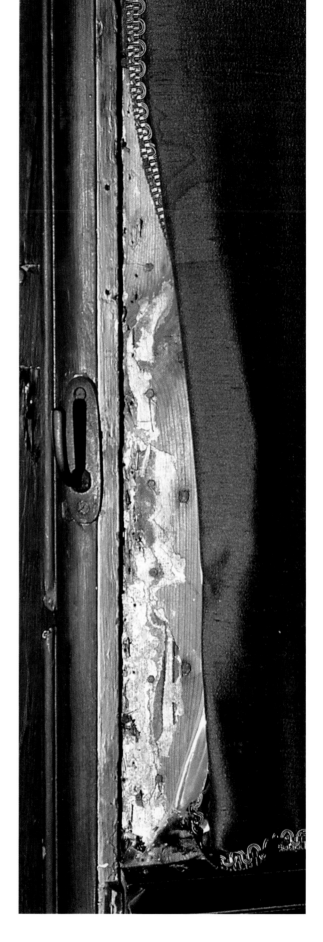

... the room where we always live, hung with a blue and white paper in stripes adorned with festoons, and a thousand plump chairs, couches and luxurious settees covered with linen of the same pattern, and with a bow-window commanding the prospect, and gloomed with limes that shade half each window, already darkened with painted glass in chiaroscuro, set in deep blue glass.[1]

As the earliest room to be used regularly as a living room the Blue Breakfast Room was decorated before any plans were afoot to use the gothic style: 'The chimney-piece and windows are not truly gothic, but were designed by Mr. W. Robinson of the Board of Works, before there was any design of farther improvements to the house.'[2] The interior was the result of remodelling rather than new building because it had been part of Chopp'd Straw Hall. The clue to the original cottage is the chimney-piece. The simple stone surround to the hearth, a remnant of the old seventeenth-century fireplace, was brought up to date by the addition of a carved timber surround by William Robinson, the first 'architect' to be employed by Walpole. Robinson was a practical man, who advised Walpole on building structure from 1748 until 1773. He does not appear to have been whimsical enough to satisfy Walpole, who at the time was still unsure of what he expected from any architect. Robinson's design for the chimneypiece, adapted from earlier designs by Gibbs and Kent, included a classical column placed either side of a Saracen's head. The Saracen was a final gothic touch. A mixture of styles was not uncommon, and a very similar surround was featured in a book published by a Twickenham builder, Batty Langley, *Gothic Architecture, Improved by Rules & Proportions*, published in 1747.

Walpole, commenting on Batty Langley's work in his *Anecdotes of Painting*, wrote:

> ...all that his books achieved, has been to teach carpenters to massacre that venerable species, and to give occasion to those who know nothing of the matter, and to mistake his clumsy efforts for real imitations, to censure the productions of our ancestors, whose bold and beautiful fabrics Sir Christopher Wren viewed and reviewed with astonishment, and never mentioned without esteem.

Walpole continued for the next fifty years to perfect a consistent gothic style throughout the house – a style that was not 'truly gothic' but was a new decorative gothic: Strawberry Hill Gothic. William Robinson was demoted to Strawberry Hill's 'Clerk of Works'. It was felt he was more suited to deal with the practicalities of finding ways for the Committee of Taste to realise their designs rather than to create those designs himself. The windows of the Blue Breakfast Room were changed for a

BELOW *Bay of the Blue Breakfast Room showing the relationship of the interior to the garden. Glass setting before resoration*

second time in the 1770s into another not 'truly gothic' style, in order to present a framed image of three 'paintings' of local views; on the left Richmond Hill, in the centre the river Thames with its busy passing traffic and Kingston Hill glimpsed from the third window, the three together forming a changing panorama of life on the river bank. New technology meant that glass was both stronger and clearer. Without the flaws found in earlier glass it became possible for someone inside a room to look out through the glass. This changed the relationship between garden and room, creating a harmony. As they grew in height the lime trees which Walpole had planted close to the house modulated the light filtering into the room and also further framed the views in the distance. The blue glass in the upper lights of these windows reflected both the blue of the water and that of the interior furnishing, and would have produced a 'watery' effect on the walls of the room.

Blue and white textiles were a popular fashionable combination reflecting a more general interest in the blue and white china coming into the country through the Dutch East India Company. In the mid-eighteenth century it became the fashion to match fabric with wall hangings. The practice is recorded by Mrs Delaney, who was almost as busy as Walpole with her correspondence, and who wrote in 1750:

> I have stripped down old stuff beds...and in their stead am putting up blue and white linen and blue and white paper hangings, ...I have done up a little apartment, hung it with blue-and-white paper, and intend a bed of blue-and-white linen – all Irish manufacture.[3]

The general demand in the period for fashionable printed furnishing fabrics was met partly by Indian imports and partly by locally produced cloth or fabric brought over from Ireland. Patterns were quickly adapted to fit the loom size and with the use of copper plates a sharper image was produced and designs could become more elaborate. Shopping was made easier by the grouping of shops in London according to their wares; mercers and drapers were to be found in Cheapside, lace and textile merchants in Paternoster Row.

The Breakfast Room had no curtains because any use of fabric on the windows would have partially concealed the Flemish glass roundels and spoiled their effect, so the 'festooning' described by

Walpole is likely to have been a design of fruit, leaves and flowers hanging in garlands on a frieze, pasted over the striped wallpaper* where it provided yet another visual link between the garden and the interior of the room. The wallpaper and linen are believed to have been of a light summery print, with blue verditer flowers highlighted by the use of a darker blue within the stripes. The impression would have been of walls covered in fabric rather than paper.

It was in this room that Walpole and his friends chose to breakfast, joined by pet spaniels and a tame red squirrel, which must have come in at the window from one of the lime trees growing outside. In the evening it was again to this room that Walpole retired with his friends to be cosy and pour over items from his Collection, presumably all grouped around the table and sharing the candlelight. The room must have seemed comfortable, contemporary and beautiful, with the colour repeated in the blue of the ornaments placed around. On a writing table stood an inlaid writing-box by Langlois, and porcelain flowers, chinoiserie figures and Sèvres blue and white flower-pots were placed over the chimney encircling a mirror which would have reflected views of the garden back into the room. Apart from the use of blue – and with the exception of a 'red velvet purse embroidered with gold and old French arms, to hold counters'[4] – everything in the room was blue or white including the china. The decorative themes chosen for the room were flowers and miniatures. The floral theme was enhanced by the flowers of the festooning and by a paper mosaic flowerpiece made for Walpole by Mrs Delaney.

Mrs Delaney was another eighteenth-century compulsive letter writer and commentator on the social scene. Seventeen years older than Walpole she records some of the same customs and practices as him but from a more conservative viewpoint, that of a dependent genteel woman.

Like Walpole, Mrs Delaney mixed with the great men of the day, meeting Reynolds and Hogarth, Wesley and Swift, and she was a friend of both Sir Joseph Banks and of Handel. She wrote about Queen Charlotte, a close friend, and of the daily family life of the King and Queen, commenting astutely on society and fashion. Gardens and their flowers were her passion and her leisure time was spent working floral motifs in fine embroidery. In the spirit of the Enlightenment she was not

*See page 151

[3] Granville, Mary, *The Autobiography and Correspondence of Mary Granville, Mrs. Delaney,* ed. Lady Llanover, 1861, Series 1, Vol. 2, p.562

[4 and 5] Walpole, Horace, *A Description of the Villa of Mr. Horace Walpole at Strawberry-Hill near Twickenham, Middlesex,* Strawberry Hill, 1784

content just to reproduce blindly, but set about producing botanically accurate copies of about one thousand plants in 'paper mosaicks', these were tiny fragments of paper which she cut and assembled with astonishing accuracy from larger sheets of paper. Walpole described her work as 'precision and truth unparalleled', and recognised in her a passion for plants which matched his own. The accuracy of her depiction of plants through minute variation of shading within each petal or leaf enables identification even today.

Miniatures were displayed around the room, grouped together in frames; some by Nicholas Hilliard and Isaac and Peter Oliver; some had a floral background: 'Robert earl of Essex, favourite of Queen Elizabeth; set in a case enamelled with flowers.'[5] The garden theme was continued still further with a painting described by Walpole as Charles II's gardener presenting the king with the first pineapple

grown in this country. The pineapple was still a rarity for the dessert table and Robert Walpole had kept '225 Pine Apple Plants' at his Chelsea home.[6]

To appreciate the deliberation with which furniture and ornaments were chosen for this room and for the Green Closet beyond, it must be remembered that these two rooms, wrapped around the corner of the house overlooking river and garden, held every painting and ornament in the house which used flowers as decoration.

The mood of the Green Closet, into which the visitors were next ushered, and the selection of green as a background colour, was as carefully composed as that of the Blue Breakfast Room; green was regarded as a significant and harmonious colour in the period. Here was a very small space which could only be entered from the Blue Breakfast Room, with two windows giving views of the road and river to the east and the garden to the south.

BELOW Seventeenth-century glass roundel of a sleeping dog, now in the Little Parlour

[6] The National Archives, Kew, C101/20, p.28

RIGHT *Seventeenth-century glass roundel of parrots with cherries from the Blue Bedchamber*

Asciotti, who had been sent on a shopping trip to Flanders to bring back all the glass he could find for thirty-six guineas – inclusive of his expenses. The shipment was varied and included pieces representing biblical stories, small grisaille figures and colourful birds and flowers. These were all small pieces, none exceeding nine inches. They were placed together in jewel-like settings by the English glazier, Palmer, and with them Walpole placed early English glass – some of the rare pieces from churches not destroyed by Cromwell. The Flemish glass came from shops, inns or the houses of prosperous merchants, most of it painted in shades of yellow, black and brown. There were several painted glass roundels by Heemskerk, whose work was already known to Walpole through roundels in the windows of the family's Chelsea house and through paintings owned by his father. Many of Walpole's favourite pieces were, however, of the more brightly coloured English glass representing coats of arms, including a special piece set in the window of his bedchamber showing the pomegranate device of Catherine of Aragon entwined with the device of Henry VIII. Illustrated botanical and ornithological books were published from about 1730 and their prints were studied and copied by craftsmen. Glaziers, among others, produced images of birds, insects and flowers which were then incorporated in windows to form part of a composite decorative feature.

The walls of the closet were hung with paintings – 141 were listed for this small room – and were divided into two main groups. Many were portraits of Walpole's family and friends such as Kitty Clive, the actress, to whom he gave a home at Little Strawberry Hill when she retired from the theatre; but the others were there to fill a gap. Walpole's Collection, including his paintings, was arranged as an integral part of the interior, essentially decoration while also demonstrating taste, connoisseurship and ancestry. The garden of Strawberry Hill had no fashionable ruins or temples, although from the east window it would have been possible to see Twickenham's own 'ruin', the obelisk at the road junction; but what was lacking in the garden was supplied by paintings hung on the walls. A copy of a Watteau conversation piece, painted by Walpole, hung beside a set of twenty-four fashionable engravings of ruins by Lucatelli, with a needle-worked landscape, an oil by Samuel Scott of a neighbouring

…in the tower beyond…is the charming closet where I am now writing to you. It is hung with green paper and water-colour pictures; has two windows; the one in the drawing looks to the garden, the other to the beautiful prospect; and the top of each glutted with the richest painted glass of the arms of England, crimson roses, and twenty other pieces of green, purple, and historic bits. I must tell you by the way, that the castle, when finished, will have two and thirty windows enriched with painted glass. In this closet, which is Mr Chute's college of arms, are two presses with books of heraldry and antiquities, Madame Sévigné's letters, and any French books that relate to her and her acquaintance…[7]

Walpole – and John Chute when he stayed in the house – both chose this space for writing and studying. The room was 'hung with green paper and water-colour pictures' to reflect the garden with its natural pleasures.[8] This was the room which held some of the most important window glass. Like most of the other glass at Strawberry Hill it had been painted in the sixteenth and seventeenth centuries by highly skilled glass painters who copied popular prints. Most of the pieces in the Green Closet, and elsewhere at Strawberry Hill, were Flemish, saved from the scrapheap by Walpole's Italian agent,

[7 and 8] Letter Horace Walpole to Horace Mann, 12 June 1753

[9] Walpole, Horace, *A Description of the Villa of Mr. Horace Walpole at Strawberry-Hill near Twickenham, Middlesex*, Strawberry Hill, 1784

[10] Du Halde, *Description géographique, historique…de l'empire de la Chine et de la Tartarie Chinoise…*, Paris, 1734

[11] Cornforth, John, *Early Georgian Interiors*, Yale University Press, New Haven & London, 2004, p.266

house and Richard Bentley's drawings of Chinese pagodas. Classical taste was pandered to through small pieces of sculpture from Herculaneum and the Lucatelli ruins, whilst Bentley's designs filled a taste for chinoiserie: 'Italian, Chinese and Gothic buildings by Mr. Bentley, in his best style' and 'A Chinese building designed and drawn by Mr. Bentley for the corner of the wood at Strawberry-hill, where the chapel now stands'.[9] Bentley's Chinese and rococo drawings were inspired in part by a publication from Paris in five volumes recording the life and costumes of the people in the various provinces of China.[10] The use of chinoiserie within a garden setting was also influenced by the designs of William Kent in the first half of the eighteenth century which had become very fashionable. Although Bentley's Chinese garden designs were never realised at Strawberry Hill, his use of ornament was freely adapted and could be seen in parts of the garden.

Richard Bentley even designed a wallpaper covered in a butterfly design for another Twickenham neighbour using a Watteau drawing as a source;[11] this was later successfully printed as a commercial wallpaper, probably by Bromwich although this is uncertain, and it is possible to speculate that it might have been intended for one of the rooms at Strawberry Hill facing the garden. Could it have been this room?

Müntz, for a short time Walpole's resident artist, painted the house and stable. Fruit and flower still-life watercolours of orange and apple blossoms painted by Walpole's mother, Catherine Shorter, hung by the window. Small objects placed about the room were further reminders of the garden, two of them especially beautiful; a Battersea enamel box decorated with a kingfisher and ducks, and a copy of Isaac Oliver's miniature of Lord Herbert of Cherbury lying on a mossy bank contemplating the poetic life and surrounded by flowers. With so many paintings around the walls it must have been difficult to catch a glimpse of the background green of the walls, and the room must have had a similar impact on visitors as the China Closet below.

The Committee of Taste met in the Green Closet to discuss their plans for the next building projects, what was 'in' and what was 'out'. They consulted manuals on heraldry deciding where arms should be placed. A special coat of arms was devised, tongue-in-cheek, and was hung in the Green Closet and recorded by Horace Walpole in *The Description*:

Edward Lord Herbert of Cherbury
Or a Miniature by Isaac Oliver in the Possession of the R.t Hon.ble the E. of Orford.
Published as the Act directs May 1.st 1797 by E. Jeffery Pall Mall.

Design for the arms of the two clubs at White's; drawn by the second lord Edgcumbe, and invented by him, Mr. G.A. Selwyn, Mr. Geo. J. Williams, and Mr. Hor. Walpole, at Strawberry-hill. The arms are as follow: Vert (for the card-table) on a chevron sable (for the hazard-table) two rouleaus of guineas in saltire between two dice proper, the chevron between 3 parolis at Pharaoh, proper; on a canton sable, a white ballotting-ball. Crest, an arm and

ABOVE *Lord Herbert of Cherbury, hand-coloured engraving*

BELOW *Seventeenth-century glass fragment showing a grasshopper, now in the Armoury at Strawberry Hill*

ABOVE *Wallpaper from Walpole's bedroom, 1757, discovered beneath nineteenth-century wallpaper hung by Lady Waldegrave. Walpole's wallpaper would have been of blue wool flocking, now oxidised to brown, on a blue ground. The overall effect in the eighteenth century would have been of Venetian cut velvet damask*

[12] Walpole, Horace, *A Description of the Villa of Mr. Horace Walpole at Strawberry-Hill near Twickenham, Middlesex,* Strawberry Hill, 1784

[13] McLeod, B., 'Horace Walpole and Sèvres Porcelain', *Apollo,* January 1998

[14] Letter Horace Walpole to Richard Bentley, 31 October 1755

hand holding a dice-box, issuant from an earl's coronet. Supporters, an old and a young knave of clubs (for the two clubs.) Motto, cog-it amor nummi. The arms surrounded by a bottle-ticket inscribed, claret, in the manner of an order.[12]

A small, green-rimmed table of Sèvres porcelain which had a design later used as a pattern for a carpet in the Round Drawing Room also stood in the room.[13] The green theming was so specific that when Walpole added two books to his 1774 inventory he did not mention the titles, authors, or contents, but simply listed 'two green books'.

All the other rooms in the South Tower were bedchambers. In 1754 Walpole discussed the completion of his own bedchamber – facing the river and decorated in blue again. It was intended to bring together memories of all his favourite people in one room. He slept there until 1757 when a new bedroom was completed on the floor above, but it was to this earlier room that he would always return to sleep when attacks of gout crippled him and made mounting a second flight of stairs unthinkable. He described the room to Richard Bentley in a letter written in May of 1754:

...The great tower is finished on the outside, and the whole whitened, and has a charming effect, especially as the verdure of this year is beyond what

I have ever seen it: the grove nearest the house comes on much; you know I had almost despaired of its ever making a figure. The bow-window room over the supper-parlour is finished; hung with a plain blue paper, with a chintz bed and chairs; my father and mother over the chimney in the Gibbons frame, about which you know we were in dispute what to do. I have fixed on black and gold, and it has a charming effect over your chimney with the two dropping points, which is executed exactly; and the old grate of Henry VIII which you bought, is within it. In each panel round the room is a single picture; Gray's, Sir Charles Williams's, and yours, in their black and gold frames; mine is to match yours; and, on each side the door, are the pictures of Mr Churchill and Lady Mary, with their son, on one side, Mr Conway and Lady Ailesbury on the other. You can't imagine how new and pretty this furniture is. – I believe I must get you to send me an attestation under your hand that you knew nothing of it, that Mr Rigby may allow that at least this one room was by my own direction.

It is in this room, completed, as he told Bentley, to his own design, that the way he viewed himself can be seen. He presented himself in his bedroom as a patron of the arts, just as his father had been viewed before him. In Ecchardt's portrait of him, Strawberry Hill forms a gothic backdrop, and he holds in his hands the inventory he compiled of Houghton Hall, listing Robert Walpole's great collection, the *Aedes Walpolianae*. His portrait hangs beside one of Thomas Gray, whose poetry he had arranged for publication, and another of Richard Bentley, who designed much of Strawberry Hill as well as providing the illustrations for Gray's poems. To these men he acted as patron. To the craftsmen brought in to advise and work on the building he also became a patron. This was the age of great craftsmanship. In the Ecchardt painting the house is displayed as the finest gothic villa of the period in the same way as Houghton had been seen as the greatest house of the early eighteenth century. His parents' portrait was placed in a frame carved by Grinling Gibbons and hung above the chimney-piece which had been designed for Walpole by Richard Bentley; the position in which the paintings hung placed Bentley on equal footing with Gibbons. All the paintings by Ecchardt were completed in the same style showing Walpole and his friends wearing

the costume of an earlier age, in the cult style of Van Dyke's portraits; Walpole loved the seventeenth century. Doubtless the housekeeper showed the paintings, described them, and then hurried visitors along to the next room without giving them too much detail because Walpole never enlarged on his 'new and pretty' furniture.

Two of the other bedchambers were decidedly grand: the Red Bedchamber was hung with crimson paper and – as might have been expected – most of the objects within were red. Crimson Norwich damask covered the chairs and red and white flower-pots were placed decoratively around. The walls were hung, ceiling to floor, with paintings and drawings framed in the manner of another print room. Homely touches were added by the addition of an armchair which had patchwork covers,

several paintings by artists known to Walpole who had worked in Strawberry Hill and by drawings which showed local events. Bentley painted his self-portrait, with his second wife, on the shores of Jersey, and this was hung on the wall alongside a drawing of a young lady reading a copy of *The Castle of Otranto* to her friend. Two local views by Müntz jostled for wall space with mementos of Alexander Pope and a mezzotint of Walpole's favourite niece, Maria. The room was kept for John Chute's use when he was staying at Strawberry Hill, and he may have had a hand in choosing what was hung on the walls.

A second Blue Bedchamber, on the upper landing, was built for Walpole and finished in 1755. '…I am building a bedchamber for myself over the old blue-room, in which I intend to die, though not yet.'[14]

ABOVE *Sir Robert Walpole and Catherine Shorter, His First Wife, engraving after a painting by Ecchardt which hung at Strawberry Hill over Richard Bentley's chimneypiece*

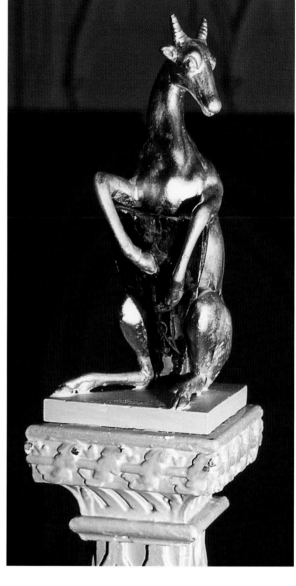

ABOVE *Henrietta Howard, Countess of Suffolk, engraving by Greatbach after a painting by Jervas in the collection of Alexander Pope which was later owned by Walpole*

ABOVE RIGHT *One of eight heraldic antelope supporters, lime wood, designed by Richard Bentley for the newel posts of the staircase*

*The cornice is now known to be Victorian

It looked out over the river and was hung with a brilliant blue flocked paper which resembled Venetian cut velvet damask – one of Bromwich's specialities. In this room textures were visually contrasted. It was not an over large room, but it was enhanced by a graceful chimneypiece adorned with vine leaves, which are also repeated in the cornice*, and by the choice of English glass set in the window. To reach the room his friends (not ticketed visitors on the housekeeper's tour) would have had to pass the eight heraldic antelope supporters holding Walpole's arms on the newel posts of the staircase. Richard Bentley designed a white bed on which two more antelope are shown on the bedposts in a watercolour, although it is uncertain if the bed was ever completed. However the design shows just how grand the room might have looked with heraldic beasts on the bed and coats of arms set within the

window. To complete the image of a family with roots back in the crusades, Walpole hung copies of Magna Carta and the death warrant of Charles I on either side of the bed. There were also some personal paintings hung around the room, mostly of theatrical works and copies of Watteau's masquerade paintings.

The Plaid Bedchamber, next door to Walpole's Blue Bedchamber, was also in the South Tower, and contained the portrait of the black sheep of the family – Henry the Jesuit, executed for treason when his plot to poison Queen Elizabeth failed. The 'plaid' used is likely to have been a combination blue and green plaid wallpaper, as all the other coloured rooms at Strawberry Hill were named after their wallpapers. It was however very unusual for a plaid or tartan fabric or wallpaper to be used in a bedchamber – it was neither fashionable nor popular in

LEFT *Design for a bed at Strawberry Hill by Richard Bentley, watercolour. It is possible that the bed was intended for Walpole's bedchamber, note the addition of the antelope supporters. Courtesy of the Lewis Walpole Library, Yale University*

mid-eighteenth-century society. Bearing in mind the Jacobite rising of 1745, and the ever present worry of a possible resurgence, it seems odd that it was chosen by Walpole*. The Scots, and all things Scottish, were decidedly unfashionable. At Richmond Lodge, another house in which the Walpole family had lived, there was also a 'plaid bed chamber', 'with Silk Plaid furniture lined with Green Silk and a Plaid coverlid'.[15] A mile downriver at Marble Hill Henrietta Howard also had a Plaid Bedchamber furnished with fabric given to her by Jonathan Swift after a trip to Ireland. Most of the rooms at Marble

Hill which overlooked the river, were decorated in green or blue like Strawberry Hill, and Henrietta and Horace were close friends, visiting each other regularly and exchanging gossip and ideas.

The housekeeper would have hurried her visitors on to the Armoury, from which point they could again view the Hall below and then be taken into Mr Walpole's favourite room, the Library. There the rainbow hues of the private rooms gave way to a great grey gothic centrepiece, made more spectacular after the colour of the bedchambers and the darkness of the stairwell and Armoury.

*During the restoration a very small fragment of blue diaper wallpaper was found

15 The National Archives, Kew, C101/20 p.40

7 The Library and the Star Chamber

'Everything in the world to tell posterity'

IN THE LIBRARY, built with extra height to increase the impression of gothic loftiness, the book presses soared upwards to be lost in a display of coats of arms on the ceiling. Wenceslaus Hollar's prints, illustrating sections of St Paul's Cathedral as it had been before being rebuilt by Christopher Wren, were kept in one of the presses. They had been published in the previous century and were used by John Chute as his source for the woodwork of the Library.[1] Chute copied one section of a print which showed the side door casing to the choir of the cathedral. By 1753, the date this wing was planned, the Committee of Taste was using the engravings of early gothic buildings to recapture their mood and significance as well as using them as pattern books and design sources. The books were ranged behind grey pierced arches made in a tracery of lime wood which had first been carved and then painted a stone colour. These provided a background through which the warmth of the books themselves with their leather bindings made the room a book-lover's delight.

After a terse reminder from Walpole that he had forgotten to calculate a depth for the shelves, Richard Bentley's fanciful design for the room was rejected in favour of John Chute's more antiquarian construction. The walls of book presses were only broken to take in a monumental, yet still delicate, chimneypiece which copied two of the great gothic

tombs: Clarence's stone tomb in Canterbury Cathedral (which held the coals) was surmounted by the spectacular canopy of John of Eltham's tomb from Westminster Abbey. The early St Paul's Cathedral, Canterbury Cathedral and Westminster Abbey were thus all brought together in an otherwise almost empty room. Held within the shelving the printed books of engravings which had been used for the design gave the room its provenance. Books furnished the room and emphasised that it was the working library of a man of letters.

Both in its design and in the selection of books the room defined Walpole's abiding interests: antiquarianism, heraldry and genealogy. Examples of his other enthusiasms in collecting were moved around the house as his interests changed. The general emptiness of the Library, for which no furniture was listed although there must have been some, would also have focused attention on what was there to be seen in paint, particularly on the ceiling. The design had been conceived by Walpole, drawn by Bentley, and painted by Jean-François Clermont, a popular French artist employed at the time in several neighbouring houses in Twickenham. His style was described by Walpole in *The Anecdotes of Painting*: 'He painted in grotesque, foliages with birds and monkeys, and executed several ceilings and ornaments of buildings in gardens.' The Library

[1] Dugdale, Sir William, *The History of St. Paul's Cathedral in London from its foundation until these times,* published by E. Maynard L.P., 1716

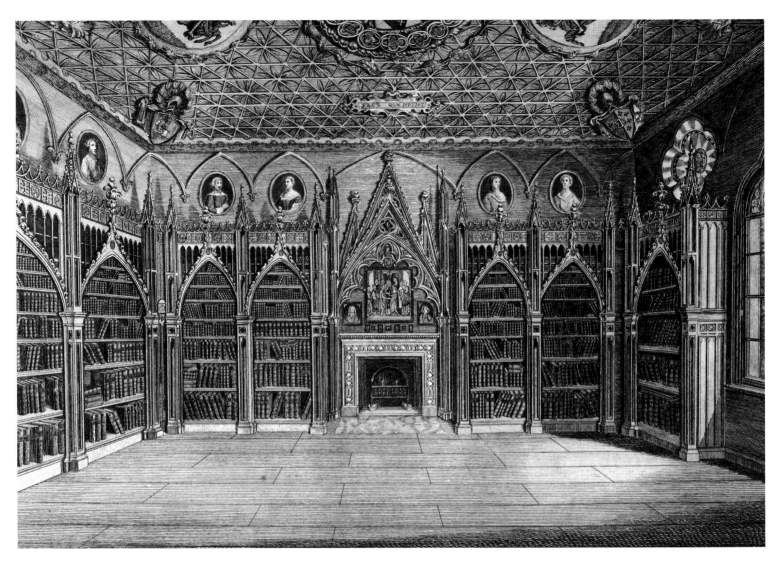

ABOVE *The Library, engraving by Godfrey*

OPPOSITE ABOVE
Sixteenth-century English glass of Queen Elizabeth I's coat of arms from the Library. This glass originally was in the window of the Closet within the Great North Bedchamber

OPPOSITE BELOW
The quarterings of the Right Hon. Horace Walpole, 4th Earl of Orford. Walpole inherited the title in 1791

[2] Letter Horace Walpole to Henry Seymour Conway, 5 August 1761

ceiling told the story of the Walpole family's heraldic antecedents from the time of the Crusades. This theme was then echoed in a band of cross-crosslets and Catherine wheels which ran round the top of the book presses. Two roundels of knights were painted on the ceiling against a mosaic background: they portrayed two Walpolian ancestors, Robsart and Fitzosbert. Walpole kept watercolours of the knights pasted into his own copy of *The Description of the Villa* and two pieces of glass set in the window show the same knights. The roundels are an example of the tight-knit theming at Strawberry Hill: each object had a place in the overall design and scheme of the house.

The room was designed and furnished, or not furnished, in a way which linked Walpole's living family to Robert Walpole's powerful position in Parliament and to historic figures of the past through the Walpole crest and thirteen family portraits. These were seen alongside painted glass

portraits of Charles I, Charles II and the royal arms of the Kings of England. His ancestor, Ludovic Robsart, who later became Lord Bourchier, acted as standard bearer to Henry V at the Battle of Agincourt and had been accorded a state burial in Westminster Abbey: he was the perfect ancestor and was portrayed on the ceiling. Knowledge and appreciation of a family's role in great events gained importance through the century, with some figures attaining cult status, among them Mary, Queen of Scots, and Charles I, whose tragic deaths fascinated Walpole. Out of the past around the room were portraits of Walpole's mother's family, the Shorters, taking pride of place amongst some of the great leaders of men – the admirals Howard and Drake hung alongside the romantic figure of Elizabeth of Bohemia, the Winter Queen. The portraits were to be read as part of the Shorter family tree. The family and the family's place in history were both significant factors in the creation of 'Strawberry

Hill Gothic' as a style. Assembling books, keeping records showing the provenance of objects, tracing genealogies, owning folios of engravings – all were part of the gothic movement.

The Library of Strawberry Hill was more than a storage space for books, it was an antiquarian's den, into which the smell of leather would have welcomed the user and where he would have been encouraged to relax and work beside a roaring fire. This alone of all the chimneypieces in the rebuilt Chopp'd Straw Hall was fashioned of stone, with a practical fire-basket and a *couvre-feu*, or fireguard, to protect the room from falling sparks or lighted coals once the reader had left.

> …I ought to write to you every day, whether I have anything to say or not. I am writing, I am building – both works that will outlast the memory of battles and heroes! Truly, I believe, the one will as much as t'other. My buildings are paper, like my writings, and both will be blown away in ten years after I am dead; if they had not the substantial use of amusing me while I live, they would be worth little indeed…[2]

Walpole was an organised reader. Books were carefully categorised and each volume had a special place within the Library with both shelf and press numbers. He had a habit of annotating his books and correcting the printed text; today these marginalia might be considered of greater interest than the books themselves. Müntz painted him sitting in an armchair by the window, surrounded by books, with the river behind him and with one of his spaniels at his feet. Classical ossuaries can be seen standing either side of the window. The implication is that the Walpoles could trace their ancestry back to ancient Rome.

Although Walpole's original intention when he bought Strawberry Hill may have been to use it as an occasional home for entertaining his friends and amusing himself, while he would spend most of the year comfortably in his London house, it is clear that the house soon dictated how his time, and his money, would be spent. This room was only one of several libraries in Strawberry Hill, the others were built as the number of volumes grew. The frequency of letters written from the house, together with the building of other libraries eventually holding over 7,000 books which were catalogued in 1763, all bear out the frequency of his visits. It was this room, the main library, which should be seen as a writer's

room, quiet and serene, noise held back through plain undecorated soundproof doors, reference material and inspirational volumes placed around: the *Aedes Walpolianae*, incunabula, 'Sir Julius Caesar's travelling library, containing 44 small volumes in Latin',[3] folios of works by Hogarth, Bunbury, Vertue, Tenniers, drawings by Müntz and Samuel Scott, three volumes of the engravings of Hollar, Richard Bentley's designs for Gray's poems, twelve folios containing prints of famous pre-Georgian Englishmen, his father's pocket book, designs and plans drawn for him by John Chute and 'The Iliad and Odyssey, the very books from which Pope made his translation: in one of the volumes is a view of Twickenham, drawn by Pope'.[4] As well as the classics Walpole loved Shakespeare and owned a Second Folio which was kept with his other most valued books in a locked cabinet. Into this same cabinet went a copy of everything published by his own printing press: it was an eclectic mix. Three of the book presses held about 800 books written either in French or about France, its literature and history; indicative of Walpole's lifelong love of France and all things French. The French also expressed interest in his writing, and when Louis XVI was imprisoned, awaiting news of his fate, he passed the time by translating one of Horace Walpole's works, *Historic Doubts on the Life and Reign of King Richard III*.

Walpole recognised the things which were important to him – art, his Collection, his family, his reputation and his place in history. On 28 June 1760 he explained to his cousin Conway: '...I have Conway papers to sort; I have lives of the painters to write; I have my prints to paste, my house to build, and everything in the world to tell posterity...' The world was to be told through letters. In them he wrote expressing his great respect and admiration for his father, while his love for his mother shines out through each anecdote he relates of her life. Some of the letters he wrote are among the finest in the English language. He especially admired Madame de Sévigné's letters, appreciating her dry wit, irony and ability to convey events succinctly to the reader.

His own style varied depending on the recipient, each series of letters on a single theme was directed to the same correspondent; when one of his correspondents died he was replaced by another to whom he corresponded on the same theme. His letters are entertaining and natural, in them his humanity and compassion are clear and his correspondents come to life. He wrote to Thomas Gray on literature, and later on antiquarianism – a subject which he also discussed with William Cole. He kept Lady Ossory informed about the happenings and gossip in Society and to Richard Bentley he related quirky events, often tongue-in-cheek. Bentley recalled that Walpole had written his letters with the greatest ease imaginable, even when guests were present in the same room and while he was speaking to other people.[5] Possibly his best letters were sent to George Montagu, seemingly spontaneous, many nonsensical, but always delightful. It was Montagu whom he directed when he was eighteen, to retain and return the letters he received, '...Mine is a life of letter writing...'.

[3] and [4] Walpole, Horace, *A Description of the Villa of Mr. Horace Walpole at Strawberry-Hill near Twickenham, Middlesex*, Strawberry Hill, 1784

Mary Berry who became his literary executrix described his method:

> …He wrote his letters as rapidly as his disabled fingers would allow him to form the characters of a remarkably legible hand. No rough draughts or sketches of familiar letters were found among his papers at Strawberry Hill: but he was in the habit of putting down on the backs of letters or on slips of paper, a note of the facts, of news, of witticisms, or of anything he wished not to forget, for the amusement of his correspondents.[6]

The letters which he wrote over a long period to Horace Mann, whom he had met for only a short period whilst on the Grand Tour, act as a political diary of the work of the government and serve as a commentary on the momentous events of the day. They appear effortless – which suggests a degree of revision. His account of the Gordon Riots, written giving varying details of the events to several of his friends as they took place over several days, while he fled from one house to another and London burnt around him, is unsurpassed as an example of a contemporary chronicle.

Walpole's position in society enabled him to be present at, or hear first hand about, the great events of the century. He recounted them both as a participant and as an onlooker. In his letter recording the funeral of George II he transports the reader to Westminster Abbey. While sitting in the abbey he must at some point have looked upwards and studied the great fan-vaulted roof; it was at around the time of the funeral that he decided to record the elaborate tracery of the roof

5 and 6 Pink, M. Alderton, ed., *The Letters of Horace Walpole*, Macmillan, London, 1938, p.xvii

---

THE FUNERAL OF GEORGE II IN WESTMINSTER ABBEY

Extract from a letter from Horace Walpole to George Montagu, written from Arlington Street, 13 November 1760.

… Do you know I had the curiosity to go to the burying t'other night; I had never seen a royal funeral. Nay, I walked as a rag of quality, which I found would be, and so it was, the easiest way of seeing it. It is absolutely a noble sight. The Prince's Chamber hung with purple and a quantity of silver lamps, the coffin under a canopy of purple velvet, and six vast chandeliers of silver on high stands had a very good effect: The ambassador from Tripoli and his son were carried to see that chamber. The procession through a line of foot-guards, every seventh man bearing a torch, the horse-guards lining the outside, their officers with drawn sabres and crape sashes, on horseback, the drums muffled, the fifes, bells tolling and minute guns, all this was very solemn. But the charm was the entrance of the Abbey, where we were received by the Dean and chapter in rich copes, the choir and almsmen all bearing torches; the whole Abbey so illuminated, that one saw it to greater advantage than by day; the tombs, long aisles, and fretted roof all appearing distinctly, and with the happiest chiaroscuro. There wanted nothing but incense, and little chapels here and there with priests saying mass for the repose of the defunct – yet one could not complain of its not being Catholic enough. I had been in dread of being coupled with some boy of ten years old – but the heralds were not very accurate, and I walked with George Grenville, taller and older enough to keep me in countenance. When we came to the chapel of Henry VII all solemnity and decorum ceased – no order was observed, people sat or stood where they could or would, the yeomen of the guard were crying out for help, oppressed by the immense weight of the coffin, the Bishop read sadly, and blundered in the prayers, the fine chapter, Man that is born of a woman, was chanted not read, and the anthem, besides being unmeasurably tedious, would have served as well for a nuptial. The real serious part was the figure of the Duke of Cumberland, heightened by a thousand melancholy circumstances. He had a dark brown adonis, and a cloak of black cloth with a train of five yards. Attending the funeral of a father, how little reason soever he had to love him, could not be pleasant. His leg extremely bad, yet forced to stand upon it near two hours, his face bloated and distorted with his late paralytic stroke, which has affected too one of his eyes, and placed over the mouth of the vault, into which in all probability he must himself so soon descend – think how unpleasant a situation! He bore it all with a firm and unaffected countenance. This grave scene was fully contrasted by the burlesque Duke of Newcastle – he fell into a fit of crying the moment he came into the chapel and flung himself back in a stall, the Archbishop hovering over him with a smelling bottle – but in two minutes his curiosity got the better of his hypocrisy and he ran about the chapel with his glass to spy who was or was not there, spying with one hand and mopping his eyes with t'other. Then returned the fear of catching cold, and the Duke of Cumberland, who was sinking with heat, felt himself weighed down, and turning round, found it was the Duke of Newcastle standing upon his train to avoid the chill of the marble. It was very theatric to look down into the vault, where the coffin lay, attended by mourners with lights. Clavering, the Groom of the Bedchamber, refused to sit up with the body, and was dismissed by the King's order…

7 Toynbee, Paget, *Journal of the Printing-Office at Strawberry Hill*, The Chiswick Press for Constable and Company Ltd. and Houghton Mifflin Company, 1923, pp.7-13

BELOW *A book written by Walpole and published by the Strawberry Hill Press*

by using it as a source for the ceiling of the Gallery he was building.

Walpole wrote several of his works in the Library, deciding in 1757 to set up his own printing press to publish only those works of which he was proud, either written by himself or by his friends. The political articles he wrote would continue to be published in London, mostly anonymously. In founding and owning a private press he never had any intention of making money. Most of the books he produced were either presented to friends as gifts or sold to bring in money for charity.

Under 1758 in the *Journal of the Printing-Office at Strawberry-hill* comes the entry:

An Account of Russia, as it was in the year 1710: written by the late Lord Whitworth.

September 29th finished Ld Whitworth's book. 700 copies printed, 600 sold, for the benefit of the Poor of Twickenham, at 3s. a vol. but deducting 3d for binding in blue paper, & 3d to the bookseller for selling them…

Work by Thomas Gray opened the Press, followed by thirty-three other full length books and several miscellaneous works which he called 'detached pieces'. Several printers were hired or fired before finally Thomas Kirgate arrived in 1765 to become printer, and later secretary and librarian. Until Kirgate's arrival Walpole did not have much luck with printers – were his standards too exacting? The following is an extract from the same *Journal* highlighting 1759 as a difficult year. On 10 February an article was published:

…Without Mr. Walpole's knowledge or approbation.
March 5th. Robinson the printer went away.
March 20th there was printed & cried about the streets of London a Grubstreet paper on Kitty Fisher: at bottom they had put (to make it sell) written and printed at Strawberry-hill.
March 29th. My new printer, Benjamin Williams, came.
May 25th. He went away.
June 19th. James Lister, a new Printer, came; staid but a week.
July 16th. The fourth Printer, Thomas Farmer, came.
July 18th. took Joseph Forrester prentice into the Printing-house.

…

1761 December 2nd. Thomas Farmer ran away for debt. I thought he had finished the two volumes [of Lucan] but he had left 19 sheets not printed off. Took one Pratt to finish the work.

Pratt lasted until 30 December 1764 when he was 'turned away'.[7]

In keeping with other rooms at Strawberry Hill a strong emphasis was placed on heraldry in the decoration of the Library. Although a rudimentary form of heraldry was in use in England by about 1150, it was the period of the Crusades which gave it real significance. Heraldry was seen as providing an inseparable link with past generations and was a statement of Englishness; it established the bearer's detailed biography and was a way of remembering

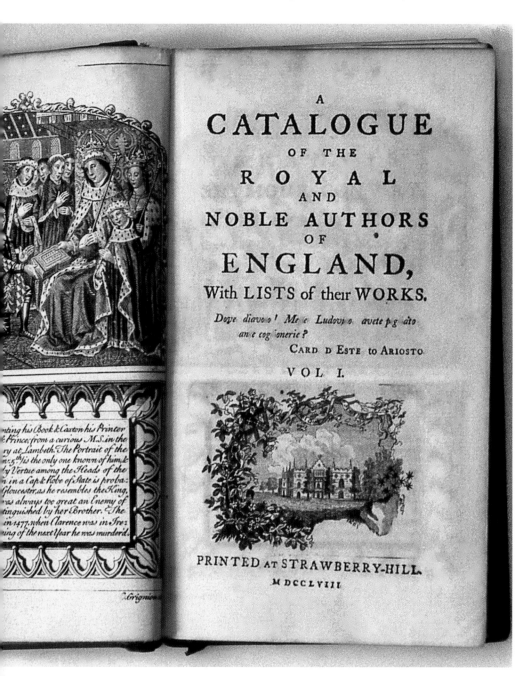

A
CATALOGUE
OF THE
ROYAL
AND
NOBLE AUTHORS
OF
ENGLAND,
With LISTS of their WORKS.

Deve diavolo! Messer Ludovico avete pigliato tante coglionerie?

CARD D ESTE to ARIOSTO

VOL I.

PRINTED AT STRAWBERRY-HILL.
MDCCLVIII

LEFT *One of Horace Walpole's bookplates*

The Walpole coat of arms was given a vantage point in most rooms, sometimes through painted *trompe l'œil* effects, and sometimes through the commission of complete sets of upper lights to a window displaying painted coats of arms, as in the Long Gallery and Little Parlour. The additions made to the arms through successive generations traced the marriages and alliances of the family and built up a web of those from whom assistance might be

BELOW *Device of a Saracen added by Lady Waldegrave to the floor of the Long Gallery in 1856 as a tribute to Horace Walpole*

and reinventing the history of a family. The practice of heraldry had grown up from necessity as part of the feudal system of the Middle Ages, enabling identification of the bearer in jousts, tournaments (as in racing colours today), and in time of war, when it became essential in the recognition of armoured knights on the field. The signs (or ensigns) were worn embroidered on tunics which partially covered the armour, thus 'coats of arms'. The same (en)sign was painted on the shield, on pennons for lances and on banners. Heraldry in England developed over a period of centuries out of the general European need to develop an easily understood symbolic language – known as Grammar – using colours, symbols, figures and devices to produce a unique identification. The use of seals on documents evolved from copies of the devices shown on the shields which instantly identified the authority of the signatory. Walpole kept a collection of coins in the Library and elsewhere had a large number of seals. (A thousand years earlier, coins, standards and shields had also all borne devices, but these were not unique to the bearer, could be changed at will and could not be regarded as a positive means of indentification.)

numerals for 1754, which was the year in which the room was completed.

This room encapsulated Walpole's two great loves, romance and history. The two were brought together in the glass setting of the Library window, which was mostly of old English glass containing a sequence displaying the arms of England in the apex of the window ogee. In his Commonplace Book of 1780 Walpole summed up epigrammatically: 'History is a Romance that is believed; Romance a History not believed – that is the Difference between them.'

One of the most romantic objects kept in the Library was a clock which had once belonged to Henry VIII. Walpole printed the following description in 1774 for his friends:

> A clock of silver gilt, richly chased, engraved, and ornamented with fleurs de lys, little heads, etc. on the top sits a lion holding the arms of England, which are also on the sides. This was a present from Henry 8th to Anne Boleyn; and since, from lady Elizabeth Germaine to Mr. Walpole. On the weights are the initial letters of Henry and Anne, within true lovers knots; at top, Dieu et mon Droit.[8]

On quitting the room, the visitors would follow Margaret down one flight of stairs, through a door on the landing, which took them out of Walpole's internal tower, but kept them within the Chopp'd Straw Hall part of the house. On the stairway the first portraits they passed recalled the reign of the Plantaganets. When they entered the Star Chamber Henry VII, the first of the Tudor kings, was seen modelled in effigy by Torreggiano. Then they passed onwards through time, to the reign of Henry VIII, which they encountered when they entered the Holbein Chamber. It was a tour through history as well as through the house and gave a unique importance to the decoration.

The Star Chamber was built over the front door and formed part of the old Chopp'd Straw Hall, when it might have been used as a bedchamber. Initially painted pink, it was quickly changed by Walpole to: '...a small anti-room, painted green, with golden stars in mosaic. It has a large window entirely of painted glass.'[9] The stars are likely to have been made in papier mâché, bought separately from the paper, and individually stuck on in a mosaic design*.

claimed through blood. A display of arms might be placed above or below paintings, on glass, produced as separate decorative objects, painted on ceramics, engraved on silver, embroidered on upholstery, overmantels, fire-poles, or screens. The display of a Saracen's head, the device of the Walpoles, achieved an effect which it is difficult to quantify today. An image of a Saracen, or Moor, on a coat of arms linked the holder with England's part in the Crusades and the fight to rescue Jerusalem. At Houghton, Robert Walpole's Saracen is flanked by two antelope; it is these antelope, heraldic supporters or protectors of Walpole's house, which pointed the way from the Entrance Hall of Strawberry Hill up the staircase, and led the way into the Library (or up to Walpole's Bed Chamber on the second floor). In the Library the roundels and lozenges on the ceiling linked the family's heraldic devices with their motto, *Fare Quae Sentiat* (do what you think) and with the gothicised Roman

The following letter was written on 4 June 1752 by Lady Luxborough to her friend William Shenstone:

…I must now beg the favour of you to instruct me about the ceiling of my bed-room, which I would have adorned a little with papier mâché and the ground painted a colour; but do not know where to get my paper-ornaments, nor how to have them fixed up: for no person hereabouts has the smallest idea of it.

Shenstone replied immediately and two days after her first letter Lady Luxborough writes again:

Your quick return to my troublesome letter gave me much pleasure, but no surprize, as you have long accustomed me to all friendly attentions on your part: but your taking down your whole ceiling to send me, merely to satisfy my impertinent curiosity, is a gallantry that quite confounds me…[10]

The chairs standing in the Star Chamber were special and very different from others in the house. In the window of his own Bedchamber Walpole had a sixteenth-century piece of religious Flemish glass which showed a strange triangular chair. The design had been copied, and a carpenter engaged to make

two similar chairs which were placed in this anteroom. Close by stood a second pair of chairs, this time Welsh arm-chairs, which had been bought at a sale of the goods of Walpole's friend, Richard Bateman. They were painted blue and white and dressed with cushions of point lace which hung decoratively over the frames.

A rich, albeit dim, colour was brought into the room by light filtered through the glass, through the use of gold stars in the decoration, through the blue and white furniture, and through all the other objects which were kept there, every piece emphasising the richness of the space. There were pieces of white Sèvres porcelain decorated with gilding of various shades and qualities of gold, two cabinets filled with coins and medals of different metals, and vases of simulated porphyry. After the gloomth and uniform grey of the Staircase, Armoury and Library the multiplicity of rich colours would have dazzled the visitors. In 1759 Walpole added a new wing, using this room as the bridge between the two. When they were ready to leave the Star Chamber the visitors entered a Passage down which they were shepherded by Margaret into the new wing. Colour and light ceased.

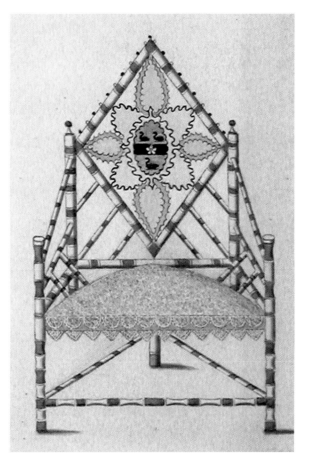

[8] Walpole, Horace, *A Description of the Villa of Horace Walpole at Strawberry-Hill, near Twickenham*, Strawberry Hill, 1774

[9] Walpole, Horace, *A Description of the Villa of Mr. Horace Walpole at Strawberry-Hill near Twickenham, Middlesex*, Strawberry Hill, 1784

[10] Luxborough, Lady, *Letters*, Dublin, 1776, p.13

8 The Trunk-ceiled Passage and the Holbein Chamber

'All is papier-mâché'

OPPOSITE *View of the obelisk from the house, eighteenth-century engraving showing a window of the Holbein Chamber in which the armorial glass and diaper-work designed by Price can be seen*

JUNE 1783 WAS A MONTH OF DOWNPOURS. In a letter written from his Berkeley Square house to his friend Lady Ossory on 20 June 1783, Walpole described a visit which took place in terrible weather:

…I had a worse woe the next night. …It rained all the time as it had done the preceeding evening…at a quarter before eight the bell rang at the gate - and behold a procession of the Duke, his two daughters, the French ambassador (on whom I had meant to sink myself), Lady Pembroke, Lord Herbert and Lord Robert. The first word M. de Guines said was to beg I would show them all I could – Imagine, Madam, what I could show them when it was pitch dark! Of all houses upon earth mine, from the painted glass and overhanging trees, wants the sun the most, besides the Star Chamber and passage being obscured on purpose to raise the gallery. They ran their foreheads against Henry VII and took the grated door of the Tribune for the dungeon of the castle. I mustered all the candlesticks in the house, but before they could be lighted up, the young ladies, who by the way are extremely natural, agreeable and civil, were seized with a panic of highwaymen and wanted to go.

The passage described by Walpole and through which Margaret now led the visitors stretched away into the darkness, lit only by a single window of amber glass at the far end. There appeared to be

*On analysis only plaster with applied wooden fretwork was found

two doors leading off to the right, one to the left; the very number of doors elongating the space. The walls were covered in a strange kind of paper which Walpole described as having a 'treillage' design*. Once again it was grey, but the overall appearance was varied by a design of lozenges pressed deep into it. This produced an embossed paper with the pattern lying proud of the wall, and to this thin timber strips were added. When the paper caught the light it would have appeared both shadowy and three dimensional, possibly looking as if it was stone. Shadows thrown from the single candlestick kept in the passage for everyday household use would have increased this illusion. However, it is unlikely that Margaret would have lit the candle in advance for her visitors peering through the gloom, nor would she have instructed one of the other servants to do so – darkness was the order of the day.

From this point on Walpole added to Strawberry Hill with different criteria in mind. By 1759 he and his spectacular Collection had outgrown their living space. New space had to be found. At the same time Strawberry Hill had to appear to be an old family house to which rooms had been added over time, as if it had been an ancestral home. The Chopp'd Straw Hall house was already bursting at the seams, with more objects being added all the time. Walpole was unable to resist attending sales, negotiating exchanges with friends and other collectors and

ABOVE *View of the 'Trunk-Cieled Passage' (sic) and the entrance to the Holbein Chamber, watercolour, courtesy of the Lewis Walpole Library, Yale University*

RIGHT *Screen in the Holbein Chamber, designed by Richard Bentley, engraving*

[1] Cornforth, John, *Early Georgian Interiors*, Yale University Press, New Haven & London, 2004, p.119

so he created the same impact in the additional rooms either by using new materials, or through the use of new technology. By so doing he gained other advantages: the work was cheaper to complete and his workmen understood what was required of them. This had not always been true in the past.

By keeping the paint used in passageways and walkways to dull, non-colours, Walpole increased the impact of colour when he used it in important rooms. By the middle of the century the production and availability of coloured pigments in paints used by workmen, and their stability when exposed to light, were greatly improved. In 1734 a list was printed in *Palladio Londonensis* giving the costs of various colours produced for these craftsmen. The most frequently used colours of 'best white lead', cream or stone, cost only 4d a pound; the so-called 'nut' colours of walnut and mahogany were around 6d a pound; gold cost 8d; olive, pea green and 'fine sky-blue mixed with Prussian blue' cost between 8d to 12d (Prussian blue had been discovered in about 1710 and only became reasonably priced in the 1730s); orange was also 12d, but 'fine deep green' was half a crown (two shillings and sixpence).[1] Therefore the use and choice of colours was not just dramatic or associative, but was a positive statement of wealth and largesse. In a period in which artificial light was normally low, strong, bright colours were generally popular.

When Margaret opened the door into the Holbein Chamber and ushered her visitors just inside, their surprise would have been immediate; it was like entering into summer sunlight after winter darkness. From the amber light of the Passage they passed into the purple glow of a most extraordinary room.

chasing objects he had heard might come on the market. In addition, he travelled in both England and France visiting other country houses, constantly refreshing his mind on changes in decorative techniques and taste, and at the same time refuelling his thirst for acquisition. The newly built rooms therefore were to house the Collection in a specific way, placing objects together thematically in order to increase their impact and enable visitors to see and appreciate them in the way Walpole intended. One Holbein drawing is beautiful; a room filled with Holbeins defies description. Adding to the old building also allowed Walpole to have larger rooms which could be erected on an axis best able to receive light at the time of day he wanted and at the strength he required. These rooms were built using the technologies of the future rather than the past. Just as he had used Bentley's modern Refectory chair to define a new design style in furniture,

It was a room of conspicuous wealth built in two halves separated by a pierced screen designed by Richard Bentley. The screen was surmounted by a jester's, or Saracen's, head and was bordered by Catherine wheels and cross-crosslets. A monumental chimneypiece, possibly Bentley's greatest achievement at Strawberry Hill, dominated the room.

Visitors were not encouraged to wander around or to examine what was displayed too closely, instead they were restrained inside the door between the state bed on one side and the wall on the other; they viewed the room as they would have viewed a set-

piece in a theatre, through a proscenium arch which was formed by the screen. What they saw through the screen was a room with walls clad in royal purple, the depth of amethyst colour reinforced by purple light coming from the red and blue glass in the upper lights of the windows; there were purple hangings, ebony furniture, and everywhere around the walls examples of Holbein's work. The effect the room made on someone entering was described by Thomas Gray, writing in September 1759 before it was completed, to Dr Wharton, one of his regular correspondents, who was another lover of gothic:

Dear Doctor,

...Mr. Walpole has lately made a new bed-chamber, which as it is in the best taste of anything he has yet done, and in your own Gothic way, I must describe a little. You enter by a peaked door at one corner of the room (out of a narrow winding passage, you may be sure) into an alcove, in which the bed is to stand, formed by a screen of pierced work opening by one large arch in the middle to the rest of the chamber, which is lighted at the other end by a bow-window of three bays, whose tops are of rich painted glass in a mosaic. The ceiling is covered and fretted in star and quatre-foil compartments, with roses at the intersections, all is papier-mâché. The chimney on your left is the high altar in the cathedral of Rouen (from whence the screen also is taken), consisting of a low surbased arch between two octagon towers, whose pinnacles almost reach the ceiling, all of nich-work; the chairs and dressing-table are real carved ebony, picked up at auctions. The hangings uniform, purple paper, hung all over with the court of Henry the VIII. copied after the Holbeins in the queen's closet at Kensington, in black and gold frames. The bed is to be either from Burleigh (for Lord Exeter is new-furnishing it, and means to sell some of his original household stuff) of the rich old tarnished embroidery; or if that is not to be had, and it must be new, it is to be a cut velvet with a dark purple pattern on a stone-colour satin ground, and deep mixed fringes and tassels.[2]

The chairs and dressing-table Gray mentioned in his letter were of seventeenth-century Indo-Portuguese manufacture, shining with polish and presenting an appearance of great age. Shortly after the room was completed in 1760 Mrs J. Henrietta Pye wrote an account of a visit she had made which was then published in an early guidebook.

Mr. Walpole's ... Represents an ancient Abby, and the Inside is quite answerable to its venerable Aspect. The Rooms and Furniture have all the noble Simplicity, yet Magnificence of Antiquity, without its decay. The State Bed-Chamber is hung with a plain Lilac Paper, and cover'd almost with Pictures, finely copied from the Originals of Holbens, in black Frames with a Gold Worm; the Chairs in this Room (and indeed throughout the whole House) are black Ebony exquisetly wrought: The Bed, which stands behind two screens of antique Carving, in the Manner of an Alcove, is made in the Form of a

Canopy, supported by four fluted Pillars of black Ebony; it is compos'd of the finest Lilac Broad Cloth, lin'd with white Sattin, and a Counterpane of white Sattin also; the whole is adorned with a tufted Fringe of black and white: At the Top is a most elegant Plume of white Ostrich Feathers, and above that another of Lilac; but the Gothic Taste is admirably preserved thro' the whole; this is call'd the Holbens Chamber. The windows are all painted, and so exquisitely, that they seem to promise a Revival of that long forgotten Art. The Library contains a fine Collection of Books, and is entirely calculated for learned Retirement and Contemplation. You are struck with a Awe at entering it, proceeding from
"The high embowed Roof,
And antique Pillars massy Proof,
And storied Windows richly dight,
Casting a dim, religious Light."[3]

As Walpole was unable to buy the Burleigh bed a new bed was commissioned from Vile, a carver, gilder and upholsterer and one of the greatest of the London cabinet makers. The bed cost Walpole ninety pounds at a time when a good, plain bed could have been bought for two guineas. By 1760

[2] *The Poems of Thomas Gray with a Selection of Letters and Essays*, J.M. Dent and Sons, London, 1912, pp.220-21

[3] Pye, Henrietta, *A Short Account of the principal seats and gardens in and about Twickenham*, London, 1760. The quotation used by Henrietta Pye is from John Milton's poem *Il Penseroso*.

cut-velvet drapery on beds was no longer the fashion, but the long folds of velvet material he chose showing the pattern and rich texture would have made an instant impact; it was recognisably an expensive luxurious bed and its separation from the rest of the room by the screen suggested that this was a state bed possibly in the French tradition.

In November Thomas Gray gave a further description of the window of the room and added some advice to Dr Wharton who was then considering buying similar glass for his own house:

> Green glass is not classical, nor ever seen in a real church-window, but where there is history painted, and there the green is remarkably bad. I propose the rich amethyst-purple instead of it. The mosaic pattern can hardly come amiss, only do not let too much yellow and scarlet come together. If I could describe the mosaic at Mr. Walpole's it would be of no use to you, because it is not merely made of squares put together, but painted in a pattern of Price, and shaded. It is as if little balaustines, or pomegranate flowers, were set four together and formed a lozenge. These are of a golden yellow, with a white pearl at the junctions, and the spaces inclosed by them are scarlet or blue. This repeated makes a diaper-work, and fills the whole top of the window…[4]

Armorial glass was placed within the diaper-work. Mr Price's reputation was high and the glazing of these windows costly. Walpole had to pay fifteen guineas for them. However, in his accounts for the same year he set down a spending of almost three times that amount, forty-two pounds, on orange trees for the garden.[5]

The papier mâché ceiling which had been designed for the room by Müntz, Walpole's artist-in-residence at the time, and described so vividly by Thomas Gray, was one example of the technical advances leapt on by Walpole because of its relative cheapness, strength and pliability. By the time the chamber was completed its use had become so widespread that woodcarvers were worried by the prospect of losing trade; even the stucco craftsmen found themselves unable to compete on cost.

It was the French who claimed to have invented the technique of making papier mâché towards the end of the seventeenth century, although a similar material, called *carta pesta*, was in use in Italy before 1600. Papier mâché reached the height of fashion

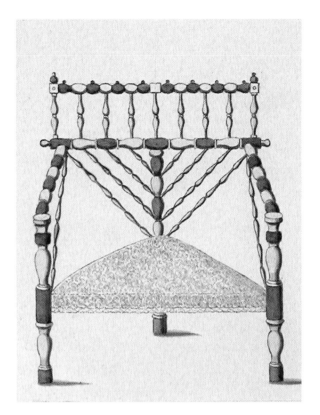

in England by the mid-eighteenth century, possibly due to the increased production of prints, books and wallpaper, all of which generated paper, or possibly due to its durability and flexibility. It was made by first pulping the fabric-based paper, mixing it with either glue and chalk, or with a flour, size and water paste, and usually giving it several coats of varnish when dry. It was then shaped and finished by giving it a coat of size. The result was very strong and rarely suffered damage. Papier mâché quickly caught on as an ornamental embellishment for ceilings, where it was used because of its lightness, strength and adaptability, it was also used for picture frames and other decorative objects. Some of the raised decorative elements, like the stars on the ceiling of the Star Chamber, which became popular in eighteenth-century interiors, were finished in moulds with intaglio designs cut into them; a process which was patented by one of Walpole's neighbours, William Brindley of Twickenham.[6]

The use of purple in the room would have suggested majesty, it was the symbol of kingship. This feeling was intensified by the portraits hanging around the walls; the visitor was invited to visit the Tudor Court. The inspiration for creating the room may well have been the acquisition of George Vertue's thirty-four tracings on to oil-paper of Holbein drawings in the possession of the king

[4] *The Poems of Thomas Gray with a Selection of Letters and Essays*, J.M. Dent and Sons, London, 1912, pp.222-23

[5] Toynbee, Paget, *Strawberry Hill Accounts*, Clarendon Press, Oxford, 1927, p.8

[6] Devoe, Shirley Spaulding, *English papier mâché of the Georgian and Victorian Periods*, Barrie and Jenkins, London, 1971, p.25

and hung in Buckingham House. To these Walpole added other original Holbein drawings which he owned. The room celebrated Holbein as the quintessential artist of the period; Henry VIII for his ability to govern and his single-minded determination to secure the succession; and England's break with Rome, through the Act of Supremacy, whereby Henry and successive monarchs became spiritually as well as temporally Defenders of the Faith. Hanging the Holbeins against a purple wallpaper displayed them to advantage.

Walpole had searched for some time before deciding on a name for his new Chamber; ten years before when he had been country house visiting with John Chute he had written to George Montagu describing some of the things they had seen on their travels:

> Dear George,
>
> If you love good roads, conveniences, good inns, plenty of postillions and horses be so kind to yourself as never to go into Sussex … our greatest pleasure was seeing Cowdry. …I was charmed with the front, and the court and the fountain, but the room called Holbein's, except the curiosity of it, is wretchedly painted, and infinitely inferior to those delightful histories of Harry the Eighth in the private apartment at Windsor. I was much more pleased with a whole-length picture of Sir Antony Brown in the very dress in which he wedded Anne of Cleves by proxy. …I have set up my staff, and finished my pilgrimages for this year. Sussex is a great damper of curiosity.
>
> Adieu![7]

As the first room in a series which together formed a suite of parade or state rooms, built at a time when there was generally a move away from building in a processional plan, the Holbein Chamber was designed to impress, first through making an initial impact and second through the sheer number of great and curious objects it housed. Until he decided to build on a further suite of rooms starting with a Gallery, this room was intended to be the final room to be shown to visitors. Many of Walpole's most important and ancient pieces of furniture were placed in the Chamber, particularly those which encapsulated the Tudor world. There was a collection of combs: 'one of ivory is extremely ancient, carved with figures, on one side representing persons bathing and going to

bed, and on the other, two men and a woman with musical instruments'.[8] Cardinal Wolsey's hat was hung by the bed, a witty way of accentuating both the Tudor and religious themes of the room.

Walpole patently enjoyed buying and owning chairs which were out of the ordinary. As well as six ebony chairs, the Holbein Chamber contained a chair which Walpole believed to have come from Glastonbury Abbey and which he described as 'very old'. Ownership of the Glastonbury Chair bestowed on him custodianship of our past and he had once placed it at breakfast for the Archbishop of Canterbury to sit upon. Another chair was made especially for the room using a pane of glass found in the Blue Breakfast Room window as a pattern; when finished the chair was dressed in purple cloth. Walpole noted that '…the height of the feet will determine the seat'. … By mixing the old with the new he increased the feeling of a house slowly evolving over the centuries and made the 'old' chairs seem still older and yet more venerable. Custom-made chairs for the house had been advocated by Thomas Gray in August 1752 when he was looking at what was available for sale:

> …The true original chairs were all sold … there are nothing now but Halsey chairs, not adapted to the squareness of a Gothic dowager's rump. And by the way I do not see how the uneasiness and uncomfortableness of a coronation chair can be any objection with you: every chair that is easy is modern, and unknown to our ancestors. As I remember, there were certain low chairs, that looked like ebony, at Esher, and were old and pretty. Why should not Mr Bentley improve upon them.[9]

The sheer number of paintings and drawings hanging in the room, as well as their quality, would have suggested to Margaret's visitors a visit to an exhibition, with the priceless nature of what they saw underlined by not being allowed to enter fully into the room. Robert Walpole had a good eye and had loved art; Horace grew up surrounded by paintings, appreciating their beauty and recognising their importance in defining an interior. For the rich, the eighteenth century was a period of consumption and of novelty; vast fortunes changed hands nightly over gambling tables with the contents of houses being offered up for auction. Attending sales of paintings or furniture and visiting exhibitions became fashionable pastimes.

[7] Letter Horace Walpole to George Montagu written from Strawberry Hill, 26 August 1749

[8] Walpole, Horace, *A Description of the Villa of Mr. Horace Walpole at Strawberry-Hill near Twickenham, Middlesex*, Strawberry Hill, 1784

[9] Letter Thomas Gray to Horace Walpole, August 1752

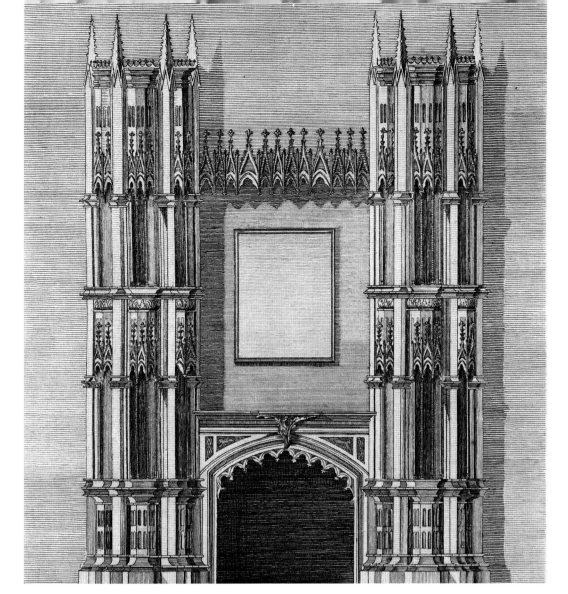

Collectors were beginning to consider the overall impact of objects in the creation of design. Horace Walpole described the practice to Horace Mann in a letter written from Strawberry Hill on 6 May 1770:

…There has lately been an auction of stuffed birds, and, as natural history is in fashion, there are physicians and others who paid 40 and 50 guineas for a single Chinese pheasant. You may buy a live one for five. After this, it is not extraordinary that pictures should be dear. We have at present three exhibitions. One West, who paints history in the taste of Poussin, gets £300 for a piece not too large to hang over a chimney. He has merit, but is hard and heavy, and far unworthy of such prices. The rage to see these exhibitions is so great, that sometimes one cannot pass through the streets where they are. But it is incredible what sums are raised by mere exhibitions of anything; a new fashion, and to enter at which you pay a shilling or half a crown. Another rage is for prints of English portraits, I have been collecting them above thirty years, and originally never gave for a mezzotinto above one or two shillings. The lowest are now a crown, most from half a guinea to a guinea. Lately I assisted a clergyman in compiling a catalogue of them; since the publication, scarce heads in books, not worth three pence, will sell for five guineas. Then we have Etruscan vases, made of earthen ware in Staffordshire, from two to five guineas; and or moulu, never made here before, which succeeds so well, that a tea-kettle which the inventor offered for 100 guineas, sold by auction for 130. In short, we are at the height of extravagance and improvements, for we do improve rapidly in taste as well as in the former. I cannot say so much for our genius.

Seen from the doorway the genius of Holbein outshone all else. The final object listed by Walpole in his description of the rooms to be seen before the visitors moved on was, 'A carpet worked by Mrs. Catherine Clive, the celebrated comedian'. Was this his invitation to visitors and guests to recognise the room as a piece of theatre and to smile with him?

9 The Long Gallery and the Round Drawing Room

'All gothicism and gold, and crimson, and looking-glass'

OPPOSITE *Detail from The Long Gallery at Strawberry Hill, engraving by Morris*

RIGHT *Ceiling of the Long Gallery reflected in a nineteenth-century mirror*

IF THE TICKETED VISITORS had been invited to view the Holbein Chamber as a spectacular piece of theatre the illusion was continued when they were ushered into the Long Gallery by Margaret. 'Richer than the roof of paradise' was Walpole's description of this grand room.[1] Everywhere the visitor looked the room was ablaze with light, and their eyes would go up to fifty-seven feet of glorious off-white and gold vaulted ceiling formed by gothic fans made out of papier mâché. The walls were hung with crimson damask; one wall contained embrasures lined with mirror while a wall of windows had been built facing the mirrored walls. The mirrors were covered in an intricate gilt fretwork like that used in the trellis-work of the garden below, and were surmounted by gilded canopies. All this came after the darkness of the passage. The intention was to astound.

By day this was a room which lifted the spirit by its beauty and unique conception; by night, lit by candles that enshadowed the embrasures with their papier mâché canopies and threw the gothic fans into wells of darkness relieved by gleams of gold, it became a magic space in which Walpole could hold entertainments. The real world was far removed from the Long Gallery. It was a room of enticement not reality. Here nothing would have surprised the eighteenth-century visitor, not even Kitty Clive descending from the ceiling sitting on a swing, lit by a spotlight of moonlight, against a backdrop of

the Thames. The use of crimson damask and gilding against a white background for the furnishing of splendid rooms was well established by the time the Long Gallery was completed, but its magnificence and elegance still astonished.

When the Library wing had been added by Walpole it was because he wanted more and larger rooms for living and for entertaining, but with the building of the Long Gallery his intention had become quite different. He began to build a great room to impress everyone who saw it – a fact made immediately apparent to any eighteenth-century visitor through his choice of crimson for the damask wall covering: crimson was recognised as the colour

[1] Letter Horace Walpole to William Mason, 11 October 1778

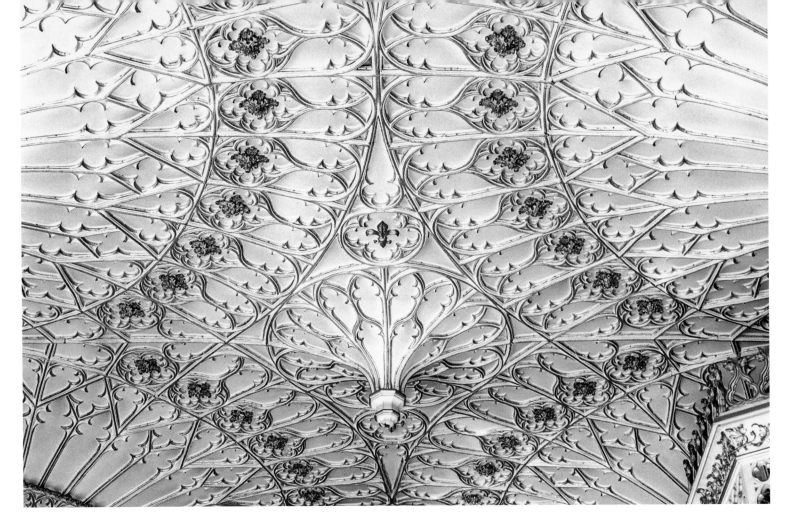

ABOVE *Detail of the fan vaulting of the Long Gallery*

[2] Letter Horace Walpole to George Montagu written from Strawberry Hill, 1 July 1763

[3] Letter Horace Walpole to Lady Hervey, 15 September 1765

of state and worked well as a background colour against which to hang pictures. The room's importance was further emphasised by the very choice of damask after the use of wallpaper for the decoration of the early rooms of the house. The change was marked and Walpole was very conscious of it, but it had not been easy to get the design right. Walpole described the uncharacteristic extravagance to George Montagu:

> Mr Chute and I intend to be with you on the 17th or 18th, but as we are wandering swains, we do not drive our nail into one day of the almanack irremovably…The journey you must accept as a great sacrifice either to you or to my promise, for I quit the gallery almost in the critical minute of consummation. Gilders, carvers, upholsterers, and picture-cleaners are labouring at their several forges, and I do not love to trust a hammer or a brush without my own supervisal. This will make my stay very short, but it is a greater compliment than a month would be at another season; and yet I am not profuse of months. Well! but I begin to be ashamed of my magnificence; Strawberry is growing sumptuous in its latter day; it will scarce be any longer like the fruit of its name, or the modesty of

its ancient demeanour, both which seem to have been in Spencer's prophetic eye, when he sung of -

> "- the blushing strawberries,
> Which lurk, close-shrouded from high-looking eyes,
> Shewing that sweetness low and hidden lies."

In truth, my collection was too great already to be lodged humbly; it has extended my walls, and pomp followed. It was a neat little house, it now will be a comfortable one, and except one fine apartment, does not deviate from its simplicity. Adieu! I know nothing about the world, care nothing about the world, and am only Strawberry's and

> Yours sincerely.[2]

As early as 1758 Walpole first mentioned building such a room in one of his letters and Richard Bentley beavered away at designs for it, which were rejected. The two men then fell out, went their separate ways, and Bentley ceased to design for Walpole, leaving John Chute to produce the next set of drawings for the Gallery. He finished them in 1761, but they too were judged unsuccessful by Walpole. Without Bentley's rococo touch the designs lacked theatre, so a new designer/architect was co-opted on to the Committee to join Walpole and Chute. Thomas Pitt was another Twickenham neighbour, a member of parliament, who had ventured into Spain on making his Grand Tour, and who had returned with an interest in Moorish architecture which he applied to the ornament of the Gallery and the chimneypiece. The room was ready to become a gothic-decorated backdrop for paintings and fashionable furniture. It is not known if the damask was of silk, which would have reflected the light as Walpole wanted, but would have detracted from the paintings themselves by its sheen, or of wool, which would have given a less lustrous sheen, but would have been more hard wearing and would also have served as a better background to the portraits. 'Norwich' was a term normally applied to wool damask.

Walpole wrote that the Glass Gallery at Chantilly had been the main design source for the room;[3] like Strawberry Hill Chantilly had been built with five windows along one wall and with recesses positioned on the opposite wall decorated with gold fretwork over looking-glass or mirror. Walpole also seems to have been influenced by the Genoese tradition, which he had noticed in palaces he had visited on his Grand Tour, of using looking-glass to create *trompe l'œil* effects. Because the mirrors of the Long Gallery at Strawberry Hill are angled within the three recessed embrasures, when walking around the Gallery an infinite number of images of the portraits and the garden are reflected, making the room into a giant display of moving pictures. All was in place to further the idea of a great room within a great house – and yet Strawberry Hill was only a small villa, cheaply built, intended by Walpole, when he first purchased it, for occasional weekend entertaining in summer.

Thomas Gray wrote describing Walpole's pleasure in his achievement in a letter to Wharton in August 1763:

>…My slumbers were disturbed the other day by an unexpected visit from Mr.Walpole, who dined with me; seemed mighty happy for the time he stayed, and said he could like to live here; but hurried home in the evening to his new gallery, which is all gothicism and gold, and crimson, and looking-glass…

In the windows overlooking the garden English painted glass commissioned from Peckitt, a glazier from York, topped the upper lights. Each window

was fitted with its own shutters; strangely these were only cheaply finished and it is possible they were only closed for security when Walpole was not in residence. At night moonlight poured in to enhance the candlelight. The candles were possibly placed on sills where they would have been reflected back through the looking-glass to become stars of light. This was the period in the building of Strawberry

ABOVE *Niche and canopy from the Long Gallery*

Hill when Walpole first commissioned sconces for holding candles instead of relying solely on portable candlesticks, and it appears likely that they might have been used in the Long Gallery, placed either side of the chimneypiece, although this is uncertain.[4] Again, light was all. Walpole described the effect in a letter to George Montagu written on 11 May 1769:

> ...Strawberry has been in great glory – I have given a festino there that will almost mortgage it. Last Tuesday all France dined there. Monsieur and Madame du Châtelet, the Duc de Liancour, three more French ladies whose names you will find in the enclosed paper, eight other Frenchmen, the Spanish and Portuguese ministers, the Holdernesses, Fitzroys, in short we were four and twenty. They arrived at two. At the gates of the castle I received them dressed in the cravat of Gibbins's carving, and a pair of gloves embroidered up to the elbows that had belonged to James I. The French servants stared and firmly believed this was the dress of English country gentlemen. After taking a survey of the apartments, we went to the printing-house where I had prepared the enclosed verses, with translations by Monsieur de Lisle, one of the company. The moment they were printed off, I gave a private signal and French horns and clarionets accompanied the compliment. We then went to see Pope's grotto and garden, and returned to a magnificent dinner in the refectory. In the evening we walked, had tea, coffee and lemonade in the gallery, which was illuminated with a thousand, or thirty candles, I forget which, and played at whisk and loo till midnight. Then there was a cold supper, and at one the company returned to town saluted by fifty nightingales, who as tenants of the manor came to do honour to their lord.

Copying elements from the palaces of France or Italy was more in the baroque tradition than the gothic. At Strawberry Hill it was ecclesiastical elements which were reflected by the fan vaulting of the ceiling, for which the source had been a section of the side-aisle of the Henry VII chapel in Westminster Abbey, by the doors which reflected the north door of St Albans Abbey and by the recesses and canopies which copied an element of design from Archbishop Bourcier's tomb in Canterbury Cathedral.[5] The use of the Robsart/Bourcier's ancestral tomb as a design source once again gave

a unity and authenticity to the overall concept. As a final statement a carpet was commissioned from the Moorfields workshops, the pattern of which was loosely reminiscent of the circular roseate elements of the ceiling. It ran the full length of the Gallery at a time when even a small carpet was a huge expense.

By the end of 1763 the Gallery was finally completed and ready to be filled with the finest furniture in the fashionable French style, hung with paintings and dressed with classical sculpture. Furniture making had become an art form by the 1760s and the furniture of the room was richly fashionable. From the middle of the eighteenth century the upholsterer had been generally replaced as the maker of furniture for the houses of the rich by craftsmen who both designed and made furniture and ornament. Their designs were frequently assembled, published and then copied by other craftsmen, which led to an increased general knowledge and interest in fashionable furniture. In the Gallery the tables and chairs were richly finished with black and gold frames; five long-stools were fashioned by Vile, who had completed a similar order for John Chute for his own house. Vile was among the greatest of the eighteenth-century cabinet makers. Four *encoignures*, or French corner cabinets, by Pierre Langlois, in black lacquer with ormolu mounts and topped by Italian marble, and two black and gold marble-topped japanned commodes also attributed to Langlois, were placed around the edge of the carpet. It is possible that the lacquerwork had been refashioned from a screen brought from China by Walpole's mother's family.[6] For the first time at Strawberry Hill a sense of fashion was apparent. The display of luxury goods spoke of a leisured lifestyle.

Entertainment was one of the driving forces behind the creation of Strawberry Hill; Walpole wanted to share the house with his friends and later with ordinary visitors, and in the sharing, to entertain them. With the building of the additional wing, which started in 1759 and included the Gallery, the Collection itself became part of this display. House and Collection combined to meet the growing Georgian desire for tourism and new experiences. Strawberry Hill fulfilled a love of spectacle, thrills and excitement, all of which could be experienced in surroundings which could later be discussed with friends. When Walpole himself appeared to receive guests, possibly dressed as recorded in his letter to George Montagu wearing a cravat carved

[4] see *The Long Gallery at Strawberry Hill*, watercolour by Paul Sandby and others, Victoria and Albert Museum, London. One sconce possibly visible.

[5] Walpole, Horace, *A Description of the Villa of Mr. Horace Walpole at Strawberry-Hill near Twickenham, Middlesex*, Strawberry Hill, 1784

[6] Hardy, John, unpublished information

out of wood by Grinling Gibbons, it would always have been with panache. He loved to entertain and at the same time to be amused by his guests. He succeeded in bringing the spirit of Vauxhall and Ranelagh Gardens to his supper parties at Strawberry Hill.

The Spring Gardens at Vauxhall had first opened in 1661, with Samuel Pepys becoming one of the early visitors, and reached their peak of fame when Jonathan Tyers took over the lease in 1728. Tyers loved innovation and the element of surprise. He created Chinese, Gothic, Turkish and other exotic buildings in the Gardens, all to be approached through a series of arches leading to an artificial waterfall.

Built to be frequented by night, the gardens were lit by over a thousand oil lamps and caged birds provided a background of birdsong. It was the place to go for entertainment and became also a show-place in which artists could display their work – this at a time when there were no public art exhibitions. The sculptor Roubiliac was commissioned by Tyers to provide a sculpture of Handel and he produced something that was not just fine but was also innovative in concept modelled with an informality suited to the Gardens. Francis Hayman and Clermont, the French artist who had worked on the Strawberry Hill Library ceiling, were both engaged to paint the supper-boxes. A Rotunda, or Music Room, was added

ABOVE *Section of fan vaulting from the Long Gallery*

in 1749. It had a painted ceiling, looking-glass around the walls, sconces for candles, with additional lighting from above provided by a chandelier holding a further seventy-two candles. The Spring Gardens presented an unreal world of pleasure with a temple at its heart dedicated to love. It built to a climax with a Cascade which, at nine o'clock each evening, revealed a moving landscape with water flowing gracefully away – achieved by releasing thin strips of tin sequentially.

Ranelagh was the more fashionable of the two pleasure gardens; it was opened in 1740 by James Lacy. It too had a large Rotunda, around which were sited a double tier of supper-boxes finely decorated, and a stage for musicians. One of the most fashionable activities advertised were the ridottos at which visitors could dance between taking supper and listening to music. It became the fashion to wear 'Van Dyck dress' – the masquerade costume which had become so fashionable and in which Walpole and his friends had chosen to be painted. It was an opportunity for everyone to dress up, perhaps wear a mask or a 'domino', a long cloak which gave the wearer anonymity. The fun aspect of the Gardens was increased through a series of Chinese buildings which were set against the austerity of a Roman style amphitheatre. Both Gardens were popular and gave rise to the production of a large number of successful prints, which in turn increased the fame of the Gardens. For the entertainments, tickets were issued; Tyers offered one thousand season tickets at one guinea apiece, the design changing annually.

In May 1749 (o.s.) Walpole visited Ranelagh and recounted his experience to Horace Mann:

>…The next day was what was called "a jubilee masquerade in the Venetian manner" at Ranelagh: it had nothing Venetian in it, but was by far the best understood and the prettiest spectacle I ever saw: nothing in a fairy tale ever surpassed it. One of the proprietors, who is a German and belongs to Court, had got my Lady Yarmouth to persuade the King to order it. It began at three o'clock, and about five, people of fashion began to go. When you entered, you found the whole garden filled with masks and spread with tents, which remained all night very commodely. In one quarter was a Maypole dressed with garlands, and people dancing round it to a tabor and pipe and rustic music, all masked, as were all the various bands of music, that were disposed in different parts of the garden, some like huntsmen with French horns, some like peasants, and a troop of harlequins and scaramouches, in the little open temple on the mount. On the canal was a sort of gondola, adorned with flags and streamers, and filled with music, rowing about. All round the outside of the amphitheatre were shops filled with Dresden china, japan, etc., and all the shopkeepers in mask. The amphitheatre was illuminated, and in the middle was a circular bower, composed of all kinds of firs in tubs, from twenty to thirty feet high: under them orange trees, with small lamps in each orange, and below them all sorts of the finest auriculas in pots; and festoons of natural flowers hanging from tree to tree. Between the arches too were firs, and smaller ones in the balconies above. There were booths for tea and wine, gaming tables and dancing, and about two thousand persons. In short it pleased me more than anything I ever saw. It is to be once more, and probably finer as to dresses, as there has since been a subscription masquerade, and people will go in their rich habits.

Although a great many plays were written in the eighteenth century the period is remembered for the actors who took London society by storm, rather than for the quality of drama. Horace's father, Sir Robert Walpole, exasperated at the persistent criticism of his government by the playwrights of the day, introduced the Licensing Act in 1737, which closed all but two 'Patent Theatres', Covent Garden and Drury Lane. Legislation brought in at the same time also meant that all new plays had to be approved by the Lord Chamberlain, thus introducing censorship. Ingenious ways were found around the Act but it stifled the writing of new drama and spectacle took the place of dialogue.

>…We have got another opera, which is liked: there was to have been a vast elephant, but the just directors designing to give the audience the full weight of one for their money, made it so heavy that at the prova it broke through the stage. It was to have carried twenty soldiers with Monticelli on a throne in the middle…[7]

Into this scenario entered David Garrick, who became a neighbour and friend of Walpole, although never an intimate one. Garrick was the same age as Walpole. He was sent, aged nineteen, to study law with Doctor Samuel Johnson at Johnson's new

[7] Letter Horace Walpole to Horace Mann, 3 March 1742 (o.s.)

academy in Lichfield. The academy was not the success they had anticipated and Johnson and Garrick left together for London, Johnson later quipping that he had only two-pence-halfpenny in his purse at the time, but that Garrick had only three-halfpence. Garrick made his name overnight appearing in the title role as Richard III, after serving only the briefest apprenticeship in a small theatre in Ipswich; as King Richard he became the great superstar of the day, the darling of Society, earning the enormous sum of £2 a night. With this money, and helped by his friends, Garrick bought a half share in the Drury Lane Theatre into which he introduced a new style of acting, more naturalistic and romantic than the established more blatant bombastic style. Confident in his own charisma, ability and stage presence, he chose to employ and work with the best actors of the day rather than follow the tradition of previous actor managers who had employed lesser known, less good performers, thereby guarding their own reputations. Charles Macklin, Peg Woffington and Kitty Clive all regularly appeared on playbills with Garrick. Good, or sometimes great, actors working together had the effect of raising the status of the theatre, and Garrick, through his continued association and friendship

with Doctor Johnson, forged links between theatre, literature and scholarship. This meant that more productions were mounted in private houses and short entertainments became a regular feature of life in the country house or out-of-town villa.

Garrick engaged the Austrian artist, de Loutherbourg, to work with him at Drury Lane designing spectacular scenery for the productions – palaces and subterranean vaults, mountains and cascades – all of which were erected on the stage. The effects were changed, scene by scene, through the use of painted scenery and through coloured and stained glass, behind which candles and lamps were placed. De Loutherbourg was producing the same effect on stage, and in Vauxhall Gardens where he was also employed, as Walpole was achieving with painted glass at Strawberry Hill. When viewing his rooms and walking through the house it would have been impossible for Margaret's visitors not to have been aware of the strong sense of theatre which Walpole had instilled there.

Kitty Clive became an even closer friend of Walpole than Garrick. She was a noted comedienne and singer, another of the darlings of eighteenth-century society regularly invited by Walpole to entertain his guests. He described one of these

ABOVE *Catherine (Kitty)*
Clive, engraving by
Greatbach after a painting
by Davidson which hung
at Strawberry Hill

[8] Letter from Lady Horatia
Waldegrave to Anne Clement,
10 October 1778, included
in *The Yale Edition of Horace*
Walpole's Correspondence

[9] Coke, Mary, *Journal*, 10
September 1774, included
in *The Yale Edition of Horace*
Walpole's Correspondence

[10] Letter Horace Walpole
to Horace Mann, 26 June
1741 (o.s.)

out for entertaining. Card tables were positioned: two for quadrille and one for whist in the Gallery, one each for whist and loo in the Round Drawing Room, and another for loo in the Great North Bedchamber, but no one played cards. Instead they spent the evening parading around the rooms. She recounts that during the evening Walpole locked her, with Miss Anne North and some others, in a room with General Fitzwilliams. She pronounced this, 'very wicked'.[8]

When gaming and gambling were the order of the evening large sums of money changed hands. In her journal of 1774 Lady Mary Coke described a visit she made to Strawberry Hill.[9] The guests assembled at about half-past four and were first served dinner before sitting down at about seven o'clock to play loo. She lost forty guineas, won it back, lost it for the second time, but finished the evening only six guineas down. This at a time when six guineas was the annual wage of a kitchen maid. Lady Mary had requested her servants to collect her at nine-thirty, but they got drunk and did not arrive until eleven. Presumably a party must have been going on below stairs in the Servants' Hall at the same time.

When they were not being professionally entertained or playing cards, both Walpole's own guests and the visitors trooping around the house behind Margaret, would have studied the paintings on the walls and looked at the objects from the Collection positioned around the Gallery. Most of these were either classical or had an element of classicism about them. The most interesting piece was a sculpture of a very large eagle described by Walpole as 'a glorious fowl'.[10] It was much travelled and had made its own Grand Tour, in reverse, from the baths of Caracalla in Rome where it had rested for over a thousand years. It was bought for Walpole by Horace Mann, who succeeded in outbidding the Pope, who had intended to add it to the Papal Treasury. It had then travelled to Genoa where it sat out the War of the Spanish Succession, and eventually reached Strawberry Hill by way of Walpole's London home where it had remained for several years. Once in Strawberry Hill it continued its travels, resting briefly in both the Library and the Refectory before being placed on a Roman plinth in the Long Gallery. The quality of the carving was remarkably fine, with feathers individually modelled to reflect light and to present an impression of movement, suggesting the bird was ruffling its

evenings to William Mason, writing to him on 11 October 1778: '…the illumination of the Gallery surpassed the Palace of the Sun; and when its fretted ceiling, which you know is richer than the roof of paradise, opened for the descent of Mrs Clive in the full moon, nothing could be more striking…' When she became elderly and impoverished he gave her a small house on the estate, Little Strawberry Hill. In return she gave him a mother-of-pearl box filled with counters and gambling chips as a gift for his Gallery. The fete at which she made her dramatic appearance from the Long Gallery ceiling was given by Walpole in honour of his nieces – the three Waldegrave sisters and Anna Maria and Laura Keppel – and from contemporary accounts was spectacular. Lady Horatia Waldegrave wrote a description of the party detailing how the suite of three rooms, which she calls 'tapestried', were set feathers before taking off in flight. The line of the feathers followed the striation within the marble, each feather slightly indented, quills exposed; the carving was left roughly hewn with a high finish only on the talons and beak. The Eagle was one of the focal points of the Gallery. In June 1791 an accident befell it which he described to Mary Berry:

> Two companies had been to see my house last week, and one of the parties, as vulgar people always see with the ends of their fingers, had broken off the end of my invaluable eagle's bill, and to conceal their mischief, had pocketed the piece. It is true it had been restored at Rome; and my comfort is, that Mrs Damer [his niece] can repair the damage – but did the fools know that? It almost provokes me to shut up my house, when obliging begets injury!

There was an increased interest in sculpture over the period with house owners commissioning portrait busts in the antique style. Walpole bought Roman portrait busts; Vespasian and Marcus Aurelius were prominently displayed in the Gallery alongside small bronzes and some ceramics.

Paintings, some hanging from a single nail, lined the walls almost covering the damask, or were hung over the mirrors flush to the fretted network. They were mostly English portraits although there were also maritime paintings, or sea-pieces and some landscapes. In the centre of the window wall hung the portrait so many of Walpole's visitors had come to see, Henry Carey, Lord Falkland, painted by Paul van Somer. This was the 'figure in white' which Walpole had described in *The Castle of Otranto*. In the novel he walked out of his frame and chased Manfred, the villain, down the length of the Gallery. Falkland is painted wearing the fashion much admired by Walpole, seventeenth-century dress, with flowing cloak, a jaunty hat topped by a curled

LEFT *The Boccapadugli Eagle which stood in the Long Gallery*

ABOVE *Henry Carey, Viscount Falkland, engraving by Brown after a painting by Harding copying the original by Vansomer which hung in the Long Gallery*

[11] Walpole, Horace, *A Description of the Villa of Mr. Horace Walpole at Strawberry-Hill near Twickenham, Middlesex,* Strawberry Hill, 1784

[12] Letter Horace Walpole to William Mason, 29 July 1773

[13] Series of correspondence between Horace Walpole and Horace Mann, 1741-49, included in *The Yale Edition of Horace Walpole's Correspondence*

ostrich feather, long pointed shoes – perhaps of silk – with double bows to fasten them, and a glove in his hand.

From his upbringing Walpole had learnt the importance of collecting paintings and he possessed an eye for hanging them to create a desired effect. As the choice of paintings is necessarily personal, Walpole is defined in his Gallery as a watcher of men, a man fascinated by character and relationships. The expected choice of paintings for a Gallery would have been of history paintings, predominantly Italian, and classical landscapes; Walpole was never predictable.

Leaving the Gallery through the great doors at the far end Margaret swept her visitors onwards past a closet in which, safely encased behind glass doors, Walpole kept his mother's collection of oriental ceramics. Margaret neither showed nor described the contents to her visitors, but led them straight into the Round Drawing Room set within the Great Tower. This was the second of the suite of crimson-clad parade rooms. It continued the theme begun in the Long Gallery, but with a very different interpretation.

The room the visitors saw was designed by Robert Adam as a drawing room after an earlier attempt to decorate and furnish it as a state bed-chamber had been abandoned. Adam's style was immediately identifiable. The symmetry of the room drew the eyes up to the segmented ceiling designed as a copy of the rose window of old St Paul's Cathedral, down to the oriel window, on to a great chimneypiece and full circle back to the door through which they had entered: from which vantage point they would be invited to look back at the Long Gallery to appreciate from a distance the intricacy and beauty of its overall design.[11] This was one of the great 'prospects' presented by Walpole for his visitors to enjoy. It seems probable that Walpole and Adam got on badly; their correspondence is terse and to the point. Adam rarely worked in the gothic style, but the Round Drawing Room with its fluid shape and beautiful proportions is a fine achievement.

> ...Mr Adam has published the first number of his 'Architecture'. In it is a magnificent gateway and screen for the Duke of Northumberland at Sion, which I see erecting every time I pass. It is all lace and embroidery, and as croquant as his frames for tables; consequently most improper to be exposed in the high road to Brentford. From Kent's mahogany we are dwindled to Adam's filigree. Grandeur and simplicity are not yet in fashion. In his preface he seems to tax Wyat with stealing from him; but Wyat has employed the antique with more judgement, and the Pantheon is still the most beautiful ediface in England. What are the Adelphi buildings? warehouses laced down the seams, like a soldier's trull in a regimental old coat.[12]

Walpole directed Adam to use an engraving of Edward the Confessor's tomb from Westminster Abbey as a source for the chimney design; Adam had the genius to produce it in scagliola which gave a brighter finish than marble. Scagliola was a technique which imitated inlaid marble or *pietra dura*, in mosaic, but was cheaper to produce. It was another form of *trompe l'œil*. The Round Drawing Room chimneypiece is the only element at Strawberry Hill to be decorated using this technique, although it was not uncommon for floors to be made in scagliola, and even furniture manufacturers made use of this false, but highly fashionable, form of inlay made possible by new technology. Walpole and Horace Mann conducted a lengthy correspondence about some tables which they wanted decorated in scagliola and which were being made in Italy by an Irish friar with the unlikely name of Fernando Enrico Hugford, and his disciple or apprentice, Don Pietro Belloni. These two were only able to work on the tables when freed from religious duties – which in practice meant that obtaining a delivery date was an impossibility. Of a pair of tables ordered by Mann for his own use only one was ever completed. However, undaunted and ever hopeful, a few years later Walpole asked Mann to order another pair of tables to give to a friend. The correspondence went back and forth between Mann, on the ground, and Walpole, in London, impatient to receive the tables, until finally Mann wrote saying they were finished at last; however, he questioned if Walpole's friend would still want them after so long a wait.[13] It may have been the cheaper option to follow but getting delivery of the finished object took time.

The workmanship of the Strawberry Hill scagliola chimneypiece was finely executed; the whole effect enhanced by viewing the surround against the

BELOW *Detail of the scagliola chimney piece designed by Robert Adam*

those of her friends.[14] Oriental lacquer was widely copied in Europe throughout the seventeenth and eighteenth centuries by both professional and amateur decorators; their pieces described as 'japanned'. The art of japanning was taught in academies for ladies and an instruction manual published for their use. The lacquer furniture at Strawberry Hill was displayed in those rooms abutting Catherine's china collection; around the walls of the Round Drawing Room stood a pair of lacquered coffers on carved and gilded legs, a boulle coffer, or trunk, lined with blue silk and a cabinet on a stand. Arranged between them stood eight carved and gilt chairs upholstered in a rich Aubusson tapestry of garlands of roses and other flowers on a white ground. The chair frames were of green and gold; bought in Paris they added both richness and colour to the room. Covering the floor was another of the Moorfields-made carpets, the design of this one copied from a small Sèvres porcelain table which stood in the Green Closet. Conventionally, settees would have been found in an eighteenth-century drawing room, and their absence is presumably due to the shape of the room. A circular table which had belonged to Walpole's parents stood in the centre of the window embrasure. Of all the rooms in Strawberry Hill this one conjured up the memory of his mother most strongly.

Aligned with the door into the room was a bow window filled with old English glass set over a wooden surbase replicating the stone tomb of Queen Eleanor in Westminster Abbey. The glass was composed of Robert Dudley's arms, those of Queen Elizabeth, with roses (presumably Tudor roses) and six special biblical pieces from Peckitt's workshops.[15] Some of Walpole's most valued paintings hung around the walls including Poussin's painting of the *Education of Venus*, two Van Dyck portraits and works by Salvador Rosa, Caracci and Paul Brill. He paid almost one hundred pounds for the gilding of the frames of the paintings and the gilding of the door and window tracery.[16] The Drawing Room became a second room in which to play cards and the room in which Walpole offered his guests tea from a Sèvres tea service bought in Paris.

There were underlying oriental elements in the room, although, with the exception of the lacquer-work, this was not immediately apparent. The collection of oriental porcelain in the China Closet between the Long Gallery and the Round Drawing

crimson Norwich damask of the walls which curved away from it on both sides. It was surmounted by a display of covered silver jars and beakers, or vases, and was further enhanced through the use of silver sconces and fire dogs. Here was the first display of silver in the house. The use of sconces was normally kept to important rooms of a Georgian house; in Strawberry Hill the combination of the additional light they shed and the display of silverware would have suggested to the visitor aspects of hospitality and gentility. It would have informed them they were approaching a climax. In front of the chimney-piece stood a pole-screen embroidered in chenille work by Lady Ailesbury, another Walpole relation. The remainder of the room was equally richly furnished, its purpose defined as a Drawing Room through the choice of damask for its hangings, tapestry for its covers and the overall richness of its furnishings, all in the fashionable French style.

Horace Walpole's mother, Catherine, had been known for her painted lacquerwork decoration of panels for furniture, made for her own home and

Room first introduced the theme which was then echoed through the use of silk, the lacquer furniture and the drinking of tea. All came from the China Trade with which his mother's family had been involved. At the beginning of the eighteenth century there was a craze for anything oriental fuelled by several illustrated accounts of experiences in the East. Oriental goods flooded into Europe, where new manufacturing techniques meant that they could be copied by European craftsmen. The style which had started out as a copy, developed a distinctive European quality inspired by the East and with imagination and whimsy became chinoiserie.

By the middle of the century the elegance of the preparation of tea and the way in which it was presented had become as important as the drink itself; it was a fashionable social ritual. Tea was generally served in the later part of the afternoon, after dinner, to the ladies, while the gentlemen lingered over their wine before the two parties met up to share an evening's entertainment. The new drink entailed new vessels in which to make and drink it and new modes of behaviour. Both black and green teas were popular and at first both were served in tea bowls which either came from China, or from Europe. When first imported the tea was generally purchased from the apothecary, and was regarded as a medicinal cure for many ailments including 'giddiness, weakness of the stomach, agues and fevers'. It was both highly priced and highly taxed, with one shilling duty levied on lawfully imported tea from the Dutch and English East India Companies and one shilling and sixpence on unlawfully, that is, smuggled, tea. The tea was the most valuable commodity of the Companies and was imported in boxes which, however tightly packed, still weighed very little. Silk was also imported by the East India traders and once again was a lightweight commodity, easy to transport. Ballast was needed to keep the ships stable especially in stormy weather, and this was partly provided by porcelain which was heavy, could be safely stored in the hold and provided a cargo which could be sold on arrival in European ports for a high price. Much of the imported oriental porcelain was made to special order; Walpole's mother had commissioned a service to be decorated with the family crest and coat of arms, complete with Saracen's head. Walpole himself bought examples of the newly fashionable French cups with handles for use at Strawberry Hill, which he called

his 'handle set' before the new terms of tea-cup and tea-set entered the vocabulary. He travelled to Paris in 1765 saying, 'I go to see French plays and buy French china.'[17] While there he bought a green teacup and saucer for his friend Henrietta Howard, paying four Louis for it. He wrote to her from Paris grumbling that his meals were both topsy-turvy and went on for too long with scarcely a break between one meal and the next, 'For my own part I receive the greatest civilities, and in general am much amused; but I could wish there was less whisk [whist], and somewhat more cleanliness.'[18]

Individual pieces of ceramics and the making of porcelain greatly interested him. To buy Sèvres he visited the factory outside Paris on three separate occasions to see the new processes. After each trip he managed to persuade his cousins to send his purchases back to England as part of their ambassadorial baggage, by-passing customs' regulations and thus evading the tax. As well as the Sèvres tea-set he owned six Chelsea cups and saucers, decorated with green landscapes on a white ground, of which he was particularly fond. Some of his many tea things, which he displayed in the China Closet on the ground floor, were listed in *The Description*. He must have loved choosing which pieces to buy and they show how catholic was his taste:

A tea-pot, milk-pot, five coffee-cups, five tea-cups and ten saucers, of white quilted china of St. Cloud.
A small tea-canister of Seve china, blue and gold, with figures on white.
A cup with a bullfinch, of modern china.
A blue and white saucer with a landscape, of fine Nankin china.
Seven old coloured octagon cups and saucers.
An old white china tea-pot with birds and flowers finely painted in Europe.
Six fine old cups, white within; without, japanned black and mother of pearl: very rare.
Six coloured handle cups and saucers, a tea-pot and sugar-dish, in shapes of leaves, of Chantilli china.
A small square brown tea-pot.
Twelve black and white tea-cups and saucers of Bow china.

After the magnificence of the Long Gallery and the Round Drawing Room, with their rich display of colour and texture, the visitors would next be taken by Margaret to see a very different room.

[14] Cholmondeley, Lady Rose, unpublished information

[15] Walpole, Horace, *A Description of the Villa of Mr. Horace Walpole at Strawberry-Hill near Twickenham, Middlesex*, Strawberry Hill, 1784

[16] Toynbee, Paget, *Strawberry Hill Accounts*, Clarendon Press, Oxford, 1927

[17] Letter Horace Walpole to George Montagu, 31 August 1765

[18] Letter Horace Walpole to Henrietta Howard, 20 September 1765

10 The Tribune and Beauclerc Closet

'Under lock and key'

MARGARET'S VISITORS retraced their steps past the China Closet and were led back to the Long Gallery where they were halted outside the nearest door. When Margaret opened that door for them, they were confronted – once more – by the unexpected. Before them stood a second door, apparently made up of metal bars and which, on a cursory glance in the dim light, seemed to be glazed in looking-glass to match the rest of the Long Gallery. When examined more closely this was seen to be an inner door, grated and gothic in style, through which they could catch a glimpse of a treasury beyond. This was as far as they were permitted to go; from outside they peeped in while Margaret described the wealth of objects kept within, safe from prying fingers. Margaret told her visitors that the room was called the Tribune (after the Tribuna of the Medici), or Cabinet (because it was a Cabinet of Curiosities), or the Chapel, depending on the mood of Mr Walpole. This was the very heart of the medieval castle, a vault filled with treasure. Walpole gave his reasons for restricting access to his visitors in a letter written at Strawberry Hill to Lady Ossory on 15 September 1787, in response to a question from her husband about the nature of the Collection:

> …In the list for which Lord Ossory asks, is the 'Description' of this place; now, though printed, I have entirely kept it up, and mean to do so while

I live for very sound reasons, Madam, as you will allow. I am so tormented by visitors to my house, that two or three rooms are not shown to abridge their stay. In the 'Description' are specified all the enamels and miniatures etc., which I keep under lock and key. If the visitors got the book into their hands, I should never get them out of the house, and they would want to see fifty articles which I do not choose they should handle and paw.

What the visitors could see was a towerlike room with plain painted walls of stone colour, decorated in relief by ornament picked out in gold. The shape was a quatrefoil with a square superimposed on it, about sixteen feet across at the broadest point, forming four semicircular recesses; the one facing them bearing a large oriel window, while each of the two either side had a pair of decorated inner niches. To the left of the visitors a second window let in light while to their right stood a dais surmounted by what appeared to be an altarpiece of black and gold seen amidst a host of secular objects. To the right and left of the door behind which they stood were two further niches set into the walls. The design of all the niches reflected the great pair of doors in the Gallery behind them and the effect was to create an harmonious flow between the two rooms. Looking upwards they could see another ceiling of intricate tracery made of papier mâché, this one resembling

the great East window of York Minster. In the centre of the ceiling shone a star of alabaster coloured glass, reminiscent of the great window of Burgos Cathedral. Straight ahead of the visitors the oriel window contained more fine old glass in a sequence illustrating the Life of Christ and His Apostles. The roundels were encased in a mosaic setting of eighteenth-century painted glass, which contained

elements of the rich window they had seen earlier in the Holbein Chamber. To achieve the requisite effect in the Tribune, Price, the most fashionable glass painter of the period, had been hired to fill-in and add colour to the early glass, in which only hues of yellow and brown had been used by the six-teenth-century glaziers. In the Tribune, as in the Holbein Chamber which also faced north, the

[1] Letter Horace Walpole to Horace Mann written from Strawberry Hill, 1 July 1762

mosaic of the glass was unable to give a sufficiently warm glow to the room; warmth was therefore provided by the top-lit star in the ceiling and by the carpet which had a design specially commissioned for the room, reflecting both the mosaic of the window surround and the central star of the ceiling. The combination of glass and its reflection on the carpet gave the illusion that it was the Italian midday sun which had created the floor pattern. Like the other English carpets in the house its presence was indicative of new technology and expertise coming together to produce desirable objects for Georgian gentlemen.

The construction of the Tribune, which was part of the same building scheme as the Long Gallery and the Round Room, had caused many problems. When he built the Long Gallery Walpole neither wanted a sixty foot wall without windows overlooking the main road, nor did he want to build windows in a wall which had been specifically designed to hold mirrors; the solution at which the Committee of Taste arrived was to have blind windows painted in *trompe l'œil* on the section of Gallery wall facing the road. In the construction of the Round Room the problems had been decorative and were resolved by Robert Adam. In the building of the Tribune Walpole thought to circumvent any problems by having the room prefabricated in seven ribs in central London, but the ribs were large and unwieldy and the manufacturer arranged for delivery to Strawberry Hill by way of the Thames, floating them upstream. On reaching Twickenham they became embedded in the mud and proved cumbersome and difficult to extricate and erect, eventually causing a strike among the workmen.

…I am in distress about my Gallery and Cabinet: the latter was on the point of being completed, and is really striking beyond description. Last Saturday night my workmen took their leave, made their bow, and left me up to the knees in shavings. In short, the journeymen carpenters, like the cabinet-makers, have entered into an association, not to work unless their wages are raised – and how can one complain? The poor fellows, whose all the labour is, see their masters advance their prices every day, and think it reasonable to touch their share. You would be frightened at the dearness of everything: I built out of economy, for unless I do now, in two years I shall not be able to afford it.[1]

It should be noted that Walpole's economy did not extend to cutting back on purchasing items for the Collection.

John Chute had designed most of the features within the Tribune, although the niches, or alcoves, were the work of Müntz, who was working at Strawberry Hill during this design period. The extraordinary grated door to the room was conceived by Pitt. Architecturally this room could be seen as the most innovative at Strawberry Hill, but impressive as was the design itself the focus of the room was on the Collection not the architecture: it was this which the bemused visitor was taken to see. Placed within the niches, set upon pedestals, were copies of four of the great classical sculptures: the *Venus de Medici*, the *Antinous*, the *Apollo Belvedere* and the *Farnese Flora*. In one niche stood a plaster copy of a statue of Walpole's mother from Westminster Abbey. Most of the small artefacts in the room were scaled down early copies of famous classical works. The stools covered in a pink cloth were also classical in style.

Although the room was small Walpole listed its contents in 1784 as: thirty-six sculptures or statues, ninety-two miniatures and enamels, one hundred and sixty-four paintings and drawings, and one hundred and eighty-nine other treasures. None of these were large but it is difficult to equate the sheer number of artefacts in the room with the illustration completed for Walpole, showing it as a spacious repository of art.

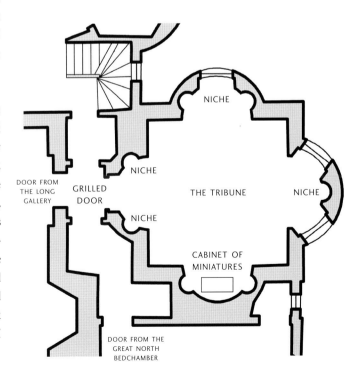

The focal point of the room, lit by the window opposite, was the dais on which stood an altar which had been built to display a Florentine box inlaid with precious stones. Above the altar hung a cabinet, made by Hallett, but designed by Walpole himself for his London home, in which he kept his unrivalled collection of miniatures and enamels. The cabinet was surmounted by three small ivory statuettes, thought by Walpole to represent the sculptor, François Duquesnoy, and the architects Inigo Jones and Andrea Palladio. Its doors were inset with ivory bas-reliefs by Grinling Gibbons. This single object with its contents epitomised Walpole's admiration for architecture, sculpture, and the artistry and workmanship of great objects created by the hands of artists and craftsmen. The cabinet with its contents was only opened by Walpole for his friends and never for Margaret's tourists.

The fact that Walpole assembled such a great collection of miniatures was partly due to his interest in portraits and the history of the people they portrayed, partly to his love of the Elizabethan period which was the golden age of the miniature, partly to his admiration for the great collection of Charles I and partly for the sheer pleasure of enjoying such exquisite workmanship. Isaac and Peter Oliver and Nicholas Hilliard were the most famous masters of the art of 'limning'. Walpole owned work by them as well as by other important miniaturists including Holbein, Cooper and Hoskins, and enamels by Petitot and Zincke. The miniature held a special place in English art: a precious object with the portrait often encased in an ivory, gold or jewelled case and with both the image and the case executed by an artist who would first have trained as a goldsmith. Generally painted in watercolour on vellum it needed to be kept safely hidden away, protected from both light and dust; it was therefore seen as a private art form. Miniatures were given as messages from one lover to another to be worn against the heart, pledges of love or friendship, painted with elaborate symbolism: many of the messages depicted in paint and understood by both lover and beloved at the time have never been deciphered. They were therefore essentially romantic objects and as such welcomed by Walpole.

The owners of all the great houses hung portraits of their ancestors on their walls, or amassed collections of miniatures, which had accumulated over a number of generations. These were often allowed to grow dusty in attics and trunks. Some of the miniatures in Walpole's cabinet were of members of his family, or were related to him through marriages within the family, and these he collected as one part of an illustrated history of his family. Others had been bought because they were exquisite examples of an artist's work.

Throughout his life Walpole took notes on both paintings and other works of art, recording what he saw as he travelled around the country. At the same time the artist George Vertue was also making notes and recording his thoughts on English artists. Vertue kept his notes in a series of thirty-nine notebooks which were bought by Walpole after his death. These became the basis of *The Anecdotes of Painting*, written and published by Walpole in five volumes. The publication became an overnight success combining an innovative approach to the appreciation of paintings and the artists who painted them with being a good read. The best of the miniaturists whose work was kept in the Tribune were given biographies in the book, with engraved copies of their portraits included as illustrations. This was the book he was working on at the time of a royal visit:

…Last Friday morning I was very tranquilly writing my 'Anecdotes of Painting': I heard the bell at the gate ring – I called out as usual, "Not at home"; but Harry who thought it would be treason to tell a lie when he saw red liveries, owned I was, and came running up, "Sir, the Prince of Wales is at the door, and says he is come on purpose to make you a visit!" There was I in the utmost confusion; undressed, in my slippers, and with my hair about my ears; there was no help, "insanum vatem aspiciet" – and down I went to receive him – him was the Duke of York. Behold my breeding of the old court; at the foot of the stairs I kneeled down and kissed his hand. I beg your uncle Algernon Sidney's pardon, but I could not let the second prince of the blood kiss my hand first. He was, as he always is, extremely good-humoured; and I, as I am not always, extremely respectful. He stayed two hours… I showed him all my castle.[2]

Four of the most treasured items in the castle were kept in the Tribune, but were only shown to friends and never mentioned by Margaret to her visitors (possibly for fear of theft or damage). They were listed in the 1784 copy of *The Description*:

A small bust in bronze of a Caligula, with silver eyes. This exquisite piece is one of the finest things in the collection, and shews the great art of the ancients. It is evidently a portrait, carefully done, and seems to represent that emperor at the beginning of his madness. It was found with some other small busts at the very first discovery of Herculaneum, which happened by digging a well for the prince d'Elboeuf, who resided many years afterwards at Florence, where it was sold on his return to France, and being purchased by sir Horace Mann, was by him sent to Mr. Walpole.

…

A magnificent missal, with miniatures by Raphael and his scholars, set in gold enamelled, and adorned with rubies and turquoises; the sides are of cornelian, engraved with religious subjects; the clasp, a large garnet. This precious prayer-book belonged to Claude queen of France, wife of Francis 1st .

…

2 Letter Horace Walpole to George Montagu written from Strawberry Hill, 14 October 1760

[3] Walpole, Horace, *The Description of the Villa of Mr. Horace Walpole at Strawberry-Hill near Twickenham, Middlesex*, Strawberry Hill, 1784. (It was later noted that Walpole called it 'La Belle des belles'.)

[4] Letter Horace Walpole to William Cole, 9 September 1776

Henry 8th's dagger, of Turkish work; the blade is of steel damasked with gold, the case and handle of chalcedonyx, set with diamonds and many rubies.

…

A most beautiful silver bell, made for a pope by Benvenuto Cellini. It is covered all over in the highest relievo with antique masks, flies, grasshoppers, and other insects; the virgin and boy-angels at top, a wreathe of leaves at bottom. Nothing can exceed the taste of the whole design, or the delicate and natural representation of the insects: the wonderful execution makes almost every thing credible that he says of himself in his life. It came out of the collection of the marquis of Leonati at Parma, and was bought by the marquis of Rockingham, who exchanged it with Mr. Walpole for some very scarce Roman medals of great bronze, amongst which was an unique medaliuncino of Alexander Severus with the amphitheatre, in the highest preservation.'[3]

Walpole, one of the original Trustees of the British Museum, never collected the fashionable 'natural' objects, such as shells, fossils or minerals, which were being bought by his friends for their own collections, but every other type of artefact seems to have been represented at Strawberry Hill. Among these were a limewood cravat carved by

Grinling Gibbons in the later part of the seventeenth century (the one Walpole had worn to amuse French visitors to Strawberry Hill); a small box containing a lock of hair cut from the head of Edward IV; a tea-cannister of straw emblazoned with the Walpole and Shorter coats of arms; a gold toothpick case; a snuff box with an image of a small dog, Tonton, given to him to accompany the gift of the dog itself, from his friend Madame du Deffand; a small box containing two petrified dates which had been found in a jar at Herculaneum, charred but still recognisable; a painting by his mother; a bronze model of the Florentine Boar; two paintings by Samuel Scott, a neighbour; and a St George painted on lapis lazuli. It was an eclectic mix. In his choice of which objects would be described or shown to visitors and which pieces of glass would be pointed out to them, he directed their judgement of him and Strawberry Hill.

After leaving the Tribune Margaret ushered her visitors next into the Great North Bedchamber, although they must all have wanted to examine the treasures more closely and to hear more of the stories which had grown up around many of them.

Only Walpole's personal friends would have been taken into the Beauclerc Closet – and then only if they were lucky. The Closet was set within a tiny tower, built in the Flemish style and looking like an illustration from a medieval Book of Hours. The tower had been added in 1776 standing beside the Round Tower where it marked the final stage of building of the main house. With its diminutive scale – only seven feet in diameter – and its pointed roof, it completed the irregular roofscape of the building. Walpole's intention in building it was outlined to William Cole in September 1776: 'I have carried this little tower higher than the round one, and it has an exceedingly pretty effect, breaking the long line of the house picturesquely, and looking very ancient.'[4]

He employed James Essex, an architect who had started his career as a carpenter in Cambridge and had gone on to work on the restoration of several cathedrals. Here at last at Strawberry Hill was a designer/architect who had a solid grounding in real gothic architecture as opposed to designers simply versed in the decorative arts. The resulting space which Essex created, modelled on Buckingham's plotting closet in Thornbury Castle in Gloucestershire, was dramatic. As well as the architectural plan, Essex was also responsible for choosing the design of 36 yards of 'Indian Blue Damask' costing eighteen guineas, which hung on the walls. The colour, fabric design and style emphasised to visitors that the purpose of this room was different from that of the other damask covered rooms; by choosing to use damask Essex and Walpole demonstrated the importance attached to this tiny space. It is believed that its fragility was emphasised by the addition of strips of thin handpainted paper covering the tacks which held the silk in place. Each strip echoed the design of a specially made piece of furniture.[5]

The Beauclerc closet was built with a very specific purpose. It was a space celebrating the work of one artist, Lady Diana Beauclerc. Lady Di, the daughter of the 2nd Duke of Marlborough, became Lady of the Bedchamber to Queen Charlotte, and married Viscount Bolingbroke, from whom she was later divorced for adultery in 1768 by Act of Parliament. Two days after the divorce was granted she married for the second time. Topham Beauclerc, a friend of Samuel Johnson, was an unusual figure for the eighteenth century with two claims to fame – or infamy: he was a grandson of Charles II and Nell Gwynn and he rarely washed. He is said to have infested all the guests at one of the great house parties at Blenheim with fleas. He said of himself, 'I have enough [fleas] to stock a parish'.[6] Beauclerc was a literary man and owned one of the largest libraries of the eighteenth century consisting of approximately 30,000 volumes; he and Walpole became friends.

Lady Di was a watercolourist and miniaturist, admired by Sir Joshua Reynolds, and invited by Josiah Wedgwood to design cameos for his new china. She was a friend of Walpole and a frequent visitor to Strawberry Hill; for him she executed seven drawings in soot-water, a cheap alternative to ink, illustrating scenes from a play which he had written. It was specifically as a home for these drawings that Walpole built the Beauclerc Closet. He explained his reason to Lady Ossory, writing to her from his house in Arlington Street on 20 June 1776:

…I am to have Mr Essex tomorrow from Cambridge to try if he can hang me on anywhere another room for Lady Di's drawings. I have turned the little yellow bedchamber below stairs into a beauty room, with the pictures I bought, along with the Cowley, at Mr

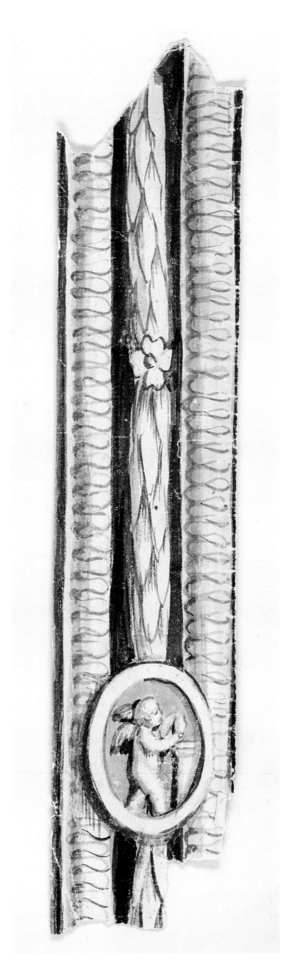

LEFT *Paper strip, possibly part of a border for the silk hanging of the Beauclerc Closet*

[5] Paper strip held in the collection of the Lewis Walpole Library, Yale University, LWL PR 16258

[6] Hicks, Carola, *Improper Pursuits, The Scandalous Life of Lady Di Beauclerk* (sic), Pan Macmillan Ltd, London, 2002, p.255

son marrying their daughter. The plot is extremely complicated; in the final scene – mercifully one might suppose – all the characters die. Although it was described as a tragedy of the highest order by Byron, it was considered unsuccessful theatrically. The drawings – which were charming rather than pornographic and were housed in the tiny secret Closet – managed to temper the bleak nature of the play's content. Walpole took his closest friends into the Closet to admire Lady Di's work, to see her portrait which hung there and to read a copy of the script. Mary Hamilton recorded her visit in a journal entry made on 21 June 1784:

> …Mr Walpole was particularly attentive to me and gave himself much trouble, as he saw I enjoyed real pleasure in looking at the pictures and other curious and beautiful works of art. He was also so obliging as to show me again (for I was here last year) the beautiful drawings of Lady Di Beauclerk [*sic*], which are in a closet built on purpose, and which he only opens for his most particular friends. These drawings are subjects taken from a play he wrote of the 'Mysterious Mother'. A tragedy I once heard read by Mr Tyghe. The story is the most horrible to be conceived, but these drawings, though they recall to mind the horrid subject, are most affectingly interesting.

The copy of the play, bound in blue tooled leather, was housed in the drawer of a specially commissioned writing table of Clay Ware which had been designed by Paul Sandby. Given the suspect purpose of this little room, it was nevertheless a fascinating and exquisite space, appearing both externally and internally the embodiment of a castle from legend or fairy tale. Once again Walpole relied on contrasts to heighten the effect he wanted: the shocking story of the play and the contents of the drawings set within the frame of a pretty, feminine, charmingly small room.

The tiny room was furnished with stools upholstered in blue damask. A tea-service of old blue and white porcelain stood on a second piece of Clay Ware: 'a tea-chest of Clay's Ware, painted with loose feathers',[7] which was itemised by Clay in his bill as, 'a tea-cade'.[8] Throughout his life strange objects and unusual methods of manufacture fascinated Walpole, and in his Commonplace Book of 1780 he noted a reminder to visit 'Wedgwoods and Clay's manufactory'. Clay Ware was produced by a strange

Lovibond's sale, but I could not place the drawings there, because I will have a sanctuary for them, not to be shown to all the profane that come to see the house, who in truth almost drive me out of my house. Adieu! Madame, remember this is summer, and that I am Methusalem. He left off writing news when he was past an hundred.

The play *The Mysterious Mother*, written in 1768, was considered to be pornographic at the time and this may have increased Walpole's desire to find a private place in which to keep a copy, together with its illustrations. The plot is built around an act of double incest: the Countess of Narbonne is warned that her son is planning to seduce a girl of good birth and decides to save the girl by taking her place in her son's bed, eventually giving birth to a daughter. She then attempts, but fails, to stop her

procedure which metamorphosed a mundane product into a glorious piece of furniture. Henry Clay had invented, and patented, a means of recycling papier mâché and converting it into a highly sought after variant of japanning or lacquer work. The process was described in 1801 by a visitor to his factory:

> Large, strong and thick cartridge paper is the material of which it is composed. Of this a wetted sheet is spread upon a flat and even board, the surface of which being pasted over, another sheet is laid upon it; being thus attached to each other, they are conveyed into an oven close adjoining, where they remain till they are dry, which strengthens their cohesion. In this manner from twelve to eighteen sheets (according to the required thickness) are pasted upon each other and dried. The pieces are then taken out of the oven, suffered to cool, and cut into the necessary forms; sawed & worked in the same manner as wood, being to the full as hard as that substance. The article of furniture being formed, it is then given to women and girls, who varnish it with black lacquer, twelve different times, being dried in ovens after every varnishing. This is the most unwholesome and disagreeable part of the process. From hence it is carried to another party of ladies, who polish it with sand and water, to take off every roughness, and give one uniform smooth surface. The fine polishers then take it, who gave it the beautiful brilliancy of its appearance, with rotten stone and rubbing of the flat hand. The painters next receive it, of whom there are two sets; one employed in delineating the little fancy patterns, the other in the more beautiful and difficult line of landscape, and figure painting. That part of the patterns which is to receive the gold, is first traced over in red paint, which having stood for some hours to dry, the leaf is put on. Part of this adhering to the painted parts, the remainder of the leaf is rubbed off, and the whole is then lackered over to secure the gilding.[9]

When the invention was patented in 1772 it was described as useful for:

> …making in paper highly varnished panels or roofs for coaches, and all sorts of wheel carriages and sedan chairs, panels for rooms, doors, and cabins of ships, cabinets, bookcases, screens, chimney-pieces, tables, tea-trays, waiters, etc.

Walpole was constantly attending sales where he bought new objects for the Collection; he found positions in the Beauclerc Closet for some of the items he was unable to resist buying, a basalt head of Jupiter Serapis from the Barbarini collection, a locket containing hair of Mary Queen of Scots, a watch and a book of psalms illustrated with twenty-one 'inimitable illuminations by don Julio Clovio, scholar of Julio Romano'. However, an ebony cabinet designed by Edward Edwards in 1783 (the source for the paper strips covering the silk wall coverings), and probably intended for the room to hold nine of Lady Di's gypsy drawings, was moved to the new state bedchamber sometime after 1784. Was it perhaps moved because there was not enough space for it in the Beauclerc Closet? Was the house finally full?

[7] Walpole, Horace, *The Description of the Villa of Mr. Horace Walpole at Strawberry-Hill near Twickenham, Middlesex*, Strawberry Hill, 1784.

[8] Toynbee, Paget, *Strawberry Hill Accounts*, Clarendon Press, Oxford, 1927 (Document 5 dated 7 May 1778, loose bill)

[9] Toynbee, Paget, op. cit., p.172

11 The Great North Bedchamber

'A very royal chamber'

BY THE MIDDLE of the eighteenth century it was usual for a suite of apartments to culminate in a bedroom rather than a drawing room or picture gallery. At the end of a very short passage, which was lit from above in a theatrical way and decorated in a daisy patterned wallpaper in monochrome, stood the Great North Bedchamber, Horace Walpole's state bedchamber and the final parade room of the house. The passage held objects presaging the great room that visitors would next enter and reminded them at the same time of those things already seen – a reprise of the early part of the tour. A painting of a scene from *The Mysterious Mother* was hanging there beside an owl made of cut paper; Walpole had a fondness for owls and recorded various purchases of them, including a set of silver castors shaped like owls. Pieces on the walls had a special significance for Walpole, the Walpole family, or were objects made or presented by friends, while yet more objects spilled over into another small closet off the passage in which Walpole placed a drawing of the genuine Castle of Otranto.

On entering the Bedchamber the visitors found themselves in a room furnished in the French style, bathed both in reflected crimson light from the damask of the walls and in amber light from the armorial glass made by Peckitt, a glass painter from Yorkshire. As the focus of the room, against the far wall and flanked by two chairs on either side, stood the bed, enriched by Aubusson tapestry hangings with festoons of flowers woven in bright colour against a pale background. This whole ensemble was further enhanced by a lining of crimson silk and decorated with ostrich plumes at the corners extending the bed upwards to meet a richly gilt ceiling. The design of the ceiling had been copied from one at John Chute's house, the Vyne, and it could be traced back still further to the decoration of the ceiling of the Court of Star Chamber within the Palace of Westminster. To enhance the effect of the tapestries six white and gold elbow chairs, made in the French style by Vile, were covered in the same fabric. Each of these had an ebony chair placed beside it. On the floor stood another carpet made at the Moorfields manufactury and a foot-carpet worked in needle-work. The combination of damask, tapestries and worked carpets indicated the importance of the room. Henrietta Pye, when she visited Strawberry Hill, referred to it as 'The Gobelin Room', confusing Gobelin and Aubusson tapestries.[1] Walpole, always interested in the techniques of manufacture, had commented adversely on tapestry design generally in his Commonplace Book of 1780, writing '...as if a tapestry-loom, when the Weavers are retird, continued to work and confounded the patterns, mixing, some it had executed before with that in the loom.'

[1] Pye, J. Henrietta, A Short View of the principal seats and gardens in and about Twickenham, London, 1775

The room itself had only been completed in 1772, following Walpole's decision to use the Round Tower Room as a drawing room and not as a state bedchamber. The internal walls had been lined with a wooden framework which gave an extra layer of warmth. A scrim, or canvas, had then been stretched over the frame, and over this the damask was hung, an expensive choice although not as costly as the best velvet would have been.

As befitted the final great room of the house, it was given a most spectacular chimneypiece, described in the 1842 Sale Catalogue as, 'The beautiful carved and gilt Chimney Piece of Portland Stone, of Gothic design, rich in effect, and very elaborate in workmanship, formed by an arch springing from two pillars, with round pediments'. Walpole had designed the chimneypiece himself using Bishop Dudley's tomb in Westminster Abbey as his source. The stone surround, unlike the timber chimneypieces of the house, was executed as a work of sculpture and richly gilded. The carving was carried out by Thomas Gayfere's workshop and was probably completed by the master mason himself who was at the same time working on the restoration of the stonework at Westminster Abbey. This would have given him an understanding of the complexity

and principles of original gothic stone carving. It was this craftsmanship and attention to detail which added a special importance to the chimney. The addition of vine leaves to the surround echoed a similar design used in Walpole's own bedroom and might also have been intended as a visual pun on the Vyne, the house which had inspired the ceiling. For the first time at Strawberry Hill a chimney-back was described in detail by Walpole and its history recorded for Margaret or other servants to relate. It was positioned so that it would be seen as part of a composite and integrated overall design. The chimney-back displayed the arms of King Henry VII, while on the wall above hung the dynastic portrait of Henry's son, Henry VIII, standing with his children, all of whom eventually ruled England;[2] thus Walpole showed those entering his State Bedchamber the whole Tudor dynasty assembled together. With them, on the chimney itself, he placed a large bust of Francis II, the weakly French husband of Mary Queen of Scots, and placed around other objects of French and English origins. The interrelated histories of both countries were repeated round the room with most of the English works hanging on the chimney-side of the room – including a portrait by Van Dyck, and another of

[2] Walpole, Horace, *The Description of the Villa of Mr. Horace Walpole at Strawberry-Hill near Twickenham, Middlesex,* Strawberry Hill, 1784

[3] Letter Horace Walpole to Lady Ossory written from Strawberry Hill, 30 June 1785

Horace's brother Robert, painted as a Knight of the Bath. It seems Walpole never tired of repositioning his Collection to achieve a more satisfactory result:

> …All this morning I have been busy in placing Henry VII in the State Bedchamber and making a new arrangement of pictures. It is really a very royal chamber now and much improved. Besides the family of Henry VIII over the chimney as before, and Queen Maintenon over one of the doors, there are Henry VII and Catherine of Braganza, on one side of the bed; Henry VIII and Henriette Duchess of Orleans on the other.[3]

Once inside the room Margaret would have closed the door behind the visitors and directed them to look back so that they might more clearly admire the workmanship of the door through which they had entered and the matching door by the window. There was no third door to a dressing room and its absence emphasised that the bedchamber had never been intended for use. The doors had been designed by John Chute in gothic style. They were gilded and surmounted by ogees. These doors were among the most elaborate in the house and held, built into the uppermost section, medallions depicting Louis XIV and Charles V. This then was the 'French' wall holding mainly French style objects. At one time a Poussin landscape hung there, alongside portraits of Madame de Maintenon, La Duchesse de Mazarin and Ninon de l'Enclos, all of them above a small French-style japanned cabinet on which was a blue and white Sèvres breakfast set decorated with a coloured border of birds and trees. Behind the second door, which was glazed in the upper-half, stood a shelved closet in which the more eclectic treasures were displayed: a collection of rare Italian faience, a silver-gilt plate illustrating the meeting of the Emperor Charles V and Francis I of France, a piece

ABOVE *Detail of the chimney piece of the Great North Bedchamber showing some of the original eighteenth-century gilding. The wallpaper is from the Baron de Stern period*

reflected back into the room through the mirror. Had he chosen to light the room only with candles placed in simple candlesticks on tables, as he had done in most of the rooms, there would only have been small individual pools of light. For this room Walpole wanted a more generous effect of light, increased by the use of gilding and looking glass, rather than gloomth. The glass set within the windows added to the rich texture and recorded the very English pedigree of the Walpole family. The objects placed under the window were also mostly English, although there were pieces of Italian faience and a Sèvres porcelain tabletop. Close by these hung Hogarth's sketch for *The Beggar's Opera*.

The windows themselves were extraordinary for Strawberry Hill and would have aroused comment. They were dressed with fashionable festooned curtains in what was possibly a deeper and richer shade of the crimson of the walls. The use of a combination of materials would have enhanced appreciation of each and given the opportunity to contrast the textures. The festoons may have been practical and could have been dropped down at night, but it is equally possible that the curtains were for dressing only – false festoon curtains were regularly used at this time.

The workmanship of Mr Peckitt, 'the man at York', on window glass generally was much admired by Gray, who wrote explaining the techniques which had been used to Dr Wharton in May 1761:

Dear Doctor,
…Mr Price here has left off business, & retired into Wales: the Person, who succeeds, does not pretend to be acquainted with all the secrets of his art. the Man at York is now in Town, exhibiting some specimens of his skill to the Society of Arts: him (you say) you have already consulted. coats of arms will doubtless be expensive (Price used to have five Guineas for a very plain one) figures much more so. unless therefore you can pick up some remnants of old painted glass, which are sometimes met with in farm-houses, little out-of-the-way churches & vestries, and even at country-glasiers shops, etc: I should advice to buy plain colour'd glass (for which they ask here in St Martin's Lane 5s: a pound, but it is sold at York for 2 or 3s:) & make up the tops of your windows in a mosaick of your own fancy. the glass will come to you in square plates, (some part of which is always wrinkled & full of little bubbles,

of silver supposedly made by Cellini, gloves which had once been worn by James I, sets of playing cards for the games of Minchiati and Taracco and King William III's spurs – all of which, together with a host of other objects, could be viewed by anyone visiting Strawberry Hill alongside a pane of glass which showed men playing cards. Surely the pack of Italian playing cards was placed close by? Horace Walpole never missed an opportunity to marry one object to the next.

Beyond the closet, on the window-wall, stood a large mirror flanked with bronze candle sconces. Branched sconces direct light upwards so that the intricate design of the ceiling would have been so you must allow for waste), any glasier can cut it into quarrels, & you can dispose the pattern & colours, red, blew, purple, & yellow (there is also green, if you like it) as well or better than the Artisan himself, & certainly much cheaper. I would not border it with the same, least the room should be too dark. nor should the quarrels of clear glass be too small (in the lower part of the window); if they are but turn'd corner-ways, it is enough to give it a gothic aspect. if there is anything to see (tho' it be but a tree) I should put a very large diamond-pane in the midst of each division.

The room the visitors saw was presented cunningly dressed with objects which they would remember after they left and would talk over later with their friends. It was also in this final great room that it became apparent to the discerning visitor that Walpole had copied ideas from other well known fashionable houses as well as from his acknowledged source of engravings. He was obviously influenced by William Kent's design for Houghton and his practice of planning a room as an entity within which the hanging of paintings became an integral part of the whole. Walpole adopted and extended this idea to produce a different mood for each room.

On the occasions when Walpole chose to use the room it was for evening entertainment of his personal guests, whom he sometimes amused with the playing of card games; the Florentine cards kept in the closet may have been used. Tarot had become popular in fifteenth-century Florence, where it was played with a deck of seventy-eight cards. In about 1530 the Florentines developed a variation which they called Minchiate, retaining most of the original tarot trumps but adding twenty new ones representing: Hope, Prudence, Faith and Charity; the four elements of Earth, Air, Water and Fire; and the twelve signs of the zodiac. Minchiate became a very popular game and was eventually preferred to tarot, with the cards used on two different levels – for card playing and for fortune telling. In his Library at Strawberry Hill Walpole kept another set of cards, quite different from the Florentine decks. This pack was used for a variation of a card trick which had the splendid name of 'The Impenetrable Secret'. The trick consisted of ten cards kept stored in a box decorated to look like a small leather-bound book. Each card contained ten sentences written

in black on one side and ten different sentences in red on the reverse. The instructions for playing are confusing: one person chooses a line from the black side of the card, the dealer taking note of an arranged code so that when the player eventually located the red card containing the chosen sentence the dealer was able to guess the sentences as if by magic. The sentences were all aphorisms with an entertaining edge, for example: 'Marrying a woman for her beauty is like eating a bird for its song', 'The gates of death are open night and day', 'Nothing is more fatal to health than over-care of it.'[4] The Impenetrable Secret entertained and astonished Society on both sides of the Atlantic.

ABOVE *Heraldic glass from the Great North Bedchamber by William Peckitt, 1772*

[4] The Impenetrable Secret (game possibly ascribed to Horace Walpole), BL C.31.b.32.1780

ABOVE *The Duchesse de Choiseul and Madame la Marquise du Deffand, engraving by Greatbach after a painting by Carmontel which hung at Strawberry Hill*

[5] Hazen, A.T., *A Bibliography of Horace Walpole*, Yale University Press, New Haven & London, 1948, p.173

[6] Watson, F.J.B., 'Walpole and the Taste for French Porcelain in Eighteenth-Century England', essay on the 250th anniversary of Walpole's birth, Yale University Press, New Haven & London, 1967

porcelain, his expenditure on ceramics must have been enormous – 130 pieces, many of them Sèvres, are listed in his inventory. For the Great North Bedchamber alone he bought snail-shaped incense burners, an elegant and rare Sèvres basket-shaped vase in blue, gold and white (which he described in his journal as 'a corbeille' and for which he paid seventy-two livres), Chantilly plates and a Villeroy ewer.

William Cole, writing in his journal about a visit to Paris made with Walpole in 1765-6 obviously thought he was being extravagant: '…I was with Mr Walpole one day at a great shop in Paris, Mr Poirier's where it [Sèvres] was sold, and saw him give 10 louis or guineas for a single coffee cup, saucer, and a little square sort of sou-coupe or under-saucer to set them on; they were indeed the highest finished things of the kind that can be conceived'. Walpole's love of porcelain is summed up in a letter written to his cousin, Conway, on 30 July 1771: 'I know the faces of every snuff-box and every teacup as well as those of Madame du Lac and Monsieur Poirier.'

Walpole chose the beautiful, the unusual, the innovative. Although Cole had been surprised at the expenditure of ten louis, or guineas, on a single cup and saucer, Walpole paid six times that sum on a blue cup and saucer decorated with batons and birds, and ninety-six livres on the square blue and white flower-tubs which he placed in the Blue Breakfast Room. A blue and white breakfast set, probably for four people, cost him a massive 114 livres. To appreciate the true extravagance of Walpole's purchases, at the same time as he was paying such high sums for relatively few pieces, the Duke and Duchess of Richmond paid only £500 – or approximately 1,000 livres – for a complete Sèvres service. Vast cargoes of French porcelain were brought into England and became so popular that George III placed an import duty of eleven guineas on each £100 spent on French and overseas porcelain, together with a second levy, estimated by weight, of ten pence per pound weight of china. This tax continued to be levied until the American War of Independence when the trade more or less dried up.[6] Walpole did not however pay tax wherever he could evade it, preferring to wait for his goods to arrive in the diplomatic bag.

To complement his pleasure in all things French, Walpole conducted a lengthy friendship and correspondence with an elderly French aristocrat,

A sales advertisement for it appeared in Benjamin Franklin's *Pennsylvania Gazette* on 11 May 1749, and George Bickham, an English engraver, advertised sets at a reduced price in January 1754 to make way for a third edition of the game which was then published in June at a higher price.[5]

On visits to Paris Walpole bought Sèvres porcelain and displayed some of these pieces in the Great North Bedchamber. Some were bought directly from the factory and others came from the fashionable *marchands-merciers* frequented by the Parisian elite. Walpole patronised three main dealers, Poirier, Du Lac and Said, all of whom set up shop in, or close to, the rue Saint Honoré. When he returned to England from Paris in 1766 he brought with him five cases containing Sèvres and Chantilly china which he had bought from Poirier, and fourteen small cases from Du Lac. Although they may not all have been filled exclusively with

Madame du Deffand. On her death she bequeathed him her dog, Tonton, who joined a long line of dogs at Strawberry Hill. His arrival was not as expected:

…I told you in my last, that Tonton was arrived. I brought him this morning to take possession of his new villa; but his inauguration has not been at all pacific. As he has already found out that he may be as despotic as at Saint-Joseph's, he began with exiling my beautiful little cat; – upon which, however, we shall not quite agree. He then flew at one of my dogs, who returned it, by biting his foot till it bled; but was severly beaten for it. I immediately rung for Margaret to dress his foot; but in the midst of my tribulation could not keep my countenance; for she cried, "Poor little thing, he does not understand my language!" – I hope she will not recollect too that he is a papist!'[7]

Walpole added a postscript two days later after receiving a reply from Conway:

I came before dinner, and find your long letter of the 3d. You have mistaken Tonton's sex, who is a cavalier, and a little of the 'mousquetaire' still; but if I do not correct his vivacities, at least I shall not encourage them like my dear old friend.

He then composed,

a Charade on my Dog Tonton. The first part is thine, the second belongs only to people of fashion; but the whole, tho doubly thine, belongs only to me.[8]

He became increasingly fond of the dog and wrote the following letter to Lady Ossory on 24 February 1789:

…I would not interrupt my news, or rather, my replies; and therefore delayed telling you that Tonton is dead – and that I comfort myself: he was grown stone deaf, and very near equally blind, and so weak that the two last days he could not walk upstairs. Happily he had not suffered, and died close by my side without a pang or a grown. I have had the satisfaction for my dear old friend's sake and his own, of having nursed him up by constant attention to the age of sixteen, yet always afraid of his surviving me, as it was scarce possible he could meet a third person who would study his happiness equally. I sent him to Strawberry and went thither on Sunday to see him buried behind the Chapel near Rosette. I shall miss him greatly – and must not

ABOVE *Walpole in his Library, engraving by Greatbach after the painting by Müntz of 1756*

have another dog – I am too old, and should only breed it up to be unhappy, when I am gone! My resource is in two marble kittens that Mrs Damer has given me of her own work, and which are so much alive that I talk to them as I did to poor Tonton – if this is being superannuated, no matter; when dotage can amuse itself, it ceases to be an evil. I fear, my marble playfellows are better adapted to me, than I am to being your Ladyship's correspondent!

The chapel, behind which Walpole buried his pets, was across the garden, and it was there, by way of the backstairs, through the Great Cloister that the visitors were next led by Margaret.

[7] Letter Horace Walpole to Henry Seymour Conway, 6 May 1781

[8] Walpole, Horace, 'Commonplace Book for 1780', Lewis Walpole Library, Yale University

12 The Garden

'lilacs and nightingales'

OPPOSITE *Detail from The Chapel in the Garden (also known as the Chapel in the Wood or Woods), engraving by Godfrey, after a watercolour by Pars, published 1784*

EMERGING FROM THE FOOT of the Round Tower the visitors found themselves in the Great Cloister. Viewed from the main road Strawberry Hill, with its apparently disparate group of ancient looking towers, pinnacles and castellations, looked like a medieval castle. However, seen from the river the view of the Great Cloister, built between 1760 and 1761 on the left of the house below the Long Gallery, gave the impression of a gothic abbey. The grey flagged Cloister had a vaulted ceiling too low to let in sunlight. To this space Walpole added eight turned Welsh chairs which he had bought at a house sale from one of his friends, and a pedestal complete with Greek inscription on which he placed an antique marble vase. Blue and white china flower pots at either end married the manufactured cloistered atmosphere with the anticipated delights of the garden.

Beyond the Cloister was the unexpected: the complete antithesis of the house. In the garden visitors and guests alike found harmony and tranquillity; it was a garden essentially English in the planting, with all seemingly natural. The garden was the romantic frame in which Walpole's Gothic Castle was set.

There was still an element of theatre, but here, out of doors, it was unobtrusive. The backdrop was the river, the wings the hills on each side and the public right-of-way along the river bank provided

an ever changing scene. Walpole was the actor-manager, overseeing all. He described the garden in a letter written from within the house:

> …This view of the castle is what I have just finished, and is the only side that will be at all regular. Directly before it is an open grove, through which you see a field which is bounded by a serpentine wood of all kind of trees and flowering shrubs and flowers. The lawn before the house is situated on the top of a small hill, from whence to the left you see the town and church of Twickenham encircling a turn of the river, that looks exactly like a seaport in miniature.[1]

Walpole had moved in six years before writing the letter, in May 1747, and had started at once to establish the mood. After completing necessary work on the house and paying three pounds two shillings and sixpence-halfpenny to a carpenter, glazier and smith, he spent a massive nine pounds and six shillings in October 1747 on planting trees to start the formation of a grove – each tree cost him one shilling and sixpence.[2] Every year he paid further large sums to Mr Ashe, a local nurseryman, for plants, and to a gardener; his account book was peppered with sums he had spent on trees. When a lover of gardens moves into a new house the garden is looked after first and ready money is spent on it, a point he explained to Mann in May 1749:

[1] Letter Horace Walpole to Horace Mann written from Strawberry Hill, 12 June 1753

[2] Toynbee, Paget, *Strawberry Hill Accounts*, Clarendon Press, Oxford, 1927

...I have made a vast plantation! Lord Leicester told me t'other day that he heard I would not buy some old china, because I was laying out all my money on trees: "Yes," said I, "my Lord, I used to love blue trees, but now I like green ones."

By June 1754 he could write to Montagu: '...It [Strawberry] is now in the height of its greenth, blueth, gloomth, honey-suckle-and seringahood.'

Walpole took pleasure in being the creator and designer of his garden, a plantsman and the first garden historian, but he had little practical knowledge when he began: 'now and then a lettuce run to seed overturns all my botany, as I have more than once taken it for a curious West Indian flowering shrub.'[3] To describe his passionate interest in the planting and the creation of a landscape Walpole coined the word 'gardenist'.

I have suggested one [a simple term] for a designer of modern gardens, and which has been approved, and will suit as well in French and English. To distinguish him from the gardener, I would call him gardenist, in French jardiniste.[4]

Having started with scant knowledge Walpole addressed himself to the garden with the same passion he gave to his coin collection, portraits or porcelain; he set out to study and understand the principles of gardening. It was to be his personal garden, which the visitors saw in their tour laid out according to his wishes. As a child he had been surrounded by rare and beautiful plants in the garden and greenhouses of the family house in Chelsea and a hand, similar to his, notes the sale details of plants from the 'Uppor Greenhouse' in the inventory compiled after his father's death.[5]

It is unclear if visitors were accompanied by the housekeeper, or another servant, although it is more probable that they were encouraged to wander by

themselves. As they left the Great Cloister they would have seen an expanse of lawn stretching down to the river, kept rolled and trim. The lawn was bordered by painted trellis, in front of which were placed orange trees in tubs. The visitors were probably directed across to the far side of the garden towards the Serpentine Walk, having been advised what to admire en route.

The Walk was deliberately designed to be winding so that it would encourage an illusion of distance and the estate would appear larger than the forty-six acres Walpole owned at the end of his life. It led from the Great Cloister, past the New Offices to the south of the house, meandering gently past the Chapel in the Woods and then continuing east towards the river through pastoral surroundings. As visitors walked they would have seen that there was nothing obviously gothic about the garden at Strawberry Hill, nor was it laid out

in any obviously planned way. Instead, Walpole's approach to the garden plan was very similar to one aspect of the house; a mixture of *sharawaggi* and contrived happenstance. He described his approach in his essay on *The History of the Modern Taste in Gardening*, which he wrote in 1770. The garden should be laid out to surprise in a very subtle way, 'where the beauty shall be great and strike the eye, but without any order or disposition of parts, that shall be commonly or easily observed'. Just as the north front of the house was planted with trees to mask parts of the building and give picturesque glimpses of the house, so the garden was planned following the principles of William Kent, to provide areas of interest and surprise. According to Walpole, Kent was the 'father of modern gardening'. By following his rules Walpole was able to screen the myriad small, temporary buildings and to hide the builders' materials which

ABOVE *View from the Terrace at Strawberry Hill, engraving by Godfrey*

3 Letter Horace Walpole to Henry Seymour Conway, 29 August 1748 (o.s)

4 Letter Horace Walpole to Duc de Nivernais, 6 January 1785

5 The National Archives, Kew, C101/20 p.27

Walpole's essay on gardening was written at the same time as he was planning to build a garden folly, the Chapel in the Woods. The Chapel was at the opposite end of the garden to the Great North Bedchamber, which was erected at about the same time.

> …I am building a small chapel too in my garden to receive two valuable pieces of antiquity, and which have been presents singularly lucky for me. They are the window from Bexhill with the portraits of Henry III and his Queen, procured for me by Lord Ashburnham. The other, great part of the tomb of Capoccio, mentioned likewise in my 'Anecdotes of Painting' on the subject of the Confessor's shrine, and sent to me from Rome by Mr Hamilton our minister at Naples…[7]

Finished by 1773 and ready for use by the following year, this small garden building, mostly attributed to John Chute, was both a garden folly and a display space for large individual pieces of Walpole's overflowing collection, many of which had some religious connotation. Thomas Gayfere, whose extensive knowledge of medieval building methods as a master mason made him the ideal choice, was employed to build it. He used brick but gave it an imposing Portland stone elevation. The Chapel was a modified octagon, surmounted by a fan-vaulted papier-mâché ceiling. Both interior and exterior were modelled after the sixteenth-century Chantry Chapel of Bishop Audley in Salisbury Cathedral.

The creation of the Chapel provided a backdrop for several individual great pieces from the Collection which Walpole had acquired and which were strategically placed to provide a climax to be reached on a garden stroll. The window glass, in a setting by Peckitt, included the roundel (from Bexhill) representing King Henry III and Queen Eleanor, which Walpole believed to be one of the oldest examples of painted glass in England. The tomb mentioned in his letter to Cole was intended for the Chapel, but was found to be too large. At this point, Horace Mann, who had provided so many of the objects for Strawberry Hill, discovered a cosmati-work shrine which had once stood in the church of Santa Maria Maggiore in Rome. It was shipped to England and placed in the apse. Walpole believed it had been made by Peter Cavalini, creator of the tomb of Edward the Confessor in Westminster Abbey, a connection which pleased him.

ABOVE *The Chapel in the Garden (also known as the Chapel in the Wood or Woods), engraving by Godfrey after a watercolour by Pars, published in 1784*

[6] Walpole, Horace, *The History of the Modern Taste in Gardening*, first printed in Vol. IV of *The Anecdotes of Painting*, Strawberry Hill, 1780

[7] Letter Horace Walpole to William Cole, 23 October 1771

must have been stowed there for the greater part of fifty years.

Groupes of trees broke too uniform or too extensive a lawn; evergreens and woods were opposed to the glare of the champain, and where the view was less fortunate, or so much exposed as to beheld at once, he blotted out some parts by thick shades, to divide it into variety, or to make the richest scene more enchanting by reserving it to a farther advance of the spectator's step. Thus selecting favourite objects, and veiling deformities by screens of plantation; sometimes allowing the rudest waste to add its foil to the richest theatre, he realised the compositions of the greatest masters in painting.[6]

He was not an overtly religious man. Perhaps the building was planned, albeit tongue-in-cheek, as a chantry chapel for Walpole himself? Considered one of the finest garden buildings of the eighteenth century in the gothic style, it functioned both as a folly and as a 'family vault'; Walpole would eventually have his pets interred there, with memorial plaques set into the wall. A gothic bench designed by Richard Bentley was installed with a head of John the Baptist by Donatello displayed on it. There was even a bronze statue of the virgin.

For the visitor completing a tour of Strawberry Hill the approach to the Chapel glimpsed through the dappled light of the Serpentine Walk would have rekindled the gothic experience after the initial natural appearance of the garden. Continuing on through the remainder of the Serpentine Walk the tour of the garden ended at the 'large seat in the

form of a shell, carved in oak, from a design by Mr. Bentley'.[8] Made in 1754 the Shell Bench was the last in a series of objects strategically placed around the garden in unexpected positions – just as objects were placed in the house – among them were a gothic iron gate with Coade stone pillars and a gothic bridge over a sunken path. The Shell Bench became a favourite resting place for ladies visiting the house; three could sit in it, or on it, at one time, and from it they would have been able to watch the river traffic, see part of the house and also glimpse the obelisk standing at the cross roads at the approach to the house.

> STRAWBERRY HILL is grown a perfect Paphos, it is the land of beauties. On Wednesday the Duchesses of Hamilton and Richmond, and Lady Ailesbury dined there….There never was so pretty a sight as to see them all three sitting in the shell; a thousand years hence, when I begin to grow old, if that can ever be, I shall talk of that event and tell young people how much handsomer the women of my time were than they will be then.[9]

The garden was planned from the start to be a continuation of the house: the views from the windows complemented the interiors, each window framing a different section of garden. When being frivolous Walpole referred to Strawberry Hill as his 'Gothic Castle', but when he was serious Strawberry Hill was his 'villa', a term which suggested the house and garden were interrelated by deliberate design. The choice of planting, colour scheme, and height of flowers and shrubs were all carefully considered. Horace Mann writing to Walpole noted in a postscript to a letter of 22 November 1760:

> …PS I have been putting up for Mr Wright, Lord Henley's nephew, some seed of an odd ivy with red leaves, which he thought very rare when he saw it in Boboli. I should think it would make a very venerable appearance through one of your painted glass windows at Strawberry Castle. I send you a few seeds enclosed, as I believe the sowing time advances.

The same skill in planting was evident looking back at the house from the garden. From each part of the garden the house could be seen from its special viewpoint with trees framing battlements, pinnacles, cloister or towers separating each area in order to increase the feeling of a medieval cluster of

castle buildings. As the weather changed the light created wells of shadow in the Cloister or sent patches of sunlight chasing around the garden from refraction on the glass. This effect was only possible because it was an asymmetric building with endless crevices, corners and crenallations, all creating shadows. Wherever possible those objects placed within the garden, Po-Yang (a pond), the Shell Bench or the Chapel, all carried the eye onwards to the next framed view. Public benches were added for visitors, natural boundaries were used and a ha-ha was added to the south of the house between a small wood and a field. On the west side a fence was built and tubs filled with plants placed alongside.

The bills for a cottage built on the estate with an additional garden (destined to become a flower garden) amounted to sixty-one pounds seven shillings and eight pence.[10] By August 1765 Walpole was inviting his friends to join him at Strawberry Hill to see this 'new cottage and garden…with which they were enchanted. It is so retired, so modest, and yet so cheerful and trim'. The thatched cottage contained two rooms, one of which became a Tea-Room and the other Walpole called a Little

ABOVE *Fragment of seventeenth-century glass from the Blue Bedchamber depicting a broody hen with her chicks*

OPPOSITE *The Shell Bench, designed by Richard Bentley, engraving by Morris*

[8] Walpole, Horace, *A Description of the Villa of Mr. Horace Walpole at Strawberry-Hill near Twickenham, Middlesex*, Strawberry Hill, 1784

[9] Letter Horace Walpole to George Montagu, 2 June 1759

[10] Toynbee, Paget, *Strawberry Hill Accounts*, Clarendon Press, Oxford, 1927

Library and had it painted green and white, presumably in reflection of the sylvan surroundings; a porch added by John Chute gave architectural interest. It was sited in a thicket of trees with stream, cascade and flower garden by the side and with a round pond in which goldfish swam. To cross the stream the gothic bridge was added, while close to the flower garden lay the kitchen garden, a rosarium and a nursery. When Walpole's cousin, Anne Damer, inherited the estate she found the Little Library damp and mouldy.

Walpole may not have been a hands-on gardener but he grew to know plants with their idiosyncrasies and loved trees. His garden assailed the senses and was planted to please the eye and create delight with scents wafting towards the house. Birdsong pleased the ear, fruit was there for the picking and the plants provided a variety of textures.

> I am just come out of the garden in the most oriental of all evenings, and from breathing odours beyond that of Araby. The acacias, which the Arabians have the sense to worship, are covered with blossoms, the honeysuckles dangle from every tree in festoons, the seringas are thickets of sweets, and the new-cut hay of the field in the garden tempers the balmy gales with simple freshness.[11]

Walpole himself was always ready with advice on horticultural matters:

My dear Sir

> You oblige me extremely by giving me this commission, and though I am exceedingly unlike Soloman in everything else, I will at least resemble him, in recommending you to the Hiram from whom I obtained my cedars of Libanus. He is by men called Christopher Gray, nurseryman at Fulham. I mention cedars first, because they are the most beautiful of the evergreen race, and because they are the dearest; half a guinea apiece in baskets. The arbutus are scarce and a crown apiece, but they are very beautiful. The lignum vitae I would not recommend to you; they stink abominably if you touch them and never make a handsome tree: the Chinese arbor vitae is very beautiful. I have a small nursery myself … out of this little parsley-bed of mine, I can furnish you with a few plants, particularly three Chinese arbor vitaes; a dozen of the New England or Lord Weymouth's pine, which is that beautiful tree we have so much admired at the Duke of Argyle's for its clean straight stem, the lightness of its hairy green, and for being feathered quite to the ground: they should stand in a moist soil, and care must be taken every year to clear away all plants and trees round them, that they may have free air and room to expand themselves. Besides these I shall send you, twelve stone or Italian pines; twelve pinasters, twelve black spruce firs; two Carolina cherries; thirty evergreen cytisus, a pretty shrub that grows very fast, and may be cut down as you please; fifty Spanish brooms; and six acacias, the genteelest tree of all, but you must take care to plant them in a first row, and where they will be well sheltered, for the least wind tears and breaks them to pieces. All these are ready, whenever you will give me directions how and when to send them. They are exceedingly small, as I have but lately taken to propagate myself; but then they will travel more safely, will be more sure of living, and will grow faster than larger. Other sorts of evergreens that you must have, are silver and Scotch firs; Virginia cedars, which should stand forwards and have nothing touch them; and above all cypresses, which I think are my chief passion: there is nothing so picturesque when they stand two or three in a clump upon a little hillock or rising above low shrubs, and particularly near buildings. There is another bit of picture of which I am fond, and that is, a larch or a spruce fir planted

[11] Letter Horace Walpole to George Montagu, 10 June 1765

[12] Letter Horace Walpole to George Montagu, 8 November 1755

[13] Letter Horace Walpole to George Montagu, 5 May 1761

behind a weeping willow, and shooting upwards as the willow depends. I think for courts about a house or winter gardens, almond trees mixed with evergreens, particularly with Scotch firs have a pretty effect, before anything else comes out; whereas almond trees, being generally planted among other trees, and being in bloom before other trees have leaves, have no ground to show the beauty of their blossoms. Gray at Fulham sells cypresses in pots at half a crown apiece; you turn them out of the pot with all their mould and they never fail...[12]

It was in the garden that Walpole was at his most natural, simply dressed, hair tied back in a queue, hatless, accompanied by one of his spaniels enjoying the sun – or thunderstorms – or deep snow – any extremity of weather, through the day and into the night:

...I am very willing to leave London...and do pass half the week at Strawberry, where my two passions, lilacs and nightingales are in full bloom. I spent Sunday as if it was Apollo's birthday; Gray and Mason were with me, and we listened to the nightingales till one o'clock in the morning.[13]

Once their tour was over and three o'clock in the afternoon reached, the visitors were expected to leave; once again the house and the garden belonged only to Walpole, his friends, servants and dogs. As he aged he continued to want to spend time at Strawberry Hill enjoying his Twickenham garden where his pleasures were simple and different from the enjoyment he received from the great estate at Houghton Hall which he had inherited with the title of 4th Earl of Orford in 1791. The pleasure he experienced in watching his guests enjoy the garden never diminished.

ABOVE *East View of the Cottage Garden at Strawberry Hill, engraving by Godfrey from a drawing by Pars, published in 1784. Note the buildings which can be glimpsed through the trees*

13 Life below stairs

'Dare one complain?'

BELOW STAIRS was Margaret's domain and no visitor would ever have ventured there. The servants had a strong sense of community and seem to have found Walpole a good employer who preferred to suffer small annoyances rather than discharge those servants who were not meeting expectations. He retained seven indoor servants for most of the time that he lived at Strawberry Hill and many of them remained with him to the end of their lives and were remembered in his will with generosity. It is not known where the men-servants slept, but Margaret, and possibly the other maidservants, were on the top floor of the house in the garrets. They were almost certainly reasonably comfortable as

Walpole paid for at least one of the servants' rooms to be wallpapered, which was quite an extravagance. Eventually, between 1790 and 1792, a service wing, the New Offices, was added to the house. It was built to accommodate the Strawberry Hill Press (although added too late to be used for the press) as well as to provide bedrooms for the servants. It stood south of the Round Tower leaving a gap before the house was reached. The New Offices were given gothic window detailing and a crenellated parapet but were constructed on a simple block plan without any of the irregularities of the main house.

The servants' lives must have been hard. Work fell into three categories: keeping Strawberry Hill

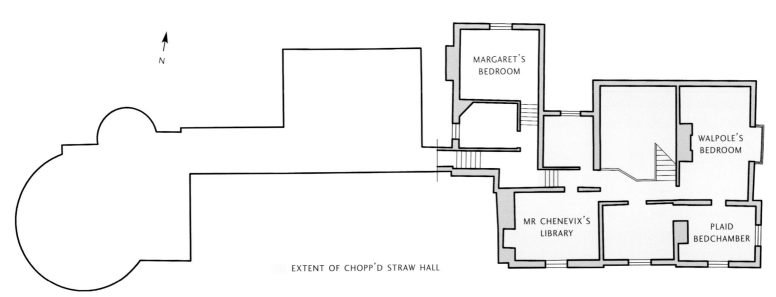

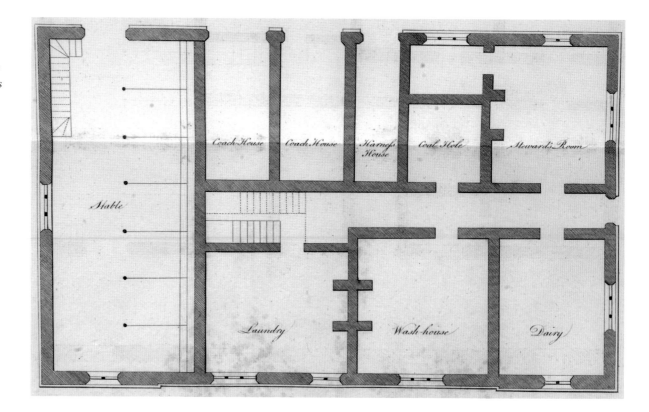

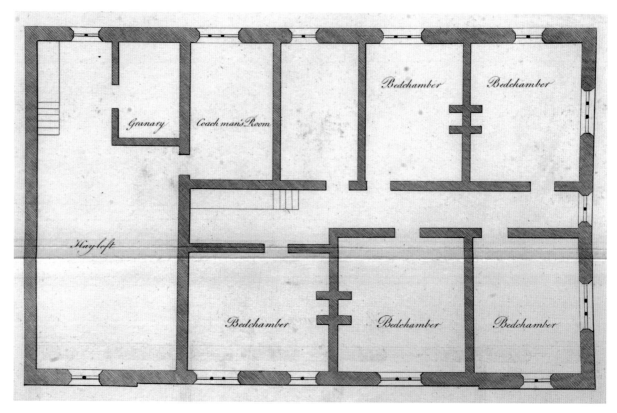

clean and fresh, the preparation and serving of food and the duties which related directly to Walpole's personal comfort and wellbeing. In addition to indoor servants, there were a large number of outdoor and garden staff, a coachman and other stable and farm workers, printing staff employed for the Strawberry Hill Press and temporary workers hired by the day when needed. Although Walpole habitually rose late he also retired late, frequently working in his Library until two in the morning.

His housekeeper, as part of her duties, had to lock both the outside doors of the house, and also interior doors, before she was able to seek her own bed in the Housekeeper's room on the second floor above the Holbein Chamber. The only room which was regularly left unlocked at night was the Library, presumably because Walpole worked there until the small hours.

In the eighteenth century no great emphasis was placed on hygiene, but keeping the house clean must have been extremely difficult given the number and fragility of the objects displayed in the rooms, the lack of light to work by, and the almost constant building work. There were also several cats and dogs in the house at any one time and they must have shed hair on carpets, rugs and fabrics. Fortunately most of the floors were of unpolished wood. A manual for training servants published in 1760 instructed them in the various methods of cleaning:

> Take some sand, pretty damp, but not too wet, and strew all over the Room, throwing it out of your hand hard, and it will fly about the Floor and lick up all the Dust and Flew. ...Take Tanzy, Mint, and Balm; first sweep the Room, then strew the Herbs on the Floor, and with a long hard Brush rub them well all over the Boards, till you have scrubb'd the Floor clean. When the Boards are quite dry, sweep off the greens, and with a dry Rubbing brush dry-rub them well, and they will look like mahogany, of a fine brown, and never want any other washing, and give a sweet smell to the Room. ...Sope is not proper for boards and sand and water shews the grain, which is the beauty of a Board.

The housemaid is also directed to:

> be sure always to have very clean feet, that you may not dirty your Rooms as soon as clean'd, nor make any Noise, but learn to walk softly, and not disturb the Family.[1]

The use of bellows was recommended for dusting small objects and paintings, but the hundreds of pieces of porcelain and pottery would all have needed regular washing and drying. In those rooms where fires were lit, hearths would have had to be cleared of ashes, relaid, the metalwork polished, the dust generated by the fires removed and the fires then relit before Walpole or his guests rose and before the sun showed up any remaining dust. The chimneys had to be swept regularly. Walpole noted in a letter:

...My present suit to you is only for a recommendatory le[tter for] a young man who is going to be entered of Trinity College, Cambridge. ...The father is one of the best and most respectable men upon earth. ...He has been long labouring to alleviate the horrid sufferings and consequential miseries of those poor victims, chimney-sweepers, and was the author of the mitigation obtained for them from Parliament last year – a plan he is still pursuing farther. He has a good fortune, and very good sense, and is one of the humblest of men.... He is a master chimney-sweeper himself; every Sunday he has his apprentices washed and cleaned, carries them to church, and then gives them a good dinner of beef and pudding.... Mr Porter, which is his name, is very apprehensive that his profession may set his son in a mortifying light, and therefore only wishes to have him well recommended to some leading man in the College who may be his protector. The lad is seventeen, and has got some Latin, designing to be of one of the three literary professions. I assure you, dear Sir, you cannot give too high a character of the father.[2]

ABOVE *Seventeenth-century glass from the Little Parlour depicting a hunting scene with dogs*

[1] Glasse, Hannah, *Servants' Directory*, 1760

[2] Letter Horace Walpole to Michael Lort written from Strawberry Hill, 5 July 1789

When the chimneys were not in use a chimney board could be put in place to exclude draughts and soot and at the same time be visually pleasing. Walpole explained to John Chute how he had put Mr Müntz to work in designing and painting such boards in 1757:

> …[Mr Müntz] has absolutely done nothing this whole summer but paste two chimney-boards. In short, instead of Claud Lorrain, he is only one of Bromwich's men.

There was always a risk of fire and many instances are recorded when Strawberry Hill was saved from fire by the valet, the dog, or by Margaret – the latter once rescued the house during the final stage of the building of the Long Gallery:

> …all my glories were on the point of vanishing last night in a flame! The chimney of the new Gallery, which chimney is full of deal-boards, and which Gallery is full of shavings, was on fire at eight o'clock. Harry had quarrelled with the other servants, and would not sit in the kitchen; and to keep up his anger had lighted a vast fire in the servants' hall, which is under the gallery. The chimney took fire; and if Margaret had not smelt it with the first nose that ever a servant had, a quarter of an hour had set us in a blaze. I hope you are frightened out of your senses for me.[3]

Candles in candlesticks were the only means of lighting the house but were another fire hazard. It can be assumed that a mixture of tallow and the more expensive wax candles would have been used; tallow for below stairs, wax for above stairs. All the burnt fragments of snuffed candles would have had to be removed each day to prevent smoking, then the residue of wax or tallow would have had to be scraped from the holder and kept for reboiling and reforming into fresh candles for further use, although it is possible that the servants might have been allowed to keep the stumps and resell them. No one over indulged in the use of candles in the eighteenth century; members of a household frequently shared a candle in the evening for reading or working and Mrs Delaney noted that even Lady Leicester at Holkham used only one candle by which to embroider each night.

The *Servants' Directory* of 1760 gives lengthy instruction on how servants should preserve fabric and other fragile objects by excluding light, which might cause the colour to fade. Light is unlikely to have been a major problem for Walpole's staff. However rooms which had already been decorated were redecorated after the Flemish glass was installed in the 1750s, which might point to early fading of fabric in the period before the light was filtered by the coloured glass.

The furniture would all have been kept under covers when Walpole was not living in the house and the covers might even have been left in place except when he was entertaining. Even the carpets and rugs would have had baize covers laid over them when not in use. The furniture would have required constant polishing with wax polish, which had first to be made by the staff. Silver had to be regularly cleaned and the objects in the Collection all maintained according to their special needs. The books too must have required attention to keep them free from dust and mould. The whole house, those who lived in it (including the household pets), the furniture, bedding, textiles and other objects all had to be kept free of infestations.

One of the ever present duties for the housekeeper and her staff was the opening and closing of the shutters. Some of the early rooms had shutters already fitted when Walpole arrived in 1747 and shutters became part of the specification for every room in the new building. Their main purpose was security, both of the Collection and of the house itself, which stood empty part of the year. The house was very close to the river and open countryside and must have presented a temptation to thieves. Lady Mary Coke's Journal for September 1785 records the hazards:

> …There is now a new species of housebreakers that go about in a coach with four horses and a pretended servant behind. Such an equipage has attempted to force their way in to Strawberry Hill not many evenings ago, but Mrs Clive as I was told had seen the equipage and from some reason suspecting the intention sent information to Mr Walpole's servants who secured the doors before the coach stopped; those on the inside [sic] tried every means to prevail with the servants to open the door but finding they could not prevail, they drove off.

In most eighteenth-century houses shutters were built to fold back on themselves and were stowed away either in the side reveals of the windows or against adjacent walls, but the shutters at Strawberry Hill were designed to run on tracks contained

[3] Letter Horace Walpole to Henry Seymour Conway, 9 September 1762

[4] Rogers, Kevin, unpublished research on the windows of Strawberry Hill

[5] West, Ian, unpublished research on the shutters of Strawberry Hill

within a void in the walls on either side; this meant that when they were open they were also invisible and did not occupy valuable wall space where paintings might be hung. The most interesting and technically advanced example was in the bay of the Round Drawing Room, where curved shutters ran along a curved track on the floor; when closed they completed the circular shape of the room.

Most of the shutters to the ground floor windows were fitted with locks and steel plates to protect them from housebreakers, and were rebated. In addition all the shutters were fitted with ring pulls to allow easy closing. In this, and in all aspects of their design, they reflected the latest technology, with every room except the Blue Breakfast Room having its own specifically designed shutters. The servants must have spent a great deal of time opening, closing and locking shutters.

Many of the windows, too, slid horizontally; an arrangement not uncommon in the eighteenth century in small dwellings where there were low ceilings and little space. This style of window was certainly included in Walpole's renovation of south-facing rooms in the earlier Chopp'd Straw Hall part of the house, probably because of the small scale of the building and to save space. Walpole then went on to use larger horizontal sliding windows in the new building of the Library. However, all of these sliding windows have a typically Walpolian twist;

instead of one window sliding across another, these windows, like the shutters at Strawberry Hill, slide into a void in the wall.[4] When open the windows were invisible and the views of the garden and river were uninterrupted.

The ogee heads to most of the windows, because of their shape, could have caused a problem, but where it was necessary aesthetically, the shutters were designed to reflect the window-head shape. In the bedrooms, where air and light were needed, some of the shutters stopped short of the head by a few inches to allow ventilation.

The Long Gallery, exquisite in almost every other way, had shutters which appear never to have been decorated on the inside face, which enforces the presumption they were only closed when the house was unoccupied.[5] Although the windows in the Great North Bedchamber were fitted with shutters, they also had ruched blinds hung above the windows, which was the only example of a fabric window treatment in the house. Fabric was expensive and cost might have been one reason for installing shutters rather than blinds in the upper rooms, but a second reason was that its use in the bedrooms might have obscured Walpole's painted glass during the day, which he would not have wanted. Understanding these facts highlights the importance attached to the use of fabric in the final great room of the house. The building of the Great

ABOVE *Seventeenth-century glass roundel from the Blue Bedchamber of a turkey and hen*

[6] Letter Horace Walpole to Mary Berry, 15 September 1795

[7] Letter Horace Walpole to Henry Seymour Conway, 28 July 1783

[8] Letter Horace Walpole to George Montagu, 18 June 1764

[9] Letter Horace Walpole to Mary Berry, 8 September 1795

[10] Will of Horace Walpole, The National Archives, Kew

North Bedchamber directly above the Servants' Hall is also important and meant that this room with its treasures was a doubly protected space.

Margaret's work about the house seemed never to be done. In addition to being Walpole's housekeeper she had to conduct the ticket holders over the house. This must have taken up an ever increasing amount of time, as Walpole relates in several of his letters. Her stories around the objects grew with time and confidence and she grew richer from receiving tips from the visitors.

> …both companies arrived within three minutes of each other and I was forced to admit both, only substituting Kirgate to conduct one set, and charging Nanny to be as tedious as she could with the other, that they might not jostle in the gallery –"Yes, yes, my Lord, I'll palaver 'em enough in the blue room"– and with such a plenary indulgence to that perpetual motion her tongue, I do not doubt but she told them ten times instead of three, "that that on the staircase, gentlemen, is the armour of Francis the First."[6]

Margaret had also to oversee the making and provision of medicinal remedies and to cope with other housekeeping emergencies.

> As I was rising this morning, I received an express from your daughter that she will bring Madame de Cambis and Lady Melbourne to dinner here tomorrow. I shall be vastly pleased with the party – but it puts Philip and Margaret to their wit's end to get them a dinner – nothing is to be had here; we must send to Richmond and Kingston and Brentford; I must borrow Mr Ellis's cook, and somebody's confectioner and beg somebody's fruit, for I have none of these of my own nor know anything of the matter – but that is Philip and Margaret's affair and not mine, and the worse the dinner is, the more Gothic Madame de Cambis will think it.[7]

At the beginning of June 1776 Walpole grumbled about some of his staff problems to Lady Ossory:

> …but it is a very serious thing to have taken an old cook as yellow as a dishclout, and have her seduced by a jolly dog of a coachman, and have her miscarry of a child and go on with a dropsy, so that she can neither employ him nor I her, nor which is worse, get rid of her. All my servants think that the moment they are useless, I must not part with them, and so I have an infirmary instead of a ménage; and those that are good for anything, do nothing but get children, so that my house is a mixture of a county and foundling hospitals…

Strawberry Hill would not have been an easy house to look after; the kitchen and store rooms were on the ground floor; there was even a time during the rebuilding when it appears there was no permanent kitchen. Day staff would have been engaged to prepare the ingredients for intricate dishes to aid the cook, but serving food must have presented huge difficulties because there was no link on the ground floor between the kitchen in the base of the Round Tower and the Refectory and Little Parlour which were both at the other end of the house and in which meals would have been served. Furniture would have had to be repositioned for dining, and food taken round the outside of the house before it could be set on the table. It must often have arrived cold. This was not an uncommon arrangement in the eighteenth century and possibly made a lot of sense given the timber and paper construction of the house and the ensuing fire risk; however it created work for the servants.

Walpole ate sparingly, dining at the old fashioned hour of four, rather than the more fashionable four-thirty or five. He preferred light dishes of chicken or pheasant to other meats, pastry in any form he found indigestible and disliked. He had a reputation for being an amusing and witty host and for providing a good table. The majority of eighteenth-century dishes were labour intensive. Syllabub we know was served to guests and was relatively easy to prepare; it was 'milked under the cows that were brought to the brow of the terrace.'[8] *The Art of Cookery Made Plain and Easy* by Hannah Glasse, first published in 1747, gives the following recipe for authentic eighteenth-century delectation:

> To make a fine Syllabub from the cow make your Syllabub of either cider or wine, sweeten it pretty sweet and grate nutmeg in, then milk the milk into the liquor; when this is done, pour over the Top half a Pint or Pint of cream, according to the Quantity of Syllabub you make. You may make this Syllabub at home, only have new Milk; make it as hot as Milk from the Cow and out of a tea Pot or any such Thing, pour it in, holding your Hand very High.

Brewing and baking would also have been part of the regular duties of the kitchen staff. Walpole rarely drank wine and an ice pail was kept beneath the table for his iced water when he dined. He completed a meal with coffee and by taking a pinch of snuff. Most of the produce would have been provided by the home farm or would have come from the kitchen garden, but keeping it fresh would have been a constant problem. Ice houses were essential and two were built at Strawberry Hill. The second and larger of them was described, with a dreadful pun, to Mary Berry, who was then living at Little Strawberry Hill: '...I have given orders for a new gigantic ice-house, that you may not want a profusion, if there should ever be such a "feel-omenon" as a hot summer.'[9] Ice was needed in large quantities both for savoury food and for the preparation of dishes for the dessert table; it was also essential for the preservation of food.

Walpole's personal needs were looked after by his valet, Philip Colomb, who became his most trusted servant. Philip was a Swiss, who could be sulky if crossed, but was invaluable to Walpole who showed his appreciation by leaving him a legacy of £1,500 (a sum approximately the same as he had paid for Chopp'd Straw Hall), an annuity of £25 and Walnut

Tree House in Twickenham. Most of the other members of the Colomb family also joined his service. Elizabeth Colomb became Strawberry Hill cook, James Colomb, a footman, and Maria, Philip's eldest daughter, was left an annuity of £6 to be paid whether she chose to remain in the service of the Walpole family or not.

A second footman, John Fitzwater, was also left a total of £60.[10] As part of his regular duties a footman would be sent to deliver by hand the many

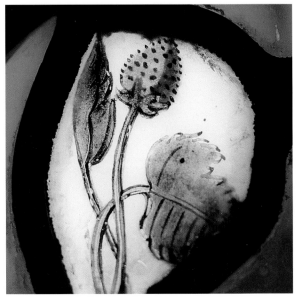

ABOVE *Seventeenth-century glass roundel of pears from a room on the second floor*

RIGHT *Seventeenth-century glass from the Armoury painted in enamel depicting a carnation*

BELOW *Fragment of seventeenth-century glass from the Armoury painted in enamel depicting a strawberry*

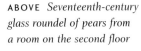

notes flowing between Walpole and his friends and neighbours, although letters were supposed to be collected by the postboy. There was no posthouse close by, which caused a problem:

I beg your Ladyship to forgive my asking you what will sound like an impertinent question: it is whether you received an answer from me, dated the 16th, to one I had the honour of receiving from you a day or two before. My reason for asking it is, that a letter I wrote on business by the same post did actually miscarry, and has given me some trouble. We have no posthouse at Twickenham, but a boy from Isleworth fetches them, and I suppose sometimes twists them to the tail of a paper-kite. If he made that use of my last to your Ladyship, perhaps you will have thought that as you gave me holidays, and told me I need not write soon, I have been flying a kite too – but my second childhood does not enable me to gambol; and if it did, you are one of the last persons from whom I would play truant.

I have been sending some layers of clove-carnations to Lady Ravensworth, for which Lady Euston wrote to me. I had not so many as I wished, the severe weather of last year having killed most of mine, and my gardener is so bad, that he does not restock me soon. I offered him an annuity some years ago, if he would leave me; but he desired to be excused, as it was not so good as his place, and he knew nobody else would take him – so I have been forced to keep him, because nobody else will.

As this is only a codicil to the letter I doubt you never received, Madam, it shall not be longer.[11]

The gardener, John Cowie, reigned outside the house battling against Walpole's love of fruit and flowers and his expectation that they could be grown in his garden and for the table. Walpole had tried to pension him off ten years before, but lost the battle:

I am sensibly obliged, my dear Lord, by your great goodness, and am most disposed to take the gardener you recommend, if I can. You are so good-natured, that you will not blame my suspense. I have a gardener that has lived with me above five and twenty years; he is incredibly ignorant and a mule. When I wrote to your Lordship, my patience was worn out, and I resolved at least to have a gardener for flowers. On your not being able to give me one, I half consented to keep my own; not on his amend-ment, but because he will not leave me. presuming on my long suffering. I have offered him fifteen pounds a year to leave me; and when he pleads that he is old and that nobody else will take him, I plead that I am old too, and that it is hard I am not to have a few flowers or a little fruit as long as I live. I shall now try if I can make any compromise with him, for I own I cannot bear to turn him adrift, nor will starve an old servant, though never a good one, to please my nose and mouth. Besides, he is a Scot, and I will not be unjust even to that tedious nation: and the more I dislike him, the less will I allow my partiality to persuade me I am in the right… . I will take the liberty of letting you know, if I can persuade the serpent that has reduced my little Eden to be as nasty and barren as the Highlands, to take a pension or a yellow ribband…[12]

Walpole's letters give the impression of a busy household with each one of the staff occupied with several things at once. He was organised, constantly correcting, updating, amending and improving his house, for much of the time with Kirgate, his printer from the Strawberry Hill Press, acting as recorder or secretary. One of Kirgate's duties was to transcribe Walpole's letters, many of which recorded the oddities of the time, the conduct of servants in other households, or the eccentricities of Walpole's Twickenham neighbours.

As Walpole aged his attacks of gout, or what he believed to be gout, became more painful and more frequent, necessitating bed or chair rest. During these periods he moved from his bedroom on the second floor into the suite of rooms on the first floor, but if he wanted to come downstairs or visit his garden he had to be carried by the footmen. He explained some of this in a letter written to Hannah More

…I must …give you a brief account [of] myself – a very poor one indeed I must give – condemned as a cripple to my couch for the rest of my days I doubt I am – though perfectly healed and even without a scar, my leg is so weak[en]ed, that I have [not] recovered the least use of it, nor can move across my chamber unless lifted and held up by two servants – this constitutes me totally a prisoner – but why should not I be so? what business had I to live to the brink of 79? and why should one litter the world at that age? Then I thank God I have vast blessings – I have preserved my eyes, ears and teeth, I have no pain left, and I would bet with any dormouse that day or night it cannot outsleep me; and when one can afford to pay for every relief or comfort or assistance that can be procured at fourscore, dare one complain?…[13]

In his last years his servants' tolerance must have been tested. Increasing frailty did not diminish Walpole's expectation of how the household should be run or how the garden should be planted. Servants and master retained a mutual respect and care for each other and for Strawberry Hill, which undoubt-edly helped to ensure its future.

BELOW *A servant at the entrance to Strawberry Hill. Detail from the watercolour on page 129*

[11] Letter Horace Walpole to Lady Ossory, written from Strawberry Hill, 28 June 1787

[12] Letter Horace Walpole to Harcourt, 18 October 1777

[13] Letter Horace Walpole to Hannah More, 29 August 1796.

14 Strawberry Hill after Walpole

'The air of an ancient abbey'

HORACE WALPOLE died in 1797 and it might well have been expected that the house would fall asleep when the last of Margaret's visitors left. But that is not what happened. A Guidebook of 1800 recounts the next stage of the house's history:

> STRAWBERRY HILL, near Twickenham, the villa of the late Earl of Orford (better known in the literary world, and often quoted in this work, as Mr. Horace Walpole) is situated on an eminence near the Thames. …In 1747, it was purchased by Mr. Walpole, by whom this beautiful structure, formed from select parts of Gothic architecture in cathedrals, &c. was wholly built, at different times. Great taste is displayed in the elegant embellishments of the ediface, and in the choice collection of pictures, sculptures, antiquities, and curiosities that adorn it; many of which have been purchased from some of the first cabinets in Europe. The approach to the house, through a grove of lofty trees; the embattled wall, overgrown with ivy; the spiry pinnacles, and gloomy cast of the buildings; give it the air of an ancient abbey, and fill the beholder with awe, especially on entering the gate, where a small oratory, inclosed with iron rails, and a cloister behind it, appear in the fore court.
>
> On entering the house, we are led through a hall and passage, with painted glass windows, into the Great Parlour, in which are the portraits of Sir Robert Walpole, his two wives and children, and other family pictures; one of which, by Reynolds, contains the portraits of the three Ladies Waldegrave, daughters of the Duchess of Gloucester. …The window has many pieces of stained glass, as have all the windows in every room. These add a richness to the rooms, which, particularly on a bright day, have a very good effect. The Gothic screens, niches, or chimney pieces, with which each room is likewise adorned, were designed, for the most part, by Mr. Walpole himself, or Mr. Bentley, and adapted with great taste to their respective situations.
>
> To enter into a minute description of the valuable collection in this villa, would exceed our limits…[1]

The house had been left, together with an annuity of £2,000 for its upkeep, to Anne Seymour Damer, daughter of Walpole's favourite cousin. Anne had grown up in and around Strawberry Hill and often stayed there with Walpole when she was young. She had an independent spirit and made her name as a sculptress. Her work was much admired by Walpole – he had her terracotta sculpture of a fishing eagle in his Library and a pair of dogs modelled by her in the Little Parlour. She moved into Strawberry Hill with her mother, Lady Ailesbury, a notable embroideress who completed various textiles for Walpole.

[1] Scatcherd, J., ed., *Ambulator or a Pocket Companion in a Tour Round London within the Circuit of twenty-five Miles,* London, 1800

RIGHT *Two layers of wallpaper with a border, found hanging in a nineteenth-century closet built in the area of Walpole's Great Cloister. The bird design on one paper can be dated to the 1850s. The birds are lifesize*

Anne Damer continued the public tours started by Walpole and even included an additional room, another Library in the upper storey of the Round Tower where Walpole had kept his folios of engravings. Very little is known about the changes she made to the house; there is a possibility that the Great Cloister was filled in around the turn of the century to provide a studio or additional living space during her stewardship. She revived the Strawberry Hill Press for special publications and there are several accounts of theatrical productions in 'The Theatre at Strawberry Hill'.[2] It is not known where in the house the theatre was set up although the Cloister or the Gallery might have been pressed into service. Towards the end of the nineteenth century a deal platform and trestles for a stage, complete with proscenium, wings and a number of 'scenes' on rollers came under the auctioneer's hammer. Together they formed a complete portable theatre.[3] No record has yet been found of when they were first purchased.

Little of Anne Damer's decoration can be positively identified. A formal terracotta coloured geometric paper, recently discovered in the Cloister, is likely to be hers, but the dating is uncertain. In 1810, after her mother's death, she decided against remaining at Strawberry Hill and passed the house to the Waldegrave family who were related to Walpole through one of 'The Three Ladies Waldegrave'.

By the time the 6th Earl Waldegrave inherited Strawberry Hill the whole estate was suffering a period of neglect and decline before it awoke with the marriage of his sons to Frances Braham. The house then entered its second important stage.

Frances Braham was the stunningly beautiful daughter of a well known society singer, John Braham. She accompanied her father to Strawberry Hill when he was giving a performance, and while wandering through the house was glimpsed by the two sons of the 6th Earl from one of the windows of the Long Gallery. Both boys fell instantly in love with her and she eventually married them both; first John, who was the illegitimate son and died shortly after the marriage, and then his brother George, the legitimate heir who became the seventh Earl Waldegrave. George had pressing financial difficulties and was a heavy drinker. He once assaulted a policeman so seriously that he was arrested and sentenced to six months imprisonment. In anger at the sentence and in an attempt to meet his debts George decided to sell the entire contents of Strawberry Hill.

So vast was Walpole's Collection that the Great Sale in 1842 took thirty-two days and raised £33,000. The Collection was dispersed to the four winds. At George's death the house was left to Frances, who went on to marry twice more; first in 1847 to

[2] Playbill for *The Fashionable Friends* performed in the Theatre, Strawberry Hill, November 1801

[3] 1883 Sale Catalogue of the Contents of Strawberry Hill

George Granville Vernon Harcourt, a Liberal MP and director of the railway, and then in 1863 to Chichester Fortescue, an Irish Whig. Both husbands were wealthy politicians and, married to them, Frances carried out extensive alterations and used the house as a centre for political entertaining; Walpole's Refectory became known as the Cabinet Room. She updated the interiors, added a new extension, grandified the exterior and modernised the approach to the house and the garden. A new wing was built between 1854 and 1856 on a grand Victorian-gothic scale. Like Walpole her intention was to create space for entertainment; a ballroom, a grand dining room, a drawing room and a billiards room were added with their necessary service areas, while in the Georgian wing Walpole's New Offices were converted into bedrooms for her guests. The new wing with its clock tower was erected in the space between the Round Tower and the New Offices, providing a link between the two Georgian buildings for the first time. The effect of this grand Victorian-gothic structure was to completely dwarf Walpole's little gothic castle. The famous profile disappeared and to remedy this Frances added a storey to both the Round and Beauclerc Towers restoring the fairytale skyline. This helped to reinstate the irregularity of the roofscape and gave a cleaner definition to the eighteenth-century house, distinguishing it from the very different Victorian gothic. Disliking Walpole's roughcast finish which

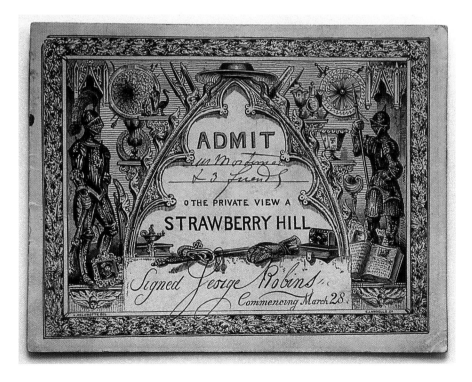

ABOVE *Gallery of Strawberry Hill, 1863 photograph by P.H.Delamotte. Reynolds' painting of The Three Ladies Waldegrave hangs at the far end*

covered the Georgian house Frances added a fashionable Roman-cement treatment to the walls and chimney pots in the style of Hampton Court. Inside, she installed better heating and by pumping gas to the house was able to use gasoliers to light important rooms. She gave lighting and decoration a contemporary twist.

The main entrance from the road was extended by glazing-in both Walpole's Little Cloister and part of the courtyard to provide a grander foyer for the reception of Victorian guests, with Minton tiles designed by Pugin. On the ground floor of the house, service and living rooms were linked by a doorway joining the Hall with the servants' corridor, thus providing internal access between the kitchen and the Refectory. For the first time in the history of Strawberry Hill hot food could be served to guests. The Great Cloister was filled in at this stage – if not earlier – and was used for bedrooms and dressing rooms. Generally more bedrooms were provided for guests and live-in servants; Frances maintained a large staff.

Throughout the house rooms were newly decorated and brought up to date. The Long Gallery floor was re-laid with a splendid wooden floor from Europe which Lady Waldegrave had seen on one of her honeymoons. In the corners she inserted brass inlays of Walpole's Saracen's head with the date 1747 (the date he had first moved into Strawberry Hill) and her own crest with the date 1856. The Blue Breakfast Room was transformed into a 'Turkish Boudoir' complete with a tented ceiling and a border of an embroidered seventeenth-century Turkish tulip design*, and there is evidence to show that she paid homage to Walpole by retaining the exact shade of blue which he had used for the room. The Boudoir was adapted to form part of a suite of private rooms for her[4] with Walpole's Blue Bedchamber above wallpapered to create a rose bower in which she slept. The state bedroom became another drawing room and was decorated with a grand French wallpaper, and all the other rooms were prettified, modernised, rehung with paintings and filled with porcelain and small objects. For the first time curtains went up in each room and rugs and carpets covered the floors. It had become a house of Victorian splendour. In the garden, she installed a fountain, a maze and did much replanting.

A further testament to Walpole was evident with the number of rooms that retained their names throughout the nineteenth century: The Holbein Chamber, The Star Chamber, The Tribune (which became a bedroom in the nineteenth century) and The (Great) North (Bed) Chamber. There is also evidence that Frances sought to retain the mood and overall colour schemes of the original eighteenth-century style and decoration of some of the rooms.

BELOW *Victorian interior of a drawing room, nineteenth-century photograph. This room linked Horace Walpole's eighteenth-century house to the newly added nineteenth-century wing (note the curtain veiling the empty fireplace)*

*See page *149*

[4] Rogers, Kevin, unpublished research

ABOVE *Victorian chimney pots copied from those at Hampton Court for Lady Waldegrave*

ABOVE RIGHT *Victorian tile by Minton designed by A.W.Pugin for Lady Waldegrave's Hall*

After her death in 1879 much of the contents of the house was put up for sale.[5] In the 'North Chamber', which must have been Walpole's Great North Bedchamber, Aubusson tapestry window curtains were auctioned and a circular-bordered rosebud patterned Aubusson carpet was included in the contents from the Round Drawing Room: this would have replaced the carpet Walpole had had woven to match his table top. Frances had picked up the theme and was able to improve on Walpole's square carpet because Victorian technology made it possible to make it circular.

After Frances's death her fourth husband, Chichester Fortescue, did not want to live at Strawberry Hill without her and the estate was broken up. In July 1883 the house was sold to Baron de

Stern, a member of a banking family. His son, Lord Michelham, inherited the property four years later and Strawberry Hill remained in their family until sold by Lord Michelham's widow in 1923. Although they lived in the house for nearly fifty years very little is known about their taste in decoration; the Ballroom was rehung with a superb shot brown silk of an oriental bird design[6] and Walpole's woodwork was varnished over to resemble mahogany.[7]

In 1923 the house was bought by The Catholic Education Council, for use by St Mary's Catholic Teacher Training College, which later became St Mary's College; they assumed the stewardship of the house. Part of the estate was sold and the land developed for housing which masked the river view for the first time. Alterations to the landscaping also removed Walpole's Serpentine Walk and Lady Waldegrave's maze as well as many of the Georgian and Victorian gothic vistas. The cottage was sold separately and the Chapel in the Woods was swallowed up by twentieth-century buildings. Although the College has maintained and protected the house generally, day to day use has taken its toll on the delicate and fragile interiors. It is an interesting fact that the fragile eighteenth-century interiors, with only a couple of exceptions, have survived better than those of the nineteenth or twentieth centuries. This is partly due to the care of those who owned the house in the generations after Walpole and partly to the superiority of the techniques used in the eighteenth-century decoration.

Walpole was not the first to use the gothic-revival style as decoration, but he was the most consistent, remaining true to the style for almost fifty years. Because the house was open to the public, and Walpole was such a good publicist, its fame spread and today the term 'Strawberry Hill Gothic' has become synonymous with a purely decorative gothic style. One hundred years later, when Frances, Lady Waldegrave, added to the house in her Victorian high-gothic style, although grander, it was still decorative rather than 'structurally' gothic. The nineteenth-century gothic revival, whether found in parliament buildings, railway stations, town halls or corporate headquarters, can all be traced back to Strawberry Hill. At the time of Frances's death it was enjoying a second heyday.

But another hundred years on, as the house became more dilapidated, it became increasingly obvious that a long term solution had to be found which would keep the house open to the public, enable it to be restored and provide a means of funding its future needs; it was too expensive to be maintained as a residence. The Strawberry Hill Trust was therefore set up as a charity in the first years

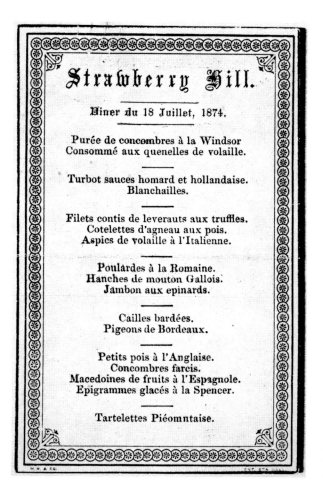

Strawberry Hill.

Diner du 18 Juillet, 1874.

Purée de concombres à la Windsor
Consommé aux quenelles de volaille.

Turbot sauces homard et hollandaise.
Blanchailles.

Filets contis de leverauts aux truffles.
Cotelettes d'agneau aux pois.
Aspics de volaille à l'Italienne.

Poulardes à la Romaine.
Hanches de mouton Gallois.
Jambon aux epinards.

Cailles bardées.
Pigeons de Bordeaux.

Petits pois à l'Anglaise.
Concombres farcis.
Macedoines de fruits à l'Espagnole.
Epigrammes glacés à la Spencer.

Tartelettes Piéomntaise.

of the new millennium to ensure a future for the house. Large sums are required to prevent further decay, conserve what remains and restore what has been lost. The World Monuments Fund in Britain placed Strawberry Hill on its Watch List as one of the one hundred most endangered buildings in the world and supported the Trust.

In 2005 Strawberry Hill was given a Heritage Lottery Fund grant which enabled the most urgent work to start. Although Strawberry Hill has always been much researched, more detailed work was carried out between 2000 and 2006 to discover and

[5] 1883 Sale Catalogue of the Contents of Strawberry Hill

[6] Rose, Peter, presentation of piece of original silk to Friends of Strawberry Hill

[7] Oestreicher, Lisa, 'The Staircase, Armoury and Hall Strawberry Hill, An investigation of their painted surfaces', unpublished thesis, RCA/V&A Conservation MA Course (Architectural Paint Studies) September 1996

lay bare the secrets of the house, many of which lie hidden within the decoration. Walpole's meticulous recording of the building and development of the house through his letters, various editions of the *Description*, commissions to artists and the Strawberry Hill account books, make it one of the best documented houses in the world. Even objects dispersed through the salerooms can often be traced through the amount of detail known about them and their lasting fame. This documentation and attention to detail ensure that accurate restoration will be carried out with sensitivity.

The restored house will be seen as an eighteenth-century gothic villa framed by eighteenth-century gardens. The garden to the south of the house will be returned, as far as possible, to its eighteenth-

LEFT *South Front of Strawberry Hill in 2007*

BELOW *Blue plaque to Horace Walpole at the entrance to Strawberry Hill*

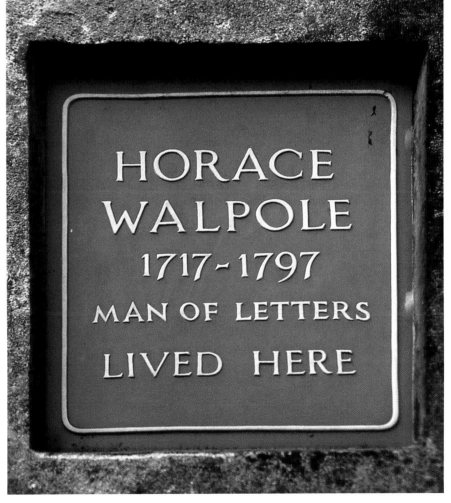

HORACE WALPOLE 1717~1797 MAN OF LETTERS LIVED HERE

Strawberry Hill is set to take its place in the world as the seminal eighteenth-century gothic revival building from which all subsequent gothic buildings can be traced. It was built over a period of fifty years as the realisation of one man's vision. That vision he described in 1784 in a letter accompanying a set of engravings. Through this letter let Horace Walpole have the last word:

...I doubt, [they] will convey no very adequate idea of it. In the first place they are but moderately executed: I could not afford to pay our principal engravers, whose prices are equal to, nay, far above those of former capital painters. In the next, as there is a solemnity in the house, of which the cuts will give you an idea, they cannot add the gay variety of the scene without, which is very different from every side, and almost from every chamber, and makes a most agreeable contrast; the house being placed almost in an elbow of the Thames which surrounds half, and consequently beautifies three of the aspects. Then my little hill, and diminutive enough it is, gazes up to royal Richmond; and Twickenham on the left, and Kingstonwick on the right, are seen across bends of the river, which on each hand appears like a Lilliputian seaport. Swans, cows, sheep, coaches, post-chaises, carts, horsemen and foot-passengers are continually in view. The fourth scene is a large common-field, a constant prospect of harvest and its stages, traversed under my windows by the great road to Hampton Court – in short, an animated view of the country. These moving pictures compensate the conventual gloom of the inside, which however, when the sun shines, is georgous, as he appears all crimson and gold and azure through the painted glass – now to be quite fair, you must turn the perspective, and look at this vision through the diminishing end of the telescope; for nothing is so small as the whole; ...I grieve that you would never come and cast an eye on it! – but are even our visions pure from annoy? Does not some drawback always hang over them? – and being visions, how rapidly must not they fleet away? Yes, yes, our smiles and our tears are almost as transient as the luster of the morning and the shadows of the evening; and almost as frequently interchanged. Our passions form airy balloons; we know not how to direct them; and the very inflammable matter that transports them, often makes the bubble burst. Adieu![8]

ABOVE *Horace Walpole, Earl of Orford, engraving by Meyer from a drawing by Lawrence. After Walpole's death this portrait was sent to his friends by Mary Berry to accompany her edited edition of his complete works*

OPPOSITE *Long Gallery of Strawberry Hill in the twenty-first century before restoration*

[8] Letter Horace Walpole to Horace Mann, 30 September 1784

century appearance, although the river view has been lost for ever. The planting will include a resited Serpentine Walk, a grove and rows of Walpole's beloved orange trees in tubs.

Within the house those rooms shown by Walpole to his ticketed visitors will be open together with some of his private rooms. Each room will be shown with the decoration reflecting as accurately as possible what was known to have been there in Walpole's time. There will be a small museum and an education block will be situated around the base of the Round Tower in the old kitchen area. There will also be a shop and tea room, without which a visit to Strawberry Hill would be incomplete.

15 Lost and found

'the little villa is grown into a superb castle'

OPPOSITE *The Little Cloister at the entrance to Strawberry Hill (see page 129 for reverse view)*

THE EXPECTATION of those visiting Strawberry Hill after the restoration is very different from that of those who visited during the period following its acquisition by the Strawberry Hill Trust and before work began. Today's visitors want to know how and why changes have been made and what has been learnt by the investigative team set up by the Trust.

> ...it is odd to say, that though my house is all the morning full of company, nobody lives so much alone. I have already this season had between seventy and fourscore companies to see my house; and half my time passes in writing tickets or excuses...[1]

The contents of Walpole's letters, *Description* and house sale catalogues had all to be weighed against evidence from new findings, the fragments and paint scrapings. There was so much documentation of how the house had been built that confirmation from the findings, rather than a reassessment, was expected. However, as elements were uncovered, questions arose which needed answers; these in turn had to be slotted into the composite restoration plan. The discoveries produced unexpected sides to Walpole's character and to Strawberry Hill. An intricate eighteenth-century plan was detected; it had been carefully thought out, detailed and efficiently executed incorporating advances in

contemporary technology. Only rarely, however, had major changes been made to the living space once the house had been completed. The best available workmen were employed by Walpole producing quality work of the highest order; nothing was done on the cheap. This philosophy was continued by the Strawberry Hill Trust.

Those who lived in Strawberry Hill after Walpole decorated on top of his fabric without destroying it, leaving hidden layers. Sections of chimneypieces had been moved and reused elsewhere and their original positions had to be traced. Paint schemes and timber floors were revealed as well as the detritus of 200 years. As the work progressed it was photographed, filmed and documented, forming an archive of the past and a reference for future historians.

Initial investigation to the Chopp'd Straw Hall section of the house revealed clues to its history and to Walpole's early alterations. Beneath the floor of his Waiting Room preliminary archaeology found brick channels, evidence of early farm buildings, which were present before the building of Chopp'd Straw Hall. When the twentieth-century pebbledash on the exterior was removed the fenestration of the early house was revealed. As part of the first alterations to this area Walpole replaced the two existing windows on the south side with one central window. Sliding shutters were

built into the wall panelling on either side of the window in what would become the Yellow Bedchamber. It is likely that here, as in so many of the rooms, he wished to make the best use of all the wall area available to display his Collection. This he achieved in part through the extensive use of sliding shutters, by dispensing with curtains, and by *trompe l'oeil* windows. Other examples of sliding windows and shutters have been found which not only slide horizontally into walls but vertically below or above the window when there was no other choice.

The removal of the pebbledash exposed many samples of Walpole's original limewashed render. This was carefully analysed and replicated so that the restored exterior would be exactly as Walpole had intended. As the scaffolding, which had covered the building for almost two years, was taken down towards the end of the restoration the brightness of the render came as a surprise; a reaction that recalled the eighteenth-century response to the whiteness of the house.

One of the best known images of the house is the garden view showing the Great Cloister. This view was lost in the nineteenth century when the arches were filled in and the Cloister was divided into small rooms. The Cloister has been reopened and the arches glazed-in to recreate the appearance of an open monastic cloister.

> ...Strawberry is in the most perfect beauty, the verdure exquisite, and the shades venerably extended. I have made a Gothic gateway to the garden, the piers of which are of artificial stone and very respectable. The round tower is finished and magnificent; and the state bedchamber proceeds fast – for you must know the little villa is grown into a superb castle...[2]

To the north of the house the Prior's Garden has been replanted with sweet smelling flowers. The Prior's Screen, separating the garden from the Little Cloister, has been rebuilt and the 'saint' which visitors pass on their way to the front door has been recast from the original. Together these elements recreate the mood of 'an ancient abbey' before entering the house.

The removal of the third floor of the Little Parlour bay, added in the 1920s, has restored the bay to the two storeys of Walpole's early design and reinstated the symmetry of the south and east elevations. The addition of gleaming white timber pinnacles together with the restored stone battlements recreate the irregularity of the roofscape.

> ...In the neighbouring city of Twickenham they talk of nothing but houses broken open and robbed. I have called my militia into my castle, and mounted cannon on the battlements...[3]

Over many years internal alterations had been made to allow changes in the way the space was used; this often resulted in the loss of the eighteenth-century gothic mood. Removal of these alterations reinstated the original feel of the house – rooms which had felt cluttered and pokey became spacious and light. The Green Closet, with the China Closet below and the Plaid Bedchamber above, had been carved up in the nineteenth and twentieth centuries to create a staircase and bathrooms. The removal of the partitioning returned the dual aspect of the windows to the surrounding gardens; large in relation to the small floor space, the windows give the rooms a contemporary feeling. Once the partitioning by the Back Stair and the Beauclerc Closet was removed, a very elegant timber archway

LEFT *Restored seventeenth-century Flemish glass titled 'Autumn – Picking Apples' from the Star Chamber*

BELOW *The Great Cloister after restoration showing the view of the garden through the glass doors*

was revealed, beautifully crafted and formed; an example of Walpole's attention to the detail of a seemingly unimportant space. Throughout the house all the later applied decoration was removed. The renaissance glass was taken down, repaired and replaced in its 1790 settings – the date to which the house has been restored, chosen because it is the date for which most evidence exists.

[2] Letter Horace Walpole to Sir Horace Mann written from Strawberry Hill, 8 June 1771

[3] Letter Horace Walpole to Lady Ossory written from Strawberry Hill, 27 October 1774

RIGHT *A reproduction of a Lely portrait set within a roundel over one of the Gallery doors*

BELOW *A gilded canopy within the Gallery*

The investigative work to the Gallery also provided surprises. The window sills had been lowered in the nineteenth century by Lady Waldegrave to give her taller windows overlooking the garden. This cut into Walpole's dado and destroyed the proportions of the Gallery. During work to return the sills to their proper eighteenth-century height, the original layout of the fretwork was exposed by the conservators which allowed new fretwork to be positioned accurately. The symmetry of the Gallery was returned. There was a similar arrangement of fretwork beneath the windows of the Great North Bedchamber. When the wall coverings were removed panelling was revealed indicating an eighteenth-century option for this fretwork to be continued around the room. Walpole, however, chose instead to run the damask from the ceiling to the skirting board.

The doors between the Gallery and the Round Room, known as the St Alban's doors, have been remade and, highly decorated and gilded, they not only complete the Gallery but also provide anticipation for what is beyond. The regilding of the Gallery and Round Room ceilings has restored the eighteenth-century magnificence to these rooms.

Paint analysis revealed a base colour of grey to both ceilings, not white as previously thought. The use of many tones of grey throughout the house is apparent, reinforcing the surprise whenever colour is introduced and heightening the effect of the gilding.

> ...I am writing to you in the bow-window of my delicious round tower with your Bianca Capello over against me, and the setting sun behind me, throwing its golden rays all around...[4]

When some sections of wallpaper were removed the remaining panelling showed 'ghostings' of objects which had once been in the house. For example, the engraving of the chimneypiece in the Yellow Bedchamber (see page 49) shows five pinnacles on top. As these had disappeared by the twentieth century there was a mystery as to whether they were originally made of timber or painted in *trompe l'oeil*. The 'ghostings' of the pinnacles on the panelling revealed they had been made of timber and applied directly to the wall above the chimney. Walpole's description of the 'festooned' wallpaper in the Blue Breakfast Room (see pages 53–54) brought to mind similar contemporary papers showing garlands of fruit, leaves and flowers over a background of stripes. The fragment which was uncovered, shows vertical festoons of ivy wrapped around the stripes. Careful removal of all the fragments of the wall-papers discovered at Strawberry Hill, together with meticulous paint and fabric analysis provide an invaluable source of information on the interiors of the house. A number of different blue papers were used in the Blue Breakfast Room possibly document-ing a search for a stable blue. The Green Closet was hung with an expensive green flocked paper. The most important discovery was of an extensive area of the eighteenth-century hand-painted paper on the staircase. The workmanship was finer and in greater detail than could have been imagined. This has been carefully conserved. Newly woven crimson damasks of wool and wool, wool and silk and silk and silk, now hang on the walls of the Gallery, Round Room and Great North Bedchamber respectively.

The alterations and decorations carried out by Lady Waldegrave and the de Stern family were reassessed. Walpole's Blue Breakfast Room had been converted into a fashionable tented room by the de Stern family at the turn of the nineteenth/twentieth centuries, possibly as a smoking room and not by Lady Waldegrave decorating in advance of fashion.

ABOVE *A view of the Gallery looking through to the Round Room; note the raised sill height*

LEFT *Chimneypiece of the Yellow Bedchamber now the Discovery Room showing paint scraping on top left. On the panelling above can be seen ghosting of wooden pinnacles. The hole to the left of the chimney is where the Victorian bell pull was sited; a glass floor tile reveals the mechanism*

[4] Letter Horace Walpole to Sir Horace Mann written from Strawberry Hill, 19 June 1771

ABOVE *View of the first floor landing of the Hall midway through the restoration showing the eighteenth-century hand-painted gothic wallpaper. The painted walls of Walpole's first Blue Bedchamber restored to their surprising original colour can be seen through the doorway*

RIGHT *The Back Stairs revealing simple fretwork on the left*

Throughout the restoration a large number of wallpapers were uncovered attributed to both families. As a result, the influence of the de Stern family is shown to have been much greater than was originally thought.

The architectural changes, together with the widespread use of grey paint, have produced an extraordinary effect. Walpole's intention in using the dark grey tone throughout the public space of the ground floor – Hall, Staircase and Great Parlour – was to reject rather than reflect light. What light there was came through painted glass with quatrefoils above the stairs, emphasising the *trompe l'oeil* painting of the walls and enhancing the feeling of being in the outer area of a castle rather than within the building. This has now been restored to Strawberry Hill and the Staircase and piers seem to be rising through a courtyard. The use of grey paint continued on some of the upper floors where, combined with gilding, light produced contrast. With the strange effect of the light enhancing the white exterior, whilst draining colour from the interior, inside and outside seem reversed.

In 2009–10 an exhibition was mounted by the Lewis Walpole Library, Yale University, The Yale Center for British Art and the Victoria and Albert Museum of objects which had been owned by Horace Walpole and placed in Strawberry Hill. It produced a reassessment of the Collection and of Horace Walpole himself, showing him to have been more deeply antiquarian than had been previously thought. In the past it had often been assumed that he bought cheaply when possible; the exhibition showed that he dug deep into his pocket when necessary to acquire the unique and the beautiful. The house had always been seen as a cabinet of curiosities, but following the exhibition it has also to be seen as a repository of the most exquisite and precious objects, all placed to further personal, historical and antiquarian interests.

Following the restoration the building looks spectacular and is as far as possible Walpole's eighteenth-century castle. But there is a difference. It is almost empty; only a few objects punctuate the space rather than hundreds of objects displayed together. This gives too great an importance to those objects which should be seen as only a part of an important documented internal landscape.

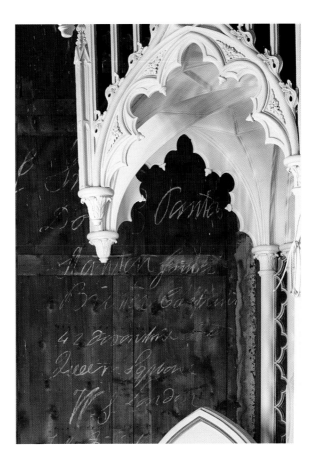

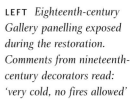

LEFT *Eighteenth-century Gallery panelling exposed during the restoration. Comments from nineteenth-century decorators read: 'very cold, no fires allowed'*

BELOW *A fragment of the festooned wallpaper found in the Blue Breakfast Room c.1753*

...PS. my tower erects its battlements bravely; my *Anecdotes of Painting* thrive exceedingly, thanks to the gout that has pinned me to my chair, think of Ariel the Sprite in a slit shoe!...[5]

[5] Letter Horace Walpole to George Montagu written from Strawberry Hill, 12 August 1760

Chronology

1698 Earl of Bradford's coachman builds Chopp'd Straw Hill

1714 Accession of George I

1717 Birth of Horatio (Horace) Walpole

1721 Sir Robert Walpole (Horace's father) appointed First Lord of the Treasury and Chancellor of the Exchequer

1727 Death of George I

1737 Death of Catherine Walpole (Horace's mother)

1738 Excavations at Herculaneum

1739 Walpole sets off on the Grand Tour

1745 The Jacobite Rising; death of Sir Robert Walpole, Lord Orford

1747 Walpole moves into Chopp'd Straw Hill; changes name to Strawberry Hill

1749 Walpole buys Strawberry Hill

1752 Britain moves from Julian to Gregorian calendar

1753 British Museum founded; start of first building scheme at Strawberry Hill

1754 Library and Refectory completed; Royal Society of Arts founded (originally Society for the Encouragements of Arts Manufactures and Commerce)

1757 Strawberry Hill Press founded and Walpole's bedroom built

1759 Holbein Chamber added

1760 Death of George II; approximate start of the Industrial Revolution

1762–64 Walpole's *Anecdotes of Painting in England* published

1763 Long Gallery and Round Tower completed and Tribune added

1764 Walpole writes and publishes *The Castle of Otranto*

1766 Captain James Cook makes round the world voyage

1768 Walpole writes *The Mysterious Mother*; foundation of the Royal Academy of Art

1769 Josiah Wedgwood founds Etruria factory

1770 Walpole writes *The History of the Modern Taste in Gardening* (published later); Great North Bedchamber added

1773 The Boston Tea Party; Chapel in the Woods completed

1774 and 1784 Publications of the *Description of the Villa*

1776 Signing of the American Declaration of Independence; Beauclerc Tower built; Yellow Bedchamber renamed the Beauty Room

1780 The Gordon Riots

1789 The French Revolution

1790–92 New Offices (service wing) built

1791 Walpole inherits title and becomes 4th Earl of Orford

1797 Death of Horace Walpole; Anne Damer inherits Strawberry Hill

1805 Battle of Trafalgar

1807 Slave trade abolished in British territories

1810 Strawberry Hill passes to the Waldegrave family

1812 Gas lighting introduced in London

1815 Battle of Waterloo ends Napoleonic Wars

1840–70 Palace of Westminster built

1842 The Great Sale

1851 The Great Exhibition

1854–56 Waldegrave Wing added

1879 Death of Lady Waldegrave; Strawberry Hill unoccupied

1883 Baron de Stern (Lord Michelham) buys Strawberry Hill

1923 Catholic Education Council buys house for St Mary's Catholic Teacher Training College

1927 Stawberry Hill becomes residence of Vincentian priests

2000 Friends of Strawberry Hill founded

2002 Strawberry Hill Trust formed

2007 Restoration programme commenced

2010 Strawberry Hill reopened, following restoration, on Horace Walpole's birthday

OPPOSITE *A view of Strawberry Hill before restoration*

Bibliography

ANON., *A Catalogue of the Contents of Strawberry Hill*, for George Robins, auctioneer, London, 1842

ANON., *A Catalogue of the Contents of the Mansion Strawberry Hill*, 1883, Printed by H. Kemstead, London

Bateman Sale Catalogue for May 3rd, Christies, 1774

BATEY, Mavis, 'Horace Walpole as Modern Garden Historian', *Garden History: The Journal of the Garden History Society*, 19:1, Spring 1991

BOYDELL, John and Josiah, *An History of the River Thames* (illustrated by Farington), London, 1796

BRACKETT, Oliver, 'English Wall-Papers of the eighteenth century', *Connoisseur*, October 1918

CHALCRAFT, Anna, *A Paper House, Horace Walpole at Strawberry Hill*, Highgate of Beverley, Beverley, 1998

CHALCRAFT, Anna and VISCARDI, Judith, *Visiting Strawberry Hill, An Analysis of the Eton Copy of 'The Description of the Villa'*, 2005

CORNFORTH, John, *Early Georgian Interiors*, Yale University Press, New Haven & London, 2004

COUTTS, Howard, 'Saint-Porchaire Ceramics', article ed. by Barbar, Daphne and Sturman, Shelley, National Gallery of Art, Washington, Hanover & London

DEVOE, Shirley Spaulding, *English papier mâché of the Georgian and Victorian Periods*, Barrie and Jenkins, London, 1971

DUGDALE, Sir William, *The History of St. Paul's Cathedral in London from its foundation until these times*, E. Maynard L.P., London, 1716

DU HALDE, *Description géographique, historique ...de l'Empire de la Chine et de la Tartarie Chinoise...*, Paris, 1734

DUNCAN, David Ewing, *The Calendar*, Fourth Estate, London, 1998

EAVIS, A., and PEOVER, M., 'Horace Walpole's painted glass at Strawberry Hill', *The Journal of Stained Glass*, Vol.XIX, No.3, 1994-5

ENTWISLE, E.A., *A Literary History of Wallpaper*, Batsford, London, 1960

ENTWISLE, E.A., *The Book of Wallpaper, A history and an appreciation*, Arthur Barker, London, 1954

FOWLER, John and CORNFORTH, John, *English Decoration in the 18th Century*, Barrie and Jenkins, London, 1974

GIROUARD, Mark, *Life in the English Country House*, Yale University Press, New Haven & London, 1978

GLASSE, Hannah, *The Art of Cookery Made Plain and Easy*, 1747

GLASSE, Hannah, *Servants' Directory*, 1760

GRANVILLE, Mary, *The Autobiography and Correspondence of Mary Granville, Mrs. Delaney*, ed. Lady Llanover, 1861

GRAY, Thomas, *Correspondence of Thomas Gray*, ed. Paget Toynbee and Leonard Whibley, Oxford, Clarendon Press, 1971

GRAY, Thomas, 'Journal of the Grand Tour', Eton College Library, ECL MS 413

GRAY, Thomas, 'Notes on a tour through France and Italy, 1739–1741, undertaken in the years 1739–1741', John Murray Archive

GRAY, Thomas, *The Poems of Thomas Gray with a Selection of Letters and Essays*, J.M. Dent and Sons, London, 1912

GUILLERY, P., 'Strawberry Hill: Building and Site: Part One: The Building', *Architectural History*, Vol. 38, Leeds, 1995

HALFPENNY, W., (and others), *The Modern Builder's Assistant*, London, 1742

HALSBAND, R., 'The Rococo in England: Book Illustrators' (mainly Gravelot and Bentley), *Burlington Magazine*, 1985

HAWKINS, L.M., *Anecdotes, Biographical Sketches and Memoirs*, 1822

HAYDEN, Ruth, *Mrs. Delany (sic), Her life and her flowers*, British Museum Press, London, 2000

HAZEN, A.T., *A Bibliography of Horace Walpole*, Yale University Press, New Haven & London, 1948

HAZEN, A.T. and KIRBY, J.P., *A Bibliography of the Strawberry Hill Press*, Yale University Press,

New Haven, 1942

HICKS, Carola, *Improper Pursuits, The Scandalous Life of Lady Di Beauclerk* (sic), Pan Macmillan Ltd, London, 2002

IDDON, J., *Horace Walpole's Strawberry Hill*, St Mary's University College, Twickenham, 1996

LANGLEY, B., *Ancient Architecture Restored and Improved*, London, 1742

LEWIS, W.S., ed., *The Yale Edition of Horace Walpole's Correspondence*, Yale University Press, New Haven, 1937–1983, Vols 1-48

LUXBOROUGH, Lady, *Letters*, Dublin, 1776

MACIVER, P., 'Jackson of Battersea', *The Connoisseur*, LXII, 1922

MAYOR, A.H., 'A Note on the Prints at Strawberry Hill', paper included in *Horace Walpole: Writer, Politician, Connoisseur*, Yale, New Haven and London, 1967

MCLEOD, B., 'Horace Walpole and Sèvres Porcelain', *Apollo*, January, 1998

OESTREICHER, Lisa, 'The Staircase, Armoury and Hall Strawberry Hill, An Investigation of their Painted Surfaces', unpublished thesis, RCA/V&A Conservation MA course (Architectural Paint Studies)', September 1996

PINK, M.Alderton, ed., *The Letters of Horace Walpole*, Macmillan, London, 1938

PLUMB, J.H., *Georgian Delights*, Weidenfeld and Nicolson, London, 1980

PYE, Henrietta, *A Short Account of the principal seats and gardens in and about Twickenham*, London, 1760

PYE, J. Henrietta, *A Short View of the principal seats and gardens in and about Twickenham*, London, 1775

RICHARDSON, Jonathan, *An Account of some of the statues, bas-reliefs, drawings, and pictures, in Italy &c.*, London, 1722

ROBERTS, W.G, ed., *Notes on a Tour Through France and Italy undertaken in the years 1739-1741 by Thomas Gray*, The Colophan Press, Carlisle, 2003

ROSOMAN, T., *London Wallpapers, Their Manufacture and Use*, English Heritage, 1992

SCATCHERD, J., ed., *Ambulator or a Pocket Companion in a Tour Round London within the Circuit of twenty-five Miles*, London, 1800

SNODIN, M., 'Strawberry Hill: Building and Site: Part Two: The Site', *Architectural History*, Vol. 38, Leeds, 1995

SNODIN, Michael, ed., with the assistance of ROMAN, Cynthia, *Horace Walpole's Strawberry Hill*, Yale University Press, New Haven and London, 2009

STRONG, Roy, *Feast, A History of Grand Eating*, Pimlico, London, 2003

STUART, Dorothy M., *Horace Walpole*, Macmillan, New York, 1927

THORNTON, Peter, *The Italian Renaissance Interior, 1400–1600*, Weidenfeld & Nicolson, London, 1991

TOYNBEE, Paget, *Strawberry Hill Accounts*, Clarendon Press, Oxford, 1927

TOYNBEE, Paget, *The Correspondence of Gray, Walpole, West and Ashton, 1734–1771*, Oxford University Press, 1915

TOYNBEE, Paget, *Journal of the Printing-Office at Strawberry Hill*, The Chiswick Press for Constable and Company Ltd and Houghton Mifflin Company, London, 1923

WAINWRIGHT, C., *The Romantic Interior*, Yale University Press, New Haven and London, 1989

WALPOLE, Horace, *A Description of the Villa of Horace Walpole*, Strawberry Hill, 1774, Storer Collection, Eton College Library, ECL Cc114

WALPOLE, Horace, 'Commonplace Book for 1780', manuscript, Lewis Walpole Library, Yale University (49, 2616)

WALPOLE, Horace, *The History of The Modern Taste In Gardening*, Ursus Press, New York, 1995

WALPOLE, Horatio, *The Works of Horatio Walpole, Earl of Orford*, Vols 1–5, London, 1798

WATSON, F.J.B., 'Walpole and the Taste for French Porcelain in Eighteenth-Century England', essay on the 250th anniversary of Walpole's birth, Yale University Press, New Haven & London, 1967

Biographies

ROBERT ADAM (1728–1792) Architect renowned for elegant sense of proportion and unified facades; set up London architectural practice with his brother James in 1758; was appointed royal architect in 1762 and became most fashionable architect in England.

LADY AILESBURY (1721–1803) (Caroline Campbell), m. 1) Charles Bruce, Earl of Ailesbury, 2) Henry Seymour Conway; mother of Anne Damer.

ASCIOTTI Walpole's agent sent to Flanders to buy glass for Strawberry Hill.

SIR JOSEPH BANKS (1743–1820) British explorer and naturalist; led Royal Society delegation on a round the world voyage with Captain Cook in 1766; made President of the Royal Society in 1778; as honorary director of the Royal Botanical Gardens at Kew he sent many botanists to countries to find new plants.

LADY DIANA BEAUCLERC (1734–1808) (Diana Spencer), m. 1) Viscount Bolingbroke, divorced 1768, 2) Topham Beauclerc; executed drawings for *The Mysterious Mother* and designs for Wedgwood.

RICHARD BENTLEY (1708–1782) Member of Committee of Taste; draughtsman and designer for Strawberry Hill; illustrated Gray's poems.

MARY AND AGNES BERRY Two sisters whom Walpole befriended in 1787. He wrote his *Reminiscences of the Courts of George I and II* for their amusement; offered them a temporary home at Little Strawberry Hill and entertained them at Strawberry Hill almost every Sunday.

THOMAS BROMWICH (–1787) Paper stainer and decorator, Master of the Guild; provided wallpapers and papier-mâché for Strawberry Hill.

HENRY CAREY, LORD FALKLAND (c. 1575–1633) Lord Deputy of Ireland, M.P., courtier, descendant from an illegitimate line from Henry VIII. His portrait hung in the Long Gallery of Strawberry Hill.

BENVENUTO CELLINI (1500–1571) Florentine sculptor, goldsmith and metalworker; was in service of Francis I, 1540–45.

MRS CHENEVIX (–1755) Toy shop keeper of the Golden Gate, Charing Cross, who rented Chopp'd Straw Hall immediately prior to Walpole.

LORD HERBERT OF CHERBURY (1582–1648) (Edward Herbert) Linguist; self-taught player of the lute; composer; English ambassador to Paris. His autobiography was printed by Horace Walpole in 1764.

JOHN CHUTE (1701–1776) Member of the Committee of Taste, great friend and gentleman architect who designed much of Strawberry Hill; owner of The Vyne.

COLLEY CIBBER (1671–1757) Actor, theatre manager and playwright; poet laureate from 1730; early resident of Chopp'd Straw Hall.

HENRY CLAY Eighteenth-century cabinet maker and inventor of Clay Ware.

JEAN-FRANÇOIS CLERMONT (1717–1807) French painter who worked in England for many years painting grotesques, foliage, birds and monkeys; returned to France in 1754.

KITTY CLIVE (–1785) Mainly comedic actress; at seventeen joined theatre company managed by Cibber; was original member of Garrick's company in 1747 and remained for 22 years; retired in 1769 to Little Strawberry Hill.

LADY MARY COKE (née Campbell) (1727–1811) Daughter of the Duke of Argyll, married Edward Coke (Viscount) 1747

REVD WILLIAM COLE (1714–1782) Antiquary, Etonian, lifelong friend of Horace Walpole.

HENRY SEYMOUR CONWAY (1719–1795) Cousin of Horace Walpole, Groom of the Chamber to George II and George III; married Caroline (Lady Ailesbury) in 1747; father of Anne Damer.

SIR DAVID DALRYMPLE (1726–1792) Lawyer, judge and historian.

ANNE DAMER (1749–1828) Sculptor, second cousin of Horace Walpole and inherited Strawberry Hill from him.

MRS DELANEY/MARY GRANVILLE (1700–1788) Lady artist, embroiderer; began making 'paper mosaicks' of flowers at the age of 72.

PHILIPPE JACQUES DE LOUTHERBOURG (1740–1812) French-born painter and stage designer; built moving panoramas (creator of the Eidophusikon) using three-dimensional sets, lighting and sound effects representing shipwrecks and natural wonders.

JOHANN AEGIDUS ECCHARDT (ECKHARDT) (–1779) German-born portrait painter; came to England in 1740; painted Walpole and Gray.

RICHARD EDGCUMBE/2ND BARON EDGCUMBE (1716–1761) Member of Walpole's Out of Town Club and life long patron of Reynolds.

EDWARD EDWARDS (1738–1806) Artist.

JAMES ESSEX THE YOUNGER (1722–1784) Architect and builder; designed Beauclerc Tower, Gothic Gates and New Offices of Strawberry Hill.

DAVID GARRICK (–1779) Actor and theatre owner; intended to study law but started writing plays and acting; took London by storm with his performance of Richard III; took half share of Drury Lane Theatre; moved to Hampton in 1754.

THOMAS GAYFERE (–1827) Master mason.

GRINLING GIBBONS (1648–1721) Woodcarver and sculptor.

JAMES GIBBS (1682–1754) Architect responsible for St Martin-in-the-Fields and other public buildings; also the Octagon at Orleans House, Twickenham.

HANNAH GLASSE (1708–1770) Author of *The Art of Cookery Made Plain and Easy*, 1747.

THOMAS GRAY (1716–1771) Poet and forerunner of the romantic movement; Etonian; accompanied Horace Walpole on the Grand Tour keeping a diary of their travels; wrote *Elegy Written in a Country Churchyard* and *Ode on the Death of a Favourite Cat*.

WILLIAM HALLETT (1707-1781) Fashionable cabinet maker of Great Newport Street, London.

MARY HAMILTON (1756-1816) First mentions Horace Walpole in her letters and journal 28 June 1783.

LAETITIA MATILDA HAWKINS (1759-1835) Twickenham resident and author; published her memoirs and five multi-volumed novels under her own name and more anonymously.

FRANCIS HAYMAN (1708-1776) Painter.

LADY HERVEY OF ICKWORTH (1700–1768) (Mary Lepell) One of the Princess's ladies-in-waiting in the Court of George I and great court beauty.

NICHOLAS HILLIARD (1547–1619) Jeweller and artist working for Elizabeth I and James I; established the English school of miniature painting.

WILLIAM HOGARTH (1697–1764) Satirical engraver and portrait painter; persuaded parliament to pass the Copyright Act of 1737 to ensure print sellers paid royalties to artists.

HANS HOLBEIN THE YOUNGER (1497–1543) German portraitist renowned for precise detail; became court painter to Henry VIII in 1536.

WENCESLAS HOLLAR (1607–1677) Bohemian engraver and watercolourist; foremost seventeenth-century engraver of topographical views; his views of London before the great fire of 1666 provided an invaluable record of the city.

HENRIETTA HOWARD, COUNTESS OF SUFFOLK (1688–1767) Mistress to the Prince of Wales, later George II, who built Marble Hill for her.

THOMAS HUDSON (1701–1779) Portrait painter trained under Jonathan Richardson; his pupils included Joshua Reynolds and Joseph Wright of Derby; he died in Twickenham.

JOHN BAPTIST JACKSON (1700–1770) Wood engraver, early printmaker and wallpaper producer.

WILLIAM KENT (1684–1748) Architect, painter, furniture designer and landscape gardener; one of the leading architects of the Palladian style; worked in London and at Houghton, Holkham and Stowe; patronised by Lord Burlington.

THOMAS KIRGATE (1734–1810) Best and most reliable of Horace Walpole's printers, working at Strawberry Hill 1765–89.

JAMES LACY Owner of Ranelagh Gardens from 1740.

BATTY LANGLEY (1696–1751) Gardener and writer; born in Twickenham; wrote *Ancient Architecture Restored* in 1742, which was reissued in 1747 as *Gothic Architecture, improved by Rules and Proportions.*

PIERRE LANGLOIS (1738–1781) French furniture maker.

MICHAEL LORT (1725–1790) D.D., Antiquary and Fellow of Trinity College, Cambridge.

LADY LUXBOROUGH (1699–1756) (Henrietta Knight), m. Robert Knight but separated nine years later; banished in 1763 to Barrels where she lived quietly, becoming the centre of a literary society.

CHARLES MACKLIN (1699?–1797) Actor-manager and dramatist.

HORACE MANN (1706–1786) English diplomat in Florence and private art dealer; supplied many objects for Strawberry Hill; great friend, distant cousin and lifelong correspondent of Walpole.

WILLIAM MASON (1725–1797) Clergyman, friend, biographer of Gray.

GEORGE MONTAGU (c.1713–1780) M.P., friend and early correspondent.

HANNAH MORE (1745–1833) Most influential member of the Society for Effecting the Abolition of the African Slave Trade; published writer from 1760s.

JOHANN HEINRICH MÜNTZ (1727–1798) Artist and designer; worked as artist in residence at Strawberry Hill.

ISAAC (d. 1617) & PETER (d. 1647) OLIVER, Father and son miniature Court painters.

LADY OSSORY (c.1738–1804) (Hon. Anne Liddell), m. 1) Duke of Grafton, 2) John Fitzpatrick, 2nd Earl of Upper Ossory.

PALMER Glazier of St Martin's Lane, provider of glass at Strawberry Hill.

WILLIAM PECKITT (1731–1795) Glass painter and glazier from York.

THOMAS PITT (1737–1793) (Baron Camelford), M.P., designer of later Moorish parts of Strawberry Hill.

ALEXANDER POPE (1688–1744) Poet, satirist and grotto designer; Twickenham resident from 1719.

WILLIAM PRICE THE YOUNGER Glass painter.

SIR JOSHUA REYNOLDS (1723–1792) Most successful portrait painter of his day; first President of the Royal Academy; knighted by George III in 1769.

JONATHAN RICHARDSON (1665–1745) Founded St Martin's Lane Academy in 1711.

WILLIAM ROBINSON (1720–1775) Architect; Secretary to the Board of Works; early architect of Strawberry Hill; Clerk of Works to the Committee of Taste; awarded commission for Somerset House but died and replaced by William Chambers.

LUDOVIC ROBSART, LORD BOURCIER Crusader knight and ancestor of Horace Walpole.

GIULIO ROMANO (1499–1546) Italian painter, architect and decorator; pupil of Raphael; helped define sixteenth-century Mannerist style.

LOUIS FRANÇOIS ROUBILIAC (1693–1762) French sculptor.

PAUL SANDBY (1730–1809) Watercolour painter and engraver.

SAMUEL SCOTT (c.1701–1772) English painter specialising in seascapes and topographical views.

GEORGE SELWYN (1719–1791) Member of Walpole's Out of Town Club.

CATHERINE SHORTER (–1737) First wife of Sir Robert Walpole and mother of Horace Walpole.

JONATHAN TYERS (1702–1767) Proprietor of Vauxhall Gardens.

GEORGE VERTUE (1683–1756) Engraver and antiquary.

WILLIAM VILE (c.1700–1767) Royal cabinet maker; work includes some of the finest English Rococo furniture.

THREE LADIES WALDEGRAVE (Lady Charlotte Maria, Lady Elizabeth Laura and Lady Anna Horatia) Walpole's great nieces; their painting by Reynolds exhibited at the Royal Academy in 1781.

SIR ROBERT WALPOLE (1676–1745) 1st Prime Minister and 1st Earl of Orford, m. 1) Catherine Shorter in 1700 and 2) Maria Skerret in 1738; Horace Walpole's father.

JAMES WYATT (1746–1813) Architect for New Offices at Strawberry Hill.

BENJAMIN WEST (1738–1820) American artist; twice elected President of the Royal Academy.

SIR CHARLES HANBURY WILLIAMS (1708–1759) Friend and wit.

GILLY WILLIAMS Member of Walpole's Out of Town Club.

MARGARET 'PEG' WOFFINGTON (c.1714–1760) Actress renowned for her impersonation of men on stage.

MARGARET YOUNG Walpole's Housekeeper and Guide to visitors.

Acknowledgements

The authors would like to give especial thanks to the following:

YALE UNIVERSITY for permission to use letters taken from the Yale edition of *Horace Walpole's Correspondence* by W.S.Lewis. We would also like especially to thank DR MARGARET POWELL and the staff of the LEWIS WALPOLE LIBRARY for their continued help and support.

MICHAEL YAUNER, CAROL OLIVER and CHRIS CAPSTICK for capturing the delights of Strawberry Hill with their photography and JOHN HARDY, KEVIN ROGERS and MICHAEL SNODIN for their generosity in sharing their information and time.

They would also like to thank KAREN BEAUCHAMP and COLE & SONS WALLPAPERS, CHRISTIES and the EARL and COUNTESS of WEMYSS AND MARCH for their kind agreement to use illustrations of material in their possession.

DUNCAN BURTON, LADY ROSE CHOLMONDELEY, MERRYL HUXTABLE, MICHAEL PEOVER, MARK SANDIFORD, IAN WEST and RAY WILLIAMS have generously shared their research and knowledge of specific subjects.

The Provost and Trustees of ETON COLLEGE, the Librarians, MICHAEL MEREDITH and NICK BAKER of College Library, ETON COLLEGE for their help and enthusiasm; the archivists of CHRISTIES and the JOHN MURRAY ARCHIVE, both of whom made eighteenth-century material available; ST MARY'S COLLEGE; the FRIENDS OF STRAWBERRY HILL and the STRAWBERRY HILL GUIDES for their kind agreement in allowing access to items in their possession, and the staff of the BRITISH LIBRARY, the BRITISH MUSEUM, the ROYAL MUSEUM OF SCOTLAND and the VICTORIA AND ALBERT MUSEUM Print Room and National Art Library for their assistance.

The authors owe an especial debt to JOHN CORNFORTH who supported the project of writing this book. He loved Strawberry Hill and enabled them to question and see afresh the rooms and their uses. After his untimely death his expertise was a continued source of inspiration through his published works, including the posthumous *Early Georgian Interiors*.

RIGHT *Illustration for Thomas Gray's 'Ode on the Death of a Favourite Cat', engraving from a drawing by Richard Bentley*

Index

Figures in *italic* indicate images.
N indicates notes in the margins.

actors, 15, 16, 86–7
Adam, Robert, 47, 91, 91N, 97, 148
Aedes Walpolianae, 12, 58, 66
Ailesbury, Lady, 58, 92, 119, 133, 134, 156
alabaster, 9, 96
altar, 98
Ambulator, 7, 7N, 133, 133N
America, 37
    War of Independence, 12, 110, 153
An Account of Russia as it was In the Year 1710, 68
ancestors, 43, 56, 60, 64–5, 69, 73, 99
Anecdotes of Painting in England, 12, 53, 63, 99,
    116, 116N, 135, 151
Anne Boleyn, Queen, 70
Anne of Cleves, Queen, 78
antelope, 36, 38, 41, 60, 60N, 60, 61N, 70
antiquarian/antiquities/antique, 26, 35, 47, 56,
    63, 65–6, 89, 113, 116, 133, 151
Arcadia, 44, 52
arches, 36, 63, 76, 85, 146
architects/architecture, 8, 10, 17, 24–5, 28, 31,
    35, 82, 97, 100, 120
    classical, 10, 17, 46–7, 57, 77, 87N, 88
    Moorish, 83
    Perpendicular, 9
    Robinson, William, 53
Arlington Street, 11, 16, 18, 23, 26, 29, 39, 65, 67,
    98, 101
armour, 35N, 39–41, 128
Armoury, 34, 35, 35N, 38–41, 43, 51, 57N, 61, 71,
    120N, 130N, 139N
art/artists, 10, 11, 32, 36, 46, 85, 98, 103, 142
Asciotti, 56, 148
Ashe, Mr, 113
Aubusson, 92, 105, 138

Back Stair *see* servants' stair
balloon, 12, 142
balustrade, 36, 38, 38, 40–1
Banks, Joseph, 54, 156
Bateman, Richard, 71, 114N
Battersea enamel, 57
battlements, 17, 25, 113, 119, 123, 133, 147, 151
Beauclerc, Lady Diana, 27, 101, 101N, 102, 102N,
    102, 156

Beauclerc, Topham, 101
Beauclerc Tower/Closet, 18, 27, 31, 95, 100,
    101, 101N, 102, 119, 135, 146N, 147, 153
beds, 20, 54, 58, 60, *61*, 75–8, 105, 107, 131
    Burleigh, 76
    by Vile, 76, 78
bedchamber, 10, 58, 60, 70–1, 76, 91, 105, 127,
    135–6
The Beggar's Opera, 108
bell (front door), 99
    (pull) 149N
    (Tribune), 100
Bentley, Richard, 9, 19, 29, 29N, 31–2, 35, 38,
    38N, 39N, 40N, 43N, *46*, 46–8, 57–8,
    58N, 59, 59N, 60N, 61N, 63, 66, 74–5, 78,
    78N, 82, 117, 119, 119N, 133, 156, 160N
Berkeley Square, 11, 20, 44N, 73
Berry, Mary, 67, 89, 128N, 129, 142N, 156
birds, 13, 25, *56*, 56–7, 63, 79, 84–5, 88,
    93, 105, 110, 113, 120–1, 128N, 134N,
    138, 142
blinds, 127
Blue Bedchamber (Walpole's early), 43–4,
    44N, 51–2, 58, 119N, 127, 128N, 131, 150N
    (Walpole's later – from 1757), 52, 56, 58–9,
    61N, 70–1, 106, 123, 127, 131, 137, 153
Blue Breakfast Room, 35, 51, 51N, 52–5, 52N, *53*,
    58, 70N, 78, 110, 127, 149, 151N
    as Turkish Boudoir, 137
Blue Room, 39, (possibly Blue Breakfast Room)
Boccapudugli Eagle, 33, 88–9, 89N, *89*
book presses, 56, 63–4, 103
books, 48, 57–8, 63, 65–6, 76–7, 79, 99, 103,
    109, 126
    botanical and ornithological, 13, 56
Borghese Villa, 25
boulle, 92
Bourchier, Lord, *see* Robsart
Boydell, John, 52
Bradford, Earl of, 16
Braham, John, 134
Brentford, 91, 128
brewing/baking, 129
Bromwich, Thomas, 36, 46–7, 57, 60, 126, 156
    trade card, *45*
    Bromwich and Legh, 47
bronzes, 89, 100
bronze saint, 18, 146

cabinet, 26, 107
    makers, 84, 76, 97
    of Curiosities, 12, 27
    of Miniatures (Hallett), 97–8, *98*
    Tribune, *see* Tribune
Caligula, 99
candelabra/candlesticks, 10, 49, 54, 67, 73, 81,
    83, 83N, 84, 108
    candles, 84, 86, 126
    candlelight, 28, 35, 73, 86
    sconces, 84N, 86, 92, 95, 108
Canterbury Cathedral, 63, 84
    Archbishop of, 78
card games, 84, 86, 88, 92, 108, 109
    loo, 88
    Minchiate, 108–9
    Taracco, 108
Cardinal Wolsey's hat, 78
Carey, Henry, Viscount Falkland, 40, 89, *89*,
    89N, 156
Caroline, Queen, 76
carpenters/plasterers, 13, 31, 71, 97, 100, 113
carpets, 20, 58, *75*, 75N, 79, 84, 92, *96*, 97, 105,
    125–6, 137, 138
    foot, 105
    Moorfields, 84, 92, 105
    rugs, 126, 137
carvers/carving, 36, 45, 63, 76–7, 82, 84,
    92, 106
castle, ancient/medieval, 18, 40, 95,
    113, 150
The Castle of Otranto, 12, 40–1, *41*, 59, 89,
    105, 153
cat, 111, 117, 125; *see* Selima
*A Catalogue of the Royal and Noble Authors of
    England*, 68
cathedrals, 9, 10, 13, 20, 76, 100, 133
Catherine, 43, 44, *see also* housekeeper
Catherine of Aragon, Queen, 56
Catherine of Braganza, Queen, 107
Catherine wheels, 64, 75
ceilings, 9, 20, 25–6, 35, 43, 45, 63–4, 71, *75*,
    77, 81, 85–6, 91, 96–7, 105, 108, 113, 116,
    127, 137, 138, 148, 149
    Long Gallery, *80*, *81*, 81N, 84, 88
    Tribune, 95, *103*
    roundels, 64, 70
Cellini, Benvenuto, 39, 100, 107–8, 156

ceramics/porcelain, 11, 23, 26–8, *27*, 70, 86, 89, 90, *92*, *93*, 101, 110, 113–14, 125, 137
    blue and white, *28*, 54, *92*, 102, 107, 110, 113
    Chelsea, 27, 93
    cups, 39, 110
    Dresden, 11, 86
    Etruscan ware, 79
    European, 27
    floral design on, 54, 113
    French porcelain, 28
    Italian faience, 107–8
    oriental, 90, 92
    Meissen (Saxon ware), 27–8
    Sèvres, 54, 58, 58N, 71, 92–3, 107, 108, 110, 110N
    tub, 18
chairs, 10, 23, 29N, 46, 53, 58, 71, *71*, 76, *76*, *77*, 78, 92, 105, 131
    armchair, 65
    armchair with patchwork, 59
    Coronation, 78
    crimson Norwich damask, 59
    ebony, 76, *76*, 78, 103, 105
    Glastonbury, 9, 78
    Halsey, low, 78
    refectory with matted bottom, 31, *31*, 32
    triangular, 71, *71*
    upholstered, 46
    Walpole/Bentley, 31–2, 74
    Welsh armchair, 71, 113, *114*, 114N
    white and gold elbow, 105
chandelier, 86
Chantilly, 83, 110
chapel, *45*, *see also* tombs
Chapel in the Woods, 21, 57, 111, *112*, 113N, 115, 116, *116*, 116N, 117, 138, 153
Charles I, King, 64
Charles II, King, 55, 64, 101
Charles V, 107
Charlotte, Queen, 27, 54, 101
Chelsea, family home in, 51, 55–6, 114
Chenevix, Mrs, 16, 28, 148; shop, 41
Chevenix, Mr, 40, 123
Cherokee Indians, 12
chimney, 126
    board, 126
    pieces, 20, *26*, 26N, 29, *30*, 32, 38, 46, 48, *49*, 53–4, 58, 59N, 60, 63, 65, 75, 79, *79*, 83, 84, 91, *91*, 92, 103, 106, *108*, 133, 145, 149, *149*
    pots, 136, *138*, 138n
    sweepers, 125
China Closet (ground floor), 21, 23–8, 24N, *26*, 39, 57; (first floor), 90, 92–3, 95, 147
Chinese/chinoiserie, 18, 23, 28, 54, 84–6, 92–3, 114N, 120
    pagodas, 57
    trade, 93
Choiseul, Duchesse de, 110, 110N
Chopp'd Straw Hall, 8, 16, 17, 21, 26, 51, 53, 65, 70, 73, 123, 127, 129, 145, 153
churches, 20, 24, 39, 56

Chute, John, 9, 46–8, *47*, 56, 59, 63, 66, 78, 82, 84, 97, 105, 116, 120, 126, 156
Cibber, Colley, 16, 156
Clarence, Duke of, 63
Clay, Henry, 103, 156
    ware, 102
Clermont, Jean-François, 63, 85, 156
Clive, Kitty, 56, 75N, 79, 81, 87–8, *88*, 126, 156
clock, 32, 70
    Julien Le Roy, 32
Cloister, Great, 44, 97N, 111, 113, *114*, 115, 119, 134, 134N, 136, 146, *147*, 147N
    possible conversion to studio, 134
    possible theatre, 134, 134N
Cloister, Little, 18, *129*, 129N, *131*, 133, 136, *144*, 145N, 146
closet, 47, 105, 108, 134N, 139N
coaches/post-chaises, 44, 103, 126, 142
coachman, 124, 128
Coade stone / artificial stone, 119, 146
coats of arms, 18, 26, 46, 54, 56–7, 60, 63, 64N, 65, 69, 70, 92–3, 100
coffee, 41, 84, 110, 129
coffee houses, 18
coins and medals, 69, 71, 100, 107, 114
Coke, Mary, 88, 126, 156
Cole, William, 41N, 66, 100, 100N, 110, 116, 116N, 156
collection/collectors, 8, 11, 12, 20, 25, 27, 33, 54, 56, 63, 66, 69, 71, 73–4, 78–9, 82, 84, 88, 90, 95, 97, 98, 100, 103, 107, 114, 116, 126, 133–4, 146, 151
Collection of all the Loose Pieces printed at Strawberry Hill, 18
colours, 47–8, 52, 54–6, 58, 74, 81–2, 97, 101, 149, 150, 150N
combs, 78
Committee of Taste, 8, 9, 29, 36, 38, 46–7, 53, 57, 63, 82, 97, 168
commodes, 84
'The Commonplace Book', 70, 103, 105, 111N
Complete Works, 28, 142N
convolvulus, 25–6
Conway, Henry Seymour, 16, 33, 38, 58, 64, 66, 93, 111, 111N, 115N, 126N, 128N, 133, 156
cook, 12, 128–9
cornice, 13, 25, 30, 45, 60
correspondence, 7, 11, 12, 23, 54, 56, 65–8, 91, 110, 130–1, 141, 145
cosmati-work, 116
costume, 10, 57, 59, 67, 84–6, 89, 90, 99, 100, 108, 121
cottage, 119, *121*, 138
country houses/great houses, 38, 74, 87, 89, 99, 109
Court of Star Chamber, 105
Covent Garden, 86
cows/cattle, 16, 28, 44, 129, 142
craftsmen, 10, 35, 37, 47, 56, 58, 77, 82, 84, 93, 97, 98, 105
cravat, 84–5, 100

Cromwell, Oliver, 9, 56
cross-crosslets, 64, 75
Crusades, 10, 60, 64, 68, 70
Cumberland, Duke of, 67
curtains, 54, 108, 137, 137N, 138, 146

dado, 148
Dalrymple, Sir David, 12, 156
damask, 49, 58N, 60, 81–3, 89, 92, 101, 105, 106, 148, 149
    crimson Norwich, 59, 81, 83, 89, 92, 105
    Indian Blue, 101–3
Damer, Anne, 7, 8, 89, 111, 120, 133, 134, *135*, 153, 157
Dart, 36
death warrant of Charles I, 60
Deffand, Madame du, 100, 100N, 110, *110*, 110N, 111
Delaney, Mrs/Mary Granville, 12, 12N, 48, 54, 54N, 55, 126, 157
Derby biscuit ware, *28*
Description of the Villa/Inventory, 18, 20, 28, 29N, 64, 93, 95, 145
    (1774), 7, 58
    (1784), 7, 20N, 52N, 54N, 56N, 57, 58N, 66, 79N, 84N, 90N, 93N, 99, 100, 103, 119N, 141
    Storer's copy, 7, 7N, 9, 9N
desserts, 28, 55, 129
diaper-work, 61N, 73N, 77
dinner/dining, 20, 25–6, 29, 40, 83–6, 88, 93, 111, 119, 125, 128–9, 131
    19th-century menu, *139*, 139N
Discovery Room *see* Yellow Bedchamber
disease/illness/ailments, 37, 41, 67, 93, 111, 128
    remedies, 128
Dixon, Cornelius, 36N
dogs, 10, 12, 43, 49, 54, 55N, 65, 100, 100N, 105N, 111, 117, 121, 125, *125*
    Rosette, *104*, 105N, 111
    sculpture by Anne Damer, 133
    Tonton, 100, *100*, 100N, 111
drawings, 7, 46, 59, 97, 102
    soot-water, 101, 103
dream, 40–1
Drury Lane, 86–7
Ducal Palace, Urbino, 25
Dugdale, 36
Durham, Bishop of, 16

Eagle, Boccapudugli, 33, 88–9, 89N, *89*
    fishing, 133
earthquake, 39
East India Company, 54
ebony/black furniture, 31, 33, 46, 49, 75–6, *76*, 78, 105
    cabinet designed by Edward Edwards, 103
Ecchardt, Johann, 46N, 51N, 58, 59N, 157
Edgcumbe, The Hon. Richard, 32, *32*, 157
Edward IV, King, 100
Edward VI, King, 9
Edward the Confessor, King, 91, 116

Edward Edwards, 35N, 103, 123N, 157
elephant, 86, *86*
Elizabeth I, Queen/Elizabethan, 10, 55, 60, 64N, 92, 98
Elizabeth of Bohemia, Queen, 64
embroidery, 54, 76, 91, 126, 133, 137
    chenille work, 92
enamels, 95, 97–9
l'Enclos, Ninon de, 107
encoignures, 84
The Enlightenment, 28, 54
entertainment/entertaining, 8, 41, 44, 65, 81, 83–4, 87, 93, 109, 135
Essex, Earl of, 55, 92
Essex, James, 47, 100, 157
exhibition/galleries, 78–9, 85, 151
explosion/powder mills, 37N, 38–9

fabric/textile, 36–7, 45–6, 48, 53–4, 58, 58N, 60–1, 70, 77, 83, 89, 90–2, 108, 125–7, 133, 148, 149
    blue and white, 54
    broadcloth, 76
    chintz, 58
    cushions, 71
    fringe, 76
    patchwork, 59
    satin, 76
    silk, 83, 90, 92–3, 103, 105, 139N
    velvet, 76–7, 106
    wool, 83
farm at Strawberry Hill, 16, 129
fashion/society, 8, 10, 16, 17, 28, 33, 41, 47, 51, 54, 60, 66–7, 78–9, 84, 86–7, 91, 109, 111
The Fashionable Friends, 134N
festino/parties, 84, 86–7
festoon/garland, 46–7, 53–4, 86, 105, 108, 120, 149, 151N
figurines, 27–8
fire, 126, 128
    basket 65
    screen (couvre-feu), 65
Fitzosbert, 64
Fitzwilliams, General, 88
flooding/downpours, 16, 43–4, 73
floors, 91, 97, 145
Florence, 35, 45, 98–100, 109
    Boboli, 119
flowers, 26, 54–7, 92, 105, 113–14, 119–21, 130, *130*, 130N, 131, 137
folly, 116–17
food, 28, 46, 54, 124, 128–9, 136
fountain(s), 24–5, 137
France/French, 9, 11, 23N, 24N, 25N, 28, 32, 41, 66, 73–4, 77, 84–5, 92, 99, 100, 105–7, 110, 114
Francis I, 35N, 39, 41, 99, 107, 128
Francis II, 106
Franklin, Benjamin, 110
fresco, 25, 27
fretwork, 45, 81, 83, 89, 148, 150N

friends, 8, 9, 12, 27, 32–3, 43–5, 54, 56, 60, 65, 68, 73, 84, 86–7, 99, 100, 102, 105, 109, 113, 119, 121
frieze, 31, 54
front door, 21, 35, 37N, 70, 129N, 146
fruit, 57, 120, 128, 130N, 131
furniture, 7, 9–10, 20, 23, 28–9, 31–3, 35, 46, 49, 54–5, 58–9, 63–4, 70–1, 74, 78, 83–4, 91–2, 101, 103, 107–8, 126
    black-japanned bureau, 32
    black leather, 23
    box, mother-of-pearl, 88
    cabinet, 92
    coffers, 92
    commodes (Langlois), 84
    dressing table, 76
    lacquerwork, 92–3
    sandalwood and ivory writing box, 49
    pier glasses, 32
    pole-screen, 92
    screen, 84

Gallery *see* Long Gallery
gambling/gaming, 78, 86, 88
games, 12, 110–11
    The Impenetrable Secret, 109N, 109–10
garden, 24–5
    at Strawberry Hill, 13, 18, 24–5, 43–4, 46, 51–2, 53N, 54–7, 60, 73, 77, 81, 83, 111, 113–21, 113N, *115*, 121N, 127, 130–1, 141–2, 146, 147, 148
    cottage garden, 119, 121N, *121*
    flower garden, 119, 120
    garden gate, 117N, *117*, 146
    gardenist, 114
    grove, 113
    ha-ha, 119
    ice house, 129
    kitchen garden, 120, 129
    lawn, 17, 113, 115–16
    Little Library, 120
    maze, 137–8
    nursery, 120
    plantation, 114
    Prior's Garden, *14*, 15N, 18, 146
    rosarium, 120
    terrace, 44, 115N, 129
gardener (John Cowie), 12, 113, 124, 130–1
Garrick, David, 87–8, 157
gas/gasoliers, 136, 153
gate at Strawberry Hill, 18, 99, *117*, 119, 133, 146
Gayfere, Thomas, 106, 116, 157
genealogy, 63, 65
Genoa, 24, 83, 88
George I, 153
George II, 12, 15, 67, 77–8, 86, 110, 153
George III, 12, 54
Georgian period, 8–10, 13, 35, 66, 77N, 84, 92, 97
ghosting, 149, 149N
Gibbons, Grinling, 58, 84–5, 98, 100, 157
Gibbs, James, 53, 157

glass, 26, 37N, 54, 168
    acquisition of, 56
    amber, 73–4, 97, 105
    armourial, 43, 56, *65*, 73, 77, 92, 105, *109*
    balaustines, 77
    blue, 52–4
    diaper work, 77
    early, 35, 116
    enamelled, 130N
    English, 60, 64, 92
    Flemish, *42*, 43N, *44*, 52, 54, 56, *70*, 70N, 126, 147N
    Heemskerk, 56
    medieval stained, 9, 37N, 43, 56, 133
    mosaic, 75–7, 96–7
    painted, 13, 29, 36, 37N, *38*, *39*, 43–4, 52–3, *55*, *56*, *57*, *70*, 73, 75–7, 83, 96, 108, *119*, 119N, *120*, 120N, *125*, 125N, 127, *128*, 128N, 130, 130N, 133, 142, 150
    Palmer, 56, 158
    Peckitt, William, 83, 92, 105, 108, 116, 158
    pomegranate flowers, 77
    Price, 73, 77, 96, 108, 158
    Renaissance, 147
    roundels, 43N, 44N, 54, 55N, 56N, 57N, 64, 70, *87*, 96, 116, *130*, 130N, 133, 142, *147*
    sources, 56, 71, 78
    technology, 54
    Thomas Gray's description of, 76–7, 108–9
Glasse, Hannah, 125N, 129, 157
    Servants' Directory, 125N, 126, 129
    The Art of Cookery Made Plain and Easy, 129
glaziers, 13, 56, 109
gloomth, 9, 13, 38–9, 41, 53, 71, 73, 108, 114, 133
Gloucester, 39
    Cathedral, 35
    Duchess of, 133
The Gobelin Room, 105
gold/gilding/gilders, 9, 10, 32, 45, 58, 71, 76, 81, 83–4, 92, 95, 99, 103, 105–8, 108N, 130, 142, 148, *148*
The Gordon Riots, 12, 67, 153
gothic, 13, 18, 43–4, 76, 100, 113, 141, 147
    Adamesque, 91
    architecture, 9, 17, 20, 28–9, 30, 46, 52, 63, 73, 91, 95, 100, 106–7, 123, 133
    bridge, 120
    Castle, 113, 119, 135
    English buildings, 9
    fans/vaults, 25, 81, 82N, 84, *85*, 113, 116
    furniture, 31, *31*, 32–3
    garden, 13, 116–17, 119
    horror, 40–1
    Moorish ornament, 83
    Movement, 64–5, 114N
    Revival, 7, 135, 139, 142
    sources, 10, 26, 46, 63, 91
    story, 40–1
    Strawberry Hill Gothic, 9, 10, 53, 64–5, 139, 150N
    wallpaper, 35–6, 45, 150, *150*

gout, 39, 41, 58, 131, 151
Grand Tour, 9, 11, 23–5, 45, 47, 67, 83, 88, 153
Gray, Christopher, 120–1
Gray, Thomas, 11, 19, 23, 23N, 24, 24N, 25, 25N, 36, 36N, 58, 66, 68, 75, 75N, 77–8, 78N, 83, 108, 121, 157
    journal, 23–4
    poems, 76N
Great North Bedchamber, 25, 51, 64N, 88, 97N, 100, 105, 106N, 107, 107, 107N, 108N, 110, 116, 127–8, 137–8, 148, 149, 153
    chimneypiece, 106–7, 108, 109
Great Parlour see Refectory
Great Tower, see Round Tower
Green Closet, 39, 44, 51, 51N, 52, 55–6, 92, 147, 149
greenhouse, 114
guests, 18, 87–8, 92, 109, 113, 121, 125, 129, 135–6
guidebooks (general), 18, 23–4, 52, 76

Hall, 17, 21, 23, 33, 35, 36N, 37, 38, 38N, 40, 40, 41, 43–4, 51, 61, 70, 133, 136, 138N, 139N, 150, 150
Hallett, William, 31, 98, 157
Hamilton, Mary, 26, 28–9, 157
Hampton Court, 15–16, 136, 138N, 142
Harry, 43, 99, 126
Hawkins, Laetetia Matilda, 10, 41N, 157
Hayman, Francis, 85, 157
Heemskerk, Maerten van, 56
Henry III, King, 116
Henry V, King, 64
    Battle of Agincourt, 64
Henry VII, King, 70, 73, 84, 106–7
    Chapel of, 67
Henry VIII, King, 9, 36, 56, 58, 70, 76, 78, 100, 106–7
heraldry, 26, 56–7, 60, 63–4, 64, 68–70
Herbert, Lord of Cherbury, 57, 57, 156
Herculaneum, 11, 57, 99, 100, 153
Heritage Lottery Fund, 139
Hervey, Lady, 82N, 157
highwaymen, 12, 73
Hilliard, Nicholas, 55, 99, 157
Historic Doubts on the Life and Reign of King Richard III, 12, 66, 87
history, 12, 43, 45, 56, 64, 66, 70, 77, 98, 106
The History of the Modern Taste in Gardening, 12, 115–16, 116N, 153
Hogarth, William, 54, 66, 108, 157
Holbein Chamber, 39, 51, 70, 73, 73N, 74, 74, 75, 78, 81, 96, 125, 137, 153
    chimneypiece, 38, 75–6, 79
Holbein, Hans, 74–9, 99, 157
Hollar, Wenceslaus, 63, 66, 157
horror, 40–1
Houghton Hall, 10, 12, 16, 58, 70, 109, 121
Hounslow Heath, 38–9
housekeeper, see servants

Howard, Henrietta, Countess of Suffolk, 15, 60, 61, 93, 93N, 157
Hudson, Thomas, 32, 157

ice, 129
    house, 129
The Impenetrable Secret, 109–10
Indian pictures/prints, 47–8, 54
innovation at Strawberry Hill, 9, 17, 31, 35, 45, 51, 136
inventory, 13, 20, 23, 110, 114
Isleworth, 130
Italy/Italian, 9, 11, 13, 23N, 24N, 25N, 26–7, 41, 45–6, 56–7, 77, 84, 90–1, 97, 108

Jackson, John Baptist, 45–6
    Venetian prints, 45–7, 49N, 149, 157
James I, King, 84, 108
japanning, 32, 35, 84, 86, 92, 103, 107
Jersey, 43, 46, 59
Jervas, Charles, 60
John of Eltham, 63
Johnson, Dr Samuel, 86–7, 101
Journal of the Printing-Office at Strawberry-hill, 68, 68N

Kent, William, 53, 57, 91, 109, 115, 158
Keppel, Anna Maria and Laura, 88
King's College Cambridge, 9, 11
Kingston, 16, 44, 54, 128, 142
Kirgate, Thomas, 68, 128, 131, 158
kitchen, 126, 128, 136, 142
kite, 130
knights, 64, 69

lacquer, 92–3, 103
    black, 84
Langley, Batty, 53, 158
Langlois, Pierre, 54, 84, 158
lantern, 35, 39, 44
laudanum, 41
library, 16, 101
    Robert Walpole's, 24
Library, Strawberry Hill (main), 29, 32, 32N, 39, 51, 61, 62, 63, 64, 65, 68, 70–1, 76, 81, 85, 88, 105N, 109, 111N, 124, 127, 133, 153, 159
    Little, 119–20
    in Round Tower, 134
Licensing Act, 86
light, 9–10, 18, 25–6, 32, 35–6, 38, 39N, 40, 43, 46–7, 52, 54, 71, 73–5, 83–4, 86, 92, 95, 108, 117, 125–6, 150
    artificial, 74, 136
    blue, 9, 54
lime trees/lime wood, 38, 53–4, 63
limewash, 146
Little Parlour, 18, 21, 24, 35, 39, 43–7, 52, 52N, 69, 125N, 128, 133, 146
Little Strawberry Hill, 56, 88
locks, 39, 95, 127, 127, 127N

loggias, 20, 25
London, 7, 12, 15, 16, 20, 36–7, 39, 45, 54, 67–8, 76N, 97, 105N, 121, 133N
    St Martin's Lane, 108
Long Gallery, 9, 25, 39, 40, 51, 69, 69N, 73, 78, 80, 81, 81, 81N, 82, 83, 83, 83N, 84, 85, 85N, 90, 92, 95, 97, 97N, 113, 126, 128, 134, 136, 136N, 142, 142N, 148, 148, 149, 149, 151N, 153, 168
    ceiling, 67, 82N, 84N, 88–9
    floor, 136–7
looking glass, 10, 28, 54, 81, 83, 86, 89, 95, 97, 108
Lort, Michael, 125N, 158
lottery ticket, 32
Louis XIV, King, 107
Louis XVI, King, 66
de Loutherbourg, Philippe Jacques, 87, 157
lozenges, 73, 77
Lucatelli prints, 56–7
Luxborough, Lady, 45, 45N, 71, 158

Mabland, 43
Magna Carta, 60
Marble Hill, 15, 61
mahogany, 91
Manfred, 40, 89
Mann, Horace, 11, 12, 16, 23, 25, 36, 44, 46N, 52, 52N, 56, 67, 79, 86, 86N, 88, 90–1, 96N, 97, 99, 113, 113N, 116, 119, 142N, 158
Mason, William, 9N, 81N, 88, 90N, 121, 158
masquerade, 86
    masks, 86
    'domino', 86
marchands-merciers, (Poirier, du Lac and Said), 110
marginalia, 65
marriage/matrimony, 20
Mary, Queen of Scots, 64, 103, 106
Michelham, Lord, 138
Middle Ages/medieval, 69, 116, 119
minatures, 26, 54–5, 95, 97–9, 101
monasticism (cloisters/abbeys), 10, 13, 17–8, 76, 113, 133, 146
money, 4, 10–12, 20, 33, 36, 56, 65, 68, 74, 76–7, 79, 86–8, 92–3, 97, 101, 108, 110–14, 119–21, 127, 129–31, 133–4, 142
Montagu, George, 46, 46N, 67, 78, 78N, 82, 82N, 84, 85, 93N, 99N, 114, 119N, 120, 120N, 128N, 158
More, Hannah, 131, 131N, 158
mosaic, 45–6, 64, 70, 76–7, 91, 96–7, 108
motto (Fare Quae Sentiat), 70
Müntz, Johann Heinrich, 25, 47N, 57, 59, 65–6, 77, 97, 111N, 126, 158
music, 44, 52, 84, 86
The Mysterious Mother, 12, 102, 105, 153

neighbours, 130–1
New Offices, 115, 123–4, 124, 135, 153
Newcastle, Duke of, 67

newel post, 38, 41, 60, *60*, 60N
Newton, Sir Isaac, 16
niche, 24, 26, 26N, 39, 41, 46, 76, 95, 97, 133
Noah, 16, *42*, 43, 43N, 44
Norfolk, 11
North, Anne, 88
Northumberland, Duke of (Sion House), 91
novel, 40–1
    gothic, 41

obelisk, 56, 73N, 119
Ode on the Death of a Favourite Cat, 19, *19*
ogee, 17, 18, 107, 127
oil lamp, 85
Old St Paul's Cathedral, 9, 63N, 91
Oliver, Isaac, 55, 57, 99, 158
Oliver, Peter, 55, 99, 158
'Onuphrio Muralto', 41, 41N
opera, 86
orange trees, 24, 77, 86, 115, 142
Oratory, 18, 133
oriental, 92–3
ormolu, 84
Ossory, Lady, 20N, 39, 41N, 44N, 66, 73, 95, 101, 106N, 111, 128, 130, 131N, 158
ossuary, 65
ostrich feathers, 76, 105

paint, 74, 145, 149, 150
painted effects, 29
paintings, 7, 10–12, 18, 20, 23–5, 32, 32N, 47–8, 51–2, 54–57, 59–60, 70, 76, 78–9, 82–4, 88–90, 97, 99–102, 105, 107, 109, 116, 125, 127, 133, 137
    in perspective, 24–5
    classical, 91
    history paintings, 90
    landscape paintings, 25, 89, 90, 103
    seascapes, 25, 89
Palazzo del Te, 25
Palladio, Andrea, 98
Palladio Londonensis, 74
Palmer, *see* glass
panelling, 146, 148, *149*, *151*
pantomime, 28
paper, 10, 28, 36–7, 45, 46–7, 55, 65, 68, 70–1, 77, 101, 103, 105, 128
paper mosaics, 54–5
papier mâché, 9, 70, 73, 75N, 76, 77, 77N, 81, 95, 103, 116
    carta pesta, 77
parade/state rooms, 78, 88, 91, 105
Paris, 16, 28, 32, 45, 57, 92–3, 110
parliament, 64, 125
    Palace of Westminster, 105
    Acts of, 15, 16, 83, 86, 101
    Walpole as Member of, 11
    political entertaining, 135
    politics, 40, 67–8
Pars, William, 15N, 113N, 116N, 120N
passage(s), 38, 41, 43, 45, 74, 76, 105, 106N, 133

patents, 77
pattern books, 63
pebbledash, 145, 146
Peckitt, William, *see* glass
pergola, 25
piers, 150
pineapples, 55
pinnacles, 17, 43, 49, 52, 76, 113, 119, 133,146N, 147, 149, 149N
Pitt, Thomas, 47, 83, 97, 158
Plaid Bedchamber, 60–1, 123, 147
Plantaganets, 70
planting, 13, 25, 119
plants in pots, 18, 86, 113, 119, 121
playbills, 87
plays, 86, 93, 101–2
pole-screen, 92
Pope, Alexander, 15, 16, 16N, 59, 60N, 84, 158
    grotto, 84
Pope, The, 88, 100
    Papist, 111
portraits, 32–3, 48, 59, 64, 70, 77, 83, 89, 98–9, 102, 103, 106, 114, 133, 148N
    see Henry Carey, Lord Falkland
post/postboy, 130
Poussin, Nicholas, 92, 107
Po-Yang, 119
Price, William, *see* glass
Prince Arthur's tomb, 35–6, 38
print room(s), 47, 48N, 59
printing house, 84
    printers, 68
prints/engravings, 9, 10, 20, 33, 36, 38, 46–9, 56, 63, 65, 77, 79, 86, 91, 99, 109, 134, 142, 149
    woodblock prints, 45
Prior's Garden, *14*, 15N, 18, 146
private rooms, 43, 46, 61
Protestant Hanoverians, 10, 12
    break with Rome, 78
public/tours, 17, 18, 20, 27, 41, 49, 51, 51N, 55, 60, 76, 81, 84, 95, 121, 128, 134, 142
    tourists, 7
Pugin, Augustus Welby, 136, 138N
puzzles, 41
Pye, Henrietta, 76, 76N, 105, 105N

quatrefoil, 17, 35, 76, 95, 150

rags, 36–7
railway, 37, 139
Ranelagh Gardens, 85–6
Red Bedchamber, 51, 59
Refectory (Great Parlour), 21, 23, 28, *29*, 30, *30*, 31–2, 35, 39, 43, 51, 74, 88, 128, 133, 135–6, 145, 150, 153
religion, 116–17
restoration, 145, 146, 147N, 150, 151, 153, 168
Reynolds, Joshua, 10N, 29N, 32, 32N, 33, 54, 101, 102N, 133, 136N, 158
Rheims, 9
rheumatism, 20

Richardson, Jonathan, 23–4, 24N, 25, 48, 158
Richmond, 15–16, 128, 142
    Bridge, 12
    Duke and Duchess of, 110, 119
    Hill, 16, 44, 51, 54
    Lodge, 61
    Park, 16, 44
ridotto, 86
roads, 37, 97, 113, 119, 136
Robinson, William, 53, 158
Robsart, Ludovic (known also as Terry Robsart, became Lord Bourchier), 36, 84, 158
rococo, 46, 57, 82
romance, 41, 46, 70
Romano, Giulio, 25, 27, 103, 158
Rome, 13, 25, 65, 78, 86, 88–9, 116
Rotunda, 85–6
Roubiliac, Jean François, 85, 158
Rouen, 9, 38, 38N, 76
Round Drawing Room, 39, 51, 58, 81, 88, *90*, 91–2, 97, 106, 127, 138, 148, 149
Round Tower/Great Tower, 17, 58, 91, 100, 113, 119, 123, 128, 134–5, 142, 146, 146N, 149, 151, 153
route, 13, 18, *21*, *51*, 51N
ruins, 56
rules for visiting, 18, 20, 23

Sackville, Lord John, 16
St Albans Abbey doors, 84, 148
St Mary's College/St Mary's Catholic Teacher Training College, 138, 153
Saint-Porchaire Ewer, 26, *26*, 27, *27*
saints in glass, 37N, 38
sales/auctions, 73, 76, 78–9, 103, 113, 114N, 138
    catalogues, 7, 145
    1842 sale, 106, 134, 135, 135N, 141, 153
        ticket, *135*
    1883 sale, 134, 134N, 139N, 141
Salisbury Cathedral, 116
Saracen/Saracen's head, 53, *69*, 70, 75, 93, 137
scagliola, 91, 91N
scale, 10, 38, 46
sconces, *see* candlesticks
Scott, Samuel, 56, 66, 100, 158
screen(s), 10, *74*, 75–7, 84, 103, 133, 146
sculptures/sculptors, 11, 23–4, 24N, 57, 84, 88, 89, 97, 98, 106, 111, 117, 133
seals, 69
security, 83
Selima, 18, 19, *19*, *160*, *see* cats
Selwyn, George, 32, *32*, 158
serendipity/surprise, 9, 38, 52
Serpentine Walk/Wood, 113, 115, 117, 138, 142
servants, 12, 18, 21, 28–9, 44, 73, 84, 88, 106, 114, 121, 123–9, 131, 131N, 136
    servants' bedrooms, 123; servants' corridor, 21, 136; servants' door, 18, 21, *129*, 129N, 131; servants' hall, 88, 126, 128; servants' stair, 51, 97N, 111, 147, *150*, 150N, 168
    coachman, 126, 128

cook, 128–9

gardener *see* gardener (John Cowie)

housekeeper, 13, 18, 21, 23, 28, 35, 51, 51N, 59–61, 114, 125–6

valet, 126

Catherine, 43–4

Elizabeth (Colomb), 129

Harry, 43–4, 99, 126

James (Colomb): footman, 129

John (Fitzwater): footman, 129

Louis, 43–4

Margaret Young, *see* Young

Maria (Colomb), 129

Peter, 43–4

Philip (Colomb), 128–9

settees/couches, 29, 53, 92

black leather, 23

pink gingham case covers, 29

Sévigné, Madame de, 56, 66

Shakespeare, William, 66, 87

sharawaggi, 37, 115

Shell Bench, 117, *118*, 119, 119N

Shenstone, William, 45, 71

shields, 36, 69

shopping, 54, 56, 86

Short Notes of My Life, 16

Shorter, Catherine (Lady Walpole), *11*, 23, 57–8, *59*, 64, 66, 84, 92–3, 97, 100, 133, 153, 158

shutters, 83, 126, 126N, 127

sill, 148, 149

silver, 126

by Cellini, 107–8

slavery, 12

snuff, 129

box, 100, *100*, 100N, 110

South Tower, 51–2, 56, 58

Spain, 83–4

Spitalfields, 10

stable, 57

staircase, 17, *34*, 35, 35N, 36, 38, 38N, 39, 40, 40N, 41, 60, 60N, 70, 71, 128, 139, 150

Star Chamber, 51, 56N, 63, 70–1, 71N, 73, 77, 137

stars (golden), 70–1, 76–7, 96–7

State Bedchambers, 76, 103, 106, *see also* Holbein Chamber and Great North Bedchamber

Stern, Baron de, 108N, 138, 145, 149, 153

stone, 38, 65

Portland, 116

stone colour/grey, 36, 38, 45–6, 63, 74, 76, 95, 149, 150

stools, 87

blue damask, 102

long (by Vile), 84

stories/storytelling, 10, 20, 40, 100

strawberry, 16, *130*, 130N

Strawberry Hill

early house, 8, 53, 145

at turn of 18th/19th century, 133–4

19th century, *17*, *133*, 134–5, 146–9, 151N

20th century, 138, *140*, 147, 149, 152

21st century and future, 139, 141–2, 151, 168

additions to, 71, 73, 81, 82, 97, 100, 135–7

ballroom, 135–8

building of, 13, 16–17, 39, 53, 97, 145

castle, 13, 35, 38–9, 41, 56, 73, 84, 99, 102, 113, 135, 145–7, 151

clock tower, 135

decoration of, 30–1, 35–9, 44–6

gothicising (sources and influences), 9, 10, 23–6, 46, 52, 63–4, 83–4, 91, 100–1, 106

intention in purchase of, 65

modern convenience, 29

on Walpole's death, 133

as Otranto, 40–1

owners other than Walpole, 8, 149

parade or state rooms,*see* listings for: Holbein Chamber, Long Gallery, Round Drawing Room, Great North Bedchamber

plans of, 21, *51* ,*97*, *123*, *124*, 168

purchase of land, 17

service wing, 123–8

site and entrance, 15–18, 145N

staff employed on estate, 124

symmetry and irregularity, 17–18, 37–8, 47, 146N, 147

toy house, 46

use of heraldry in, 68–70

views of, *2*, *6*, *8*, *13*, *14*, *15*, *21*, *72*, *114*, *122*, *129*, *131*, *146*

Strawberry Hill Accounts, 7, 77, 77N, 93N, 103, 113, 113N, 119N, 141

Strawberry Hill Press, 7, 12, 18, 66, 68, 68N, 84, 123–4, 131, 134, 153

Strawberry Hill Trust, 139, 145, 153, 168

stream, 120

Stuart Court, 48–9

stucco, 28, 45–6, 77

paper, 45

supper parties, 18, 25, 46, 84–6, 88

sweetmeats, 28

Swift, Jonathan, 61

syllabub, 129

symmetry, 10, 17, 91, 146N, 147, 148

lack of, 18, 37, 119

tables, 28–9, 46, 49, 84, 91, 92, 102–3, 128–9, 138

card, 57, 88

hazard, 57

refectory, *31*, 33

Sèvres, 58, 92

scagliola, 91

writing, 54

tapestry, 92, 105, 138

taste, 10, 56, 74, 76, 133

tax/duty, 37, 93, 110

tea, 37, 40, 84, 86, 92

bowl, *92*

cannister, 100

chest/caddy, 102

tea-room, 119

serving tea, 92–3

technology/techniques, 8–9, 35, 37, 45, 47, 54, 74, 77, 86, 91, 93, 97, 102–3, 105, 108, 127, 138, 145

Thames, River, 9, 16, 21, 25, 37, 43–4, 51–2, 54–5, 58, 60, 65, 81, 97, 113, 115, 119, 126–7, 133, 138, 142

theatre at Strawberry Hill, 134,134N

theatre/drama, 9, 18, 25, 35, 39–41, 56, 60, 70, 73, 75, 79, 81–2, 85–7, 88, 101–2, 105, 113, 116

theft/housebreakers, 99, 126–7

The Three Ladies Waldegrave, *22*, 29N, *32*, *32*, 88, 133–4, 136N, 159

The Three Princes of Serendip, 38

tickets, 18, 20, 23, 35, 41, 51, 81, 86, 128, 145

tiles

Dutch, 23

Minton floor, 136, 138, *138*

terracotta floor, 26, 27, 38, 41

Titian, 45–6

tombs, 10, 20, 35–8, 46, 63, 84, 91–2, 116–7

Torreggiano, 70

toy-shop/china shop, 16, 28

traffic, 12, 44, 54

travel, 12

treasures, 23, 95, 97

trellis-work, 24–6, 81, 115

Tribune (Cabinet), 39, 51, 73, *94*, 95N, *96*, 97, *97* (diagram), 99–100, 103N, 137, 145

trompe l'oeil, 18, 23–5, *32*, 38, 49, 69, 83, 91, 97, 149

Trunk-ceiled Passage, 51, 71, 73, *74*, 76, 81

Tudor (paperstainer), 36, 38

Tudor period, 9, 77–8, 92, 106

tulip vase, 17th century, *28*

Turkish:

buildings, 85

work, 100

sheep, 43–4

Twickenham, 12, 15–6, 32–3, 39, 53, 56–7, 63, 66, 68, 76N, 77, 83, 97, 105N, 113, 121, 129, 130–1, 133, 142, 147

Tyers, Jonathan, 85–6, 159

upholsterers, 36, 52, 76, 82, 84

Van Dyke, Anthony, 49, 59, 86, 92, 106

Vauxhall Gardens (Spring Gardens), 85–7

Vertue, George, 11, 66, 77, 99, 159

Venice, 45, 58N, 60, 86

vestibule, 36

Victorian Drawing Room, 137N, *137*

Victorian period, 8–9, 60N, 77N, 135, 137, 149N

Vile, William, 76, 84, 105, 151

villa, 9, 20, 25, 52, 58, 83, 87, 111, 119, 133, 141, 145–6

Vincentian Order/Catholic education, 8, 138, 153

vine leaves, 60, 106
vines, 24
visitors, 7, 9, 18, 20–1, 23, 25, 33, 35, 39, 41, 43, 46, 57, 59, 61, 71, 73, 75, 77–8, 81, 84, 88, 91, 95, 97, 99–101, 105, 107, 109, 111, 113–15, 117, 119, 121, 128, 133, 145
    royal, 10, 9
The Vyne, 48

wages, 97
Waiting Room, 18, 21, 23, 26, 43, 145
Waldegrave family, 8, 134, 153
    6th Earl, 134
        John (illegitimate), 134
    7th Earl (George), 134
Waldegrave, Frances Lady (née Braham), 8, 69N, 134, 135, 135, 135N, 136, 138, 138N, 139, 145, 148–9, 153
        husbands: John, 134; George, 134; George Granville Vernon Harcourt, 135; Chicester Fortescue, 135, 138
Wales, Prince of, 99
wallpaper, 24, 36, 48, 52, 58, 82, 101, 106, 123, 134, 139, 139N, 149
    architectural, 25, 149
    battens, 36–7
    Blue Breakfast Room, 53, 149, 151
    blue, 58, 149
    blue and white, 23, 24N, 53–4
    borders, 37, 47–8, 101, 101N, 134N
    chinoiserie style, 25
    choice of colour, 52, 58
    copied from engravings, 35–6, 45–6, 48
    cutting a new block, 36
    daisy pattern, 105, 106N
    designs, 36
    early papers in distemper, 47
    embossed, 73
    festooning, 53–4, 149, 151
    flocked, 58, 60
    French, 137
    geometric, 134
    gothic, 33, 35–6, 45–6, 150N
    Gray, Thomas, advises on, 36, 76
    Green Closet, 55–6, 149
    grey-spotted, 48
    Hall, 25, 33, 35–8
    hanging, 37
    Holbein Chamber, 75
    in oil, 45–6
    lining with textile, 37
    Little Parlour, 45–6
    monochromatic, 105, 106N
    mosaic, 45, 70, 71
    nineteenth-century, 134N, 137, 150
    paper used, 36–7
    paperstainers, 13, 36, 38, 47
    plaid, 60–1
    print rooms, 47, 48, 48N, 59
    purple, 76
    Red Bedchamber, 59

Refectory, 28–9
relationship to textile printing, 45, 53–4
Star Chamber, 70
Stern, Baron de, 108N
stucco, 28–9, 31–2, 45–6
taxation, 37
treillage, 73
trompe l'oeil, 35, 38, 150
Trunk-ceiled Passage, 73
Waiting Room/Early Hall, 23
Waldegrave, 58N, 60, 150
Walpole's Early Bedchamber, 58
Walpole's Bedchamber from 1757, 58, 58N, 60
woodblock printing, 45–6
Yellow Bedchamber/later Beauty Room, 47–8
Venetian cut velvet damask, 58N, 60
wallpaper designers, workers and suppliers:
    Bentley, Richard: butterfly design 57; general designs, 35–6, 38, 46
    Bromwich, Thomas, 36, 45N, 46, 57, 60
    Bromwich and Legh, 47
    Jackson, John Baptist, 45–7, 48N
    Tudor, 38
Walnut Tree House, 129
Walpole Cabinet, 97N, 98, 98, 98N
Walpole family, 10, 26, 32, 47, 51, 56, 64, 66, 84, 92, 99, 105, 108, 117
Walpole, Henry (the Jesuit), 60
Walpole, Horace, 10, 50, 104, 111, 142, 145
    antiquarian, 35, 63, 65, 151
    Arcadian influences, 51–2
    authorises visits, 18, 20
    as builder/designer, 82–3
    buys glass, 38–9, 56
    buys land, 17
    Castle of Otranto, 41, 89
    choice of paintings, 56–7
    chooses wallpaper, 35–8, 45
    collector, 20, 26–8, 54–7, 63, 73–4, 88–90, 93, 97–100, 103, 110, 114
    Committee of Taste, 29, 46–7, 168
    compiles inventory, 18, 20
    contemporary purchases, 32
    death, 133
    description of, 10–11, 121, 129
    dream, 40–1
    entertaining, 44, 81–4, 87–8, 109
    everyday living, 53–4
    gardenist, 113–21, 131
    genealogy, 60, 63–4
    Grand Tour, 24–5
    health, 12, 39, 41, 131
    heraldry, 26, 70
    income, 11
    influences, 8–9
    intention in buying Chopp'd Straw Hall, 65
    interests, 60, 63
    letter writing, 12, 66–7
    (as) master, 123, 128

(as) patron, 32–3, 58
perception of gothic, 10
position in society, 67
sets up Strawberry Hill Press, 68
uses new techniques, 35
view of himself, 58
will, 12
works, 12
(as) writer, 33, 41, 56, 102–3
Walpole, Mary, 33
Walpole, Robert, 1st Earl of Orford, 11, 12, 16, 23, 29, 55–6, 58, 59, 64, 66, 70, 78, 86, 92, 114, 133, 153, 159
    inventory, 23–4, 29, 55–6, 58, 114
watercolours, 13, 20, 23, 39N, 40N, 56, 60, 64, 99, 101
Watteau, Antoine, 56–7, 60
weapons, 36, 39, 41, 100
weather, 43–4, 73, 121, 130
Wedgwood, Josiah, 27, 101, 153
West, Benjamin, 79, 159
Westminster Abbey, 9, 46, 63–4, 67, 84, 91–2, 106, 116
    Henry VII Chapel, 67
Wharton, Thomas, 36N, 75, 77, 83, 108
whist, 88, 93
will, 128N, 129, 133
William and Mary, King and Queen, 108, 127N
Williams, Sir Charles Hanbury, 58, 159
Williams, Gilly, 32, 32, 159
windows, 145, 149
    Great North Bedchamber, 108, 109, 127
    lancet, 18, 26, 31
    Long Gallery, 81, 134
    ogee, 18, 31, 70, 127
    oriel, 95–6
    quatre-foil, 17, 35, 150
    shutters, 126–7, 146
    sliding, 127, 146
    trompe l'oeil, 18, 25, 97, 146
    views from, 25, 56, 119
Windsor, 78
wine, 86, 93, 129
Woffington, Peg, 87, 159
women, 12, 37, 54
Worcester Cathedral, 35, 38
workmen/tradesmen, 13, 30, 36, 46, 74, 82, 91, 97, 113, 115–16, 145
The World, 28
The World Monuments Fund in Britain, 139
Wren, Christopher, 53, 63
writers, 15, 41
Wyatt, James, 47, 91, 159

Yellow Bedchamber (Beauty Room), 35, 43, 47, 48, 49N, 101, 146, 149, 153, 159
York, Duke of, 99
York Minster, 96
Young, Margaret, 18, 20, 39, 44, 70, 73–4, 78, 81, 87–8, 90, 93, 95, 98–100, 106–7, 111, 123, 126, 128, 133, 159, see also housekeeper

Picture Credits

ILLUSTRATIONS COURTESY OF:

Duncan Burton, 45
The Provost and Fellows of Eton College, 9
John Hardy, 28 top
Trustees of the National Museums of Scotland, 27
Friends of Strawberry Hill, 2, 46, 151 top
Strawberry Hill Trust, 144, 149, 151 below
The Earl and Countess of Wemyss and March,
    89 left
The World Monuments Fund in Britain, 140,
    143, 152
The Lewis Walpole Library, Yale University, 29, 31,
    37, 39–40, 61, 71, 74 left, 75, 77, 90, 96, 98,
    100–101, 107, 114, 129, 131

PHOTOGRAPHS BY:

Authors, 148 below, 150 top
Chris Capstick, 1, 6, 8, 10–11, 13–15, 17, 19, 21–22, 26,
    30, 32–34, 47–50, 59, 60 left, 62, 64, 65 below,
    72, 74 right, 79–80, 88, 89 right, 92, 94, 102,
    104, 110–12, 115–18, 121–22, 124, 132, 135–37, 139
    left, 142, 159, 160
Richard Holttum, 149 top
Angelo Hornak, 140, 143, 152
JED, 89 left
Carol Oliver, 24, 28 below, 36, 41, 46, 57 top, 66,
    68–69, 76, 106, 109, 135 right, 138, 141
Mark Sandiford, 151 below
Terry Smith, 146
Richard Spires, 144
Brian Whitehead, 147, 148 top, 149 below, 150 below
Michael Yauner, 38, 42, 44, 52–53, 55–56, 57 below,
    58, 60 right, 65 top, 70, 81–83, 85, 87, 91, 103,
    108, 119–20, 125, 127–28, 130, 134, 139 right

NOTES TO THE REVISED EDITION

The final chapter in this edition describes research and discoveries made during the restoration. The opportunity has also been taken to make some small corrections to the original text and the captions have been brought up to date to reflect the movement of glass and similar objects to their original and present positions.

In the first edition various terms were used which were in common use in spoken and academic written material about Strawberry Hill at the time of writing. They have not been changed here (other than in the new chapter) but it should be noted that following the restoration the decision has been made by the Strawberry Hill Trust to revert to the eighteenth-century text seen on Walpole's plans of the house of 1781. Two terms in particular have been affected: the 'Gallery' previously referred to as the 'Long Gallery' and the 'Back Stair' also called the 'Servants' Stair'. In addition the term 'Committee of Taste', which has been in use for approximately 150 years, is now known not to have been the term used by Walpole himself who named his group 'The Committee'.